Stripping, Sex, and Popular Culture

Dress, Body, Culture

Series Editor: **Joanne B. Eicher,** ***Regents' Professor, University of Minnesota***

Books in this provocative series seek to articulate the connections between culture and dress which is defined here in its broadest possible sense as any modification or supplement to the body. Interdisciplinary in approach, the series highlights the dialogue between identity and dress, cosmetics, coiffure and body alternations as manifested in practices as varied as plastic surgery, tattooing, and ritual scarification. The series aims, in particular, to analyze the meaning of dress in relation to popular culture and gender issues and will include works grounded in anthropology, sociology, history, art history, literature, and folklore.

ISSN: 1360-466X

Previously published in the Series

Helen Bradley Foster, *"New Raiments of Self": African American Clothing in the Antebellum South*
Claudine Griggs, *S/he: Changing Sex and Changing Clothes*
Michaele Thurgood Haynes, *Dressing Up Debutantes: Pageantry and Glitz in Texas*
Anne Brydon and Sandra Niessen, *Consuming Fashion: Adorning the Transnational Body*
Dani Cavallaro and Alexandra Warwick, *Fashioning the Frame: Boundaries, Dress and the Body*
Judith Perani and Norma H. Wolff, *Cloth, Dress and Art Patronage in Africa*
Linda B. Arthur, *Religion, Dress and the Body*
Paul Jobling, *Fashion Spreads: Word and Image in Fashion Photography*
Fadwa El Guindi, *Veil: Modesty, Privacy and Resistance*
Thomas S. Abler, *Hinterland Warriors and Military Dress: European Empires and Exotic Uniforms*
Linda Welters, *Folk Dress in Europe and Anatolia: Beliefs about Protection and Fertility*
Kim K.P. Johnson and Sharron J. Lennon, *Appearance and Power*
Barbara Burman, *The Culture of Sewing*
Annette Lynch, *Dress, Gender and Cultural Change*
Antonia Young, *Women Who Become Men*
David Muggleton, *Inside Subculture: The Postmodern Meaning of Style*
Nicola White, *Reconstructing Italian Fashion: America and the Development of the Italian Fashion Industry*
Brian J. McVeigh, *Wearing Ideology: The Uniformity of Self-Presentation in Japan*
Shaun Cole, *Don We Now Our Gay Apparel: Gay Men's Dress in the Twentieth Century*
Kate Ince, *Orlan: Millennial Female*
Nicola White and Ian Griffiths, *The Fashion Business: Theory, Practice, Image*
Ali Guy, Eileen Green and Maura Banim, *Through the Wardrobe: Women's Relationships with their Clothes*
Linda B. Arthur, *Undressing Religion: Commitment and Conversion from a Cross-Cultural Perspective*
William J.F. Keenan, *Dressed to Impress: Looking the Part*
Joanne Entwistle and Elizabeth Wilson, *Body Dressing*
Leigh Summers, *Bound to Please: A History of the Victorian Corset*
Paul Hodkinson, *Goth: Identity, Style and Subculture*
Michael Carter, *Fashion Classics from Carlyle to Barthes*
Sandra Niessen, Ann Marie Leshkowich and Carla Jones, *Re-Orienting Fashion: The Globalization of Asian Dress*
Kim K. P. Johnson, Susan J. Torntore and Joanne B. Eicher, *Fashion Foundations: Early Writings on Fashion and Dress*
Helen Bradley Foster and Donald Clay Johnson, *Wedding Dress Across Cultures*
Eugenia Paulicelli, *Fashion under Fascism: Beyond the Black Shirt*
Charlotte Suthrell, *Unzipping Gender: Sex, Cross-Dressing and Culture*
Yuniya Kawamura, *The Japanese Revolution in Paris Fashion*
Ruth Barcan, *Nudity: A Cultural Anatomy*
Samantha Holland, *Alternative Femininities: Body, Age and Identity*
Alexandra Palmer and Hazel Clark, *Old Clothes, New Looks: Second Hand Fashion*
Yuniya Kawamura, *Fashion-ology: An Introduction to Fashion Studies*
Regina A. Root, *The Latin American Fashion Reader*
Linda Welters and Patricia A. Cunningham, *Twentieth-Century American Fashion*
Jennifer Craik, *Uniforms Exposed: From Conformity to Transgression*
Alison L. Goodrum, *The National Fabric: Fashion, Britishness, Globalization*
Annette Lynch and Mitchell D. Strauss, *Changing Fashion: A Critical Introduction to Trend Analysis and Meaning*
Marybeth C. Stalp, *Quilting: The Fabric of Everyday Life*

Stripping, Sex, and Popular Culture

Catherine M. Roach

Oxford • New York

First published in 2007 by
Berg
Editorial offices:
1st Floor, Angel Court, 81 St Clements Street, Oxford, OX4 1AW, UK
175 Fifth Avenue, New York, NY 10010, USA

Berg is the imprint of Oxford International Publishers Ltd.

Library of Congress Cataloguing-in-Publication Data
Roach, Catherine M., 1965-
Stripping, sex, and popular culture / Catherine M. Roach.
p. cm.
Includes bibliographical references and index.
ISBN-13: 978-1-84520-128-9 (cloth)
ISBN-10: 1-84520-128-0 (cloth)
ISBN-13: 978-1-84520-129-6 (pbk.)
ISBN-10: 1-84520-129-9 (pbk.)
1. Sex—Social aspects—United States. 2. Sex in popular culture—United States. 3. Striptease—United States. 4. Stripteasers—United States—Biography. I. Title.

HQ18.U5R62 2007
306.77—dc22 2007030715

British Library Cataloguing-in-Publication Data
A catalogue record for this book is available from the British Library.

ISBN 978 1 84520 128 9 (Cloth)
ISBN 978 1 84520 129 6 (Paper)

Typeset by Avocet Typeset, Chilton, Aylesbury, Bucks
Printed in the United Kingdom by Biddles Ltd, King's Lynn

www.bergpublishers.com

To KMM

and also to MAM,

in a lifetime of sisterhood

Contents

Acknowledgements

I didn't know I had this book in me. It developed quite suddenly. The idea to write it came about as a result of my good fortune in three areas. First, although my university degrees are all in the academic study of religion and culture and although I have a cross-appointment in the Department of Religious Studies, as well as in Women's Studies, my main appointment at the University of Alabama is in New College. This program is an interdisciplinary one wherein undergraduate students – often purple-haired and multiple-pierced – design their own majors. Not only students but faculty members as well enjoy an unusual degree of freedom from their association with New College. As my senior colleague Ed Passerini has said on many occasions, part of the reward of New College is that it allows you, indeed challenges you, "to play in many puddles." My interdisciplinary appointment grants me the latitude to pursue research topics somewhat outside the main and certainly outside the disciplinary boundaries of religious studies. Through the process of writing this book, I've come to understand more and more what Ed means and to appreciate this freedom. I thank New College for its steadfast dedication to the art of interdisciplinary teaching and research. I thank the Directors of New College, Dave Klemmack and then Jim Hall, for both being a junior professor's dream-come-true of the supportive and encouraging boss. I thank Ed, Jerry Rosenberg, Bing Blewitt, and the other visionary founders of New College for creating this special place. And I thank the students, too numerous to mention here, from several years' worth of New College seminars who helped me to think through this book's ideas and who so graciously volunteered to assist me on any field trips necessary for the research. The students of "Gender, Sexuality, and Society" in Fall 2006 were particularly astute peer reviewers of the book manuscript in its final draft.

My second piece of good fortune lies in my ongoing membership in the Interpretive and Interdisciplinary Research Group of the University of Alabama. This group of faculty from across the university gathers weekly to read and critique each other's works in progress. With members from history, American studies, women's studies, French, anthropology, social work, communications, education, psychology, law, film, and more, it is by far the most intellectually stimulating and collegial group I've encountered anywhere in academia. Several of my colleagues from this group do qualitative research using methodologies such as in-depth interview techniques. Reading their work and learning from it led me to develop my own qualitative interview-based research project, a methodology I might never have adopted without having had this possibility opened up for me by their example. In particular here, I thank Jerry Rosiek, whose work first inspired me. Whether explicating John Dewey, breaking new ground in antiracist educational research, or dry smoking the hind quarter of a Mississippi deer, Jerry's exuberant leadership of our research group has helped keep many of us afloat in the treacherous waters of the tenure track. I also thank the group as a whole for their insightful critique of drafts of this book; I benefited enormously from their feedback and encouragement.

Finally, and most importantly, this book came about because of my friendship with Marie, whose story I tell in the Introduction. Without her, I could never have written this book. Indeed, I doubt it would ever have occurred to me to do so.

Also due my sincere thanks for aid, encouragement, and critical feedback on the project are Kelley Raab, Naomi Goldenberg, Ted Trost, Russ McCutcheon, Carol Pierman, Jennifer Purvis, Kurtis Schaeffer, Ann Pellegrini, Louise Bernikow, Carmen Taylor, Michael Conaway, Andy Valvur, Maryan McCarrey, and my family members Danielle Perron Roach, Michael Roach, Diane Roach, and Joseph Roach. I also thank the staff at Berg Publishing in Oxford, UK, who graciously shepherded this book to publication. Audience members at academic conferences and lectures spurred me in my thinking while I was trying out the book's ideas (at American Academy of Religion meetings in Atlanta and Toronto, in talks in Tuscaloosa, Ottawa, Vancouver, and Halifax), and I appreciate their engagement. I am grateful to the students who transcribed interview tapes for me: Adam Beach, Christina Corley, Tiffany Self, and Christine Scott. For financial support of the research and writing time that made this book possible, I appreciate the assistance of New College, Religious Studies, the College of Arts and Sciences, and the Research Advisory Council of The University of Alabama. For providing a most collegial setting during my final year of writing while I was on sabbatical leave, I thank Farhang Rajaee and the faculty of the College of the Humanities at Carleton University in Ottawa.

Finally, to all the people who agreed to be interviewed for this project and who gave so generously of their time, I am indebted and deeply thankful. Their stories are the warp threads on which I have woven this book.

Introduction: Marie/Foxy

One of my best friends is a stripper.

We met as five-year-old girls, growing up in the same middle-class leafy suburb of Ottawa, in Canada. It was a new residential development, full of kids riding bicycles and playing in the woods down by the Ottawa River. Marie's family lived on the street behind mine. The streets formed two interlocking crescents whose pattern meant that we passed each other's house all the time. Our families stayed put for twenty-five years – indeed, mine is still there – while we went to the same Catholic elementary school; the same junior high; and then on to high school together, in a building just across the playing fields from our old elementary school. I often went with her family to their cottage on a lake in the Gatineau Hills north of the city. Because my mother wouldn't let me have a cat or a dog, their Black Lab became my surrogate pet. We both went to the University of Ottawa for our undergraduate and master's degrees, while still living at home with our families. We often took the bus downtown to campus together where we met up with another neighborhood friend, Anita, for a weekly breakfast club.

Marie and I then came down to the United States at the same time to do our Ph.D.s, hers in English literature and medieval studies at a prestigious Midwestern university and mine in religious studies at Harvard. Marie used feminist theory in her research and teaching; she was, and remains now, a self-avowed feminist. After several years studying full-time, she switched to part-time status before leaving school completely for a while to work in administration at the Gender/Women's Studies Department of her university. She then decided to resume her program full-time in order to determine once and for all if she wanted to finish her degree. Knowing that she couldn't combine school work with her administrative job, she quit her position and, for income and out of curiosity, started dancing at the local strip club (there was only one in her small town), first on the day shift and then on the more lucrative night shift. She found that she enjoyed the job and that it let her manage her expenses, while still leaving plenty of time for library research and classes. At the end of the calendar year, she made the decision that she truly didn't want to be employed in academia. So, like many other people and for a variety of reasons, Marie left her Ph.D. program. But "Foxy" kept on dancing.

Meanwhile, I finished my degree and was hired at The University of Alabama as an assistant professor. My appointment was shared between the Department of

Religious Studies and New College, an interdisciplinary liberal arts program where students design their own majors and where I teach courses in ethics and in gender studies. When we both started our new jobs Marie said to me, "Working as a stripper makes me feel much better about myself than trying to do a Ph.D. ever did." I think that even those of us who haven't worked as exotic dancers but who have emerged, intact but frayed, from the Ph.D. process can sympathize with what she means. Little I've ever done, save raise two children, has been as emotionally taxing to my sense of self. When I mention my friend's quote in academic circles, practically everyone nods his or her head.

I was at first a little shocked and quite concerned to learn that one of my best friends had become a stripper. What did it involve, I wanted to know? Why was she doing it? Was it a dangerous, seedy profession and one damaging to her self-esteem, as I initially assumed? Should I, as her friend, try to talk her out of it? Well, talk we did. We began to have long talks about stripping. And what I began to realize was that exotic dance raises all sorts of fascinating questions about gender, sexuality, sexism, feminism, consumerism, agency, power, empowerment, exploitation, and male-female relations in contemporary society. Moreover, I saw that this realm of exotic dance, at precisely the time when Marie entered the industry, was coincidentally making more and more incursions into the mainstream of popular culture. Accordingly, this book isn't just about strippers. As I did the research, I realized that the book needed to address this impact of "striptease culture" on the wider popular culture. As a result, the book is about the complexities and ambivalences of sex-positive popular culture, particularly in regards to our cultural attitudes toward the sexuality of girls and women. Or to put it another way, more and more I realized that stripping wasn't just about strippers, but was about Everywoman.

Exotic dancers are interesting because they illuminate Everywoman, as just a more curvaceously enhanced version of her. What the stripper does and the pressures she is under to look and act a certain way are the same pressures under which Everywoman operates, but in more exaggerated form. It is precisely this exaggeration that allows us to see more clearly the workings of gender. Just as Freud studied neurotics because their exaggerated psychological traits permitted him to see more easily how the mind works and thereby to develop a theory of human psychology, so too studying exotic dance allows us to see more clearly how gender works as a regulatory system that is transmitted, performed, and enforced by the culture. It is a system whereby we arrange and stratify society, act out and repress fantasy and desire, exercise and abuse power, exert and resist authority. Gender does all that and more, and exotic dance is the perfect Petri dish from which to study its workings. In the putatively sex-positive pop culture of the twenty-first century, amidst the gender upset over meanings of "masculinity" and "femininity," and in all our glorious baroque confusion over male-female gender relations, the strip club and striptease culture have become key places of experimentation and questioning in which we try to figure out what constitutes a liberated woman and an enlightened man. The chapters in the first part of this book are all devoted to an exploration of these issues by focusing on the life and work of the strippers themselves and of the stripping industry.

The book's second half then broadens the scope of inquiry to the wider popular culture and asks about the meaning and role of exotic dance in contemporary society. Chapter 5 investigates what the stripping industry reveals about the increasingly sexualized tenor of our times, wherein the stripper look has gone mainstream and exotic dance paradoxically both flourishes and is condemned. What does it mean that striptease culture is spreading like wildfire as everyone is now taking it off in the name of political protest, charity fund-raising, aerobic workout, personal empowerment, and good old-fashioned fun? Chapter 6 looks at efforts to organize dancers through unions and professional associations as the profession becomes ironically – and somewhat tragically – both more socially acceptable and more sexually hardcore (partly because of increased competition from the entry of additional young women into the industry). It examines the link to prostitution here and raises the larger question, "What makes sex ethical?" Finally, on this question of the broader social and cultural meaning of stripping, various comments by dancers and others lead me to explore in Chapter 7 whether religious scripts might provide some of this meaning. By "religious scripts," I have in mind long-standing religious narratives, myths, or archetypes that have become embedded in our wider culture and that we use to assign meaning to behavior. I am thinking here of stories about the fallen good woman (Eve), or the wicked dancing temptress (Salome, with her Dance of the Seven Veils), or the magical female being who is sexually independent and life-giving (the Goddess). In particular, I look at the connection of sex work to a type of "goddess spirituality" that finds in women's sexuality and the naked female form a playful, powerful, creative, and healing force.

My talks with Marie thus eventually led me to the idea of writing this book about stripping and its current major impact on society based on interviews with the dancers themselves. I wanted a chance to explore the complexities and ambiguities of the profession and to try to figure out this new world in which Marie had involved herself and which was increasingly intersecting with the mainstream. My goal was to explore the culture's fascination with stripping while coming to grips with my own, with neither bias nor ridicule.

The following pages are the result.

* * * *

This book is based, in part, on in-depth interviews with women who are current or former exotic dancers in the United States and Canada. The interview research was reviewed and approved by the Institutional Review Board for the Protection of Human Subjects at the University of Alabama. I interview the dancers using an open-ended questionnaire in order to elicit their stories of what they do, how they got into it, and what they think about their work. My friend Marie agreed to act as my principal informant and introduced me to many of the other dancers with whom I spoke. These women were generous with their time and quite willing to reflect on their work and its role in their lives and in society. In addition, I talk with other people identified as knowledgeable and willing informants, such as neo-burlesque performers; political organizers in the sex workers' rights movement; other sex workers such as prostitutes; strip club patrons; the boyfriends or husbands or lesbian partners of some of the dancers; and DJs and bouncers at the clubs. I interview a total of about forty people from the areas of West Palm Beach, Florida; Tuscaloosa and Birmingham, Alabama; Atlanta; San Francisco; Toronto; and Ottawa. Some of the interviews are formal, sit-down taped events of one to two hours duration, conducted in my office, at a restaurant, or interviewee's home, or by phone, and sometimes then repeated with the same person at a later date and followed up with email clarifications. Other interviews are briefer and more informal talks with people whom I meet through the clubs during the five years in which I conduct research for this book. In addition, many colleagues, friends, and even minor acquaintances also provide opinion, insight, and anecdotes whenever I mention my research topic and often end up functioning as informal interviewees themselves. The majority of people, it turns out, seem to have a stripper story to share.

To conduct these interviews, observe the dancers, and get a sense of the variety of venues within the stripping industry, I visit a total of eight clubs in the U.S. and Canada, and interview dancers from four other clubs. These clubs range from upscale urban establishments, to obscure suburban holes-in-the-wall, to lower-end local hang-outs. Each club operates in a different regulatory environment such that they vary from no-contact establishments to full-grind naked lap-dance clubs. In the book, I change the names of all of the dancers (except for Marie, who chose to use her name) and of Marie's club (Mr. Lucky's Lounge, in this book), in order to protect the confidentiality of the people whom I interview. Through the Capstone Poll (a unit of The University of Alabama that conducts survey research), I also obtain quantitative telephone survey data in 2002 from 484 representatively-chosen respondents on public perceptions about women who work as exotic dancers.

Part I

The Strip Club

–1–

Stripping: Demeaning and/or Empowering?

How I Got a Titty Rub, or My Introduction to the World of Stripping

I'm sitting in Mr. Lucky's Lounge in Florida. This is not a high-level "gentleman's club," but it's not a particularly seedy one either. Mr. Lucky's falls in the mid-range and attracts a mixed clientele of regulars, bachelor-party patrons, and tourists and businessmen. It's the end of March, and I'm spending my spring break touring the strip clubs of West Palm Beach and interviewing dancers. I'm in West Palm because this is where Marie now lives and works; it turns out that the area is a better market for dancing than was her small Midwestern college town. Marie is setting up interviews for me this week with a number of her fellow dancers. Various male colleagues at the university back in Tuscaloosa sent me off with good-natured jokes about volunteering to act as research assistants: "Bring back pictures of your trip!" they said, faking dirty-old-man snickers. When I told one of my senior colleagues how I was going to spend my spring break, he sputtered – laughing, charmed, a little shocked, jealous? – "And what would you say if I announced that?" My women colleagues have reacted differently. None has asked for photos. While apparently not interested in seeing naked women, they are interested in seeing into these women's lives. Some immediately focused on the "girl-power" theme of the project, of a woman claiming and using her sexuality for profit. Others are more skeptical. But all – including, to be fair, many of the men – see it as a legitimate women's-studies project that tells a story of contemporary women's lives and experience.

I'm aware that this project lets me get away with something that my male colleagues couldn't, and that's part of what amuses me about the book. My credentials as a feminist professor and a heterosexual woman (married, with two little boys) protect me from public charges of prurience and voyeurism to which they would be more vulnerable, unless my colleagues happened to be out gay males (which they're not). But I do wonder and worry as well: is this fair? Am I betraying feminist ideals by using that credential to legitimize the work of strippers? And am I deluding myself by denying my own vulnerability as a junior, non-tenured public university professor working on a controversial topic in a conservative and religious region of the country? When I started this project, the state's Southern

Baptist majority had just defeated a proposal to allow a lottery in Alabama; what would the good citizens of the state do if they knew that their tax dollars were helping to fund my research trip through West Palm strip clubs? These are the questions that occupied me on the plane out here, but right now, I'm just trying to sort out the gender and power dynamics of the club itself.

This is my first-ever strip club, if you don't count the establishment with male strippers that I went to years ago with a group of semi-inebriated bridesmaids on the eve of my sister-in-law's wedding to my brother (more on that later). Marie is dancing tonight, and I'm here with her boyfriend, Jeff, and Anita, another of our good friends from Canada who has joined me for this trip. Jeff is acting as our required male escort since women generally aren't allowed into most strip clubs unless accompanied by a man. Although this rule is surely illegal, many places claim that they must maintain the restriction for fear that unescorted women might be prostitutes who would pose competition for their dancers and threaten the legal status of the club. Other concerns are that such women might be lesbians whose presence could make the male patrons uncomfortable by changing the club's sexual dynamics, or even that they could be jealous wives hot on the trail of straying mates (indeed, a dancer will later tell me a story about an angry wife smashing a chair across the table where she found her husband on the receiving end of a lap dance).

Tonight is the first time that I watch Marie dance, and I'm a little nervous about being with her at work, as well as about the club itself. How will I feel about seeing her take off her clothes? How will she feel about having me watch? I've certainly seen her naked before. As life-long friends, we've been without clothes in each other's presence in any number of situations, but all of them non-sexual and more or less private, such as in the locker room at gym class or changing into bathing suits at her cottage. This is another matter entirely. I feel somewhat awkward and wonder whether my presence will discomfit her at all, although as she greets us inside the club, she seems happy to see us and very much at ease.

My first impressions of Mr. Lucky's are that it's loud, dark, and cold. The air-conditioning is up high – some say, I'm later told, to encourage nipple-puckering among the dancers. Rock music blares, controlled by the DJ in a raised and screened booth above the back corner of the stage. The lighting is low, with black lights in strategic use around the club so that many of the strippers, in their day-glow costumes, shine like beacons in a cave. Marie is in a mock-1960s flower-child outfit. Her top is a sheer peasant style with frilled cuffs and a low scoop neckline. It is patterned in large neon orange and green daisies that glow under the lights, and I'm a little surprised when I realize that I can see her breasts through it. She wears a bright orange thong and clear plastic platform shoes that lift her heels five inches off the ground. Around her upper thigh is a white garter. There are bills already folded over it.

Despite all that, Marie has a "girl-next-door" look. She's not drop-dead gorgeous with a tiny waist, huge breasts, and masses of blond hair, as in classic stripper stereotypes. She's five foot seven and has shoulder-length brown hair and deep brown eyes. Her breasts are medium-sized and natural – unlike about half the dancers in the club whose bosoms are surgically enhanced – and she has a sturdy build, with strong shoulders and back. Her make-up is fairly light, just some glittery eye shadow and lipstick. She's pretty, with smooth white skin, even features, and a big, easy smile. As we settle at a table with her, a cocktail waitress comes over to take our drink order (hugely over-priced), and I gaze around.

For the most part, Mr. Lucky's looks like any other mid-range dance bar, except that the dance floor is a raised stage and that smiling semi-naked women are everywhere. The nudity is disconcerting, disorienting. I feel a little embarrassed and even threatened at first, although the place seems perfectly safe with its big bouncers and tame clients. The men aren't running around wild as I half expected in my lurid imaginings about the club and none has approached us or even made eye contact since we entered. (This remains true in all my site visits to the clubs.) I think it's simply the strangeness of the experience that is threatening, its violation of everyday norms and conventions. I've never seen such a display of female flesh, of naked beauty, of women charmingly, indiscriminately, offering their company to men.

In the dance clubs of my (admittedly limited, nerdy, much earlier on) experience, women were often warding men off, or they were at least discriminating in terms of those men to whom they paid attention. Men chased; women chose. Of course I know it's not always like that, that women can be sexually aggressive, but still, in a world where it's the men who hoot out the windows of passing cars, I am much more accustomed to women being wary and saying no. I guess I didn't realize that the dancers were going to be so *nice* to the guys, that they were selling female charm as much as dances. I hadn't thought it through that the women would appear so happy to be naked and accommodating toward the men in the club. It makes sense: guys are a lot less likely to buy dances from a stripper who is intimidating or cold or rude. Here, I could see that pretty much any man with money – no matter how homely or boring or obnoxious – was guaranteed the time and attention of a beautiful woman offering up to him the proximity of her naked young body and the fantasy of her desire, or at least her interest in him. I began to understand the appeal of the experience.

The club's main area consists of a stage and two large seating areas spreading back from the stage's front and right sides. The décor isn't as flashy as I might have expected: the walls are painted a dark blue and the seats are upholstered in a black fabric patterned in blue and purple. Most of these seats are chairs scattered around bar tables, but the wall at the back of the club is lined with a banquette separated by dividers into a series of small alcoves where the dancers perform lap dances. A long bar is situated at the front of the club, along with the "champagne rooms" that Marie shows me later. In these tiny private chambers, smoked-glass doors swing open into a space big enough for only a loveseat, a standing silver champagne bucket, and a few square feet of dancing room. Frankly, these rooms strike me as a little sinister and seedy – just what goes on here? – although everything looks clean and in good condition.

Tonight – a rather slow Friday – there are around forty or fifty customers in the club. Except for Anita and me, they are all men. I am curious as to who they are and why they're at the club, but no one type predominates. They range in age from their twenties on up to one man who appears to be in his seventies and who is laughing at a table with a blonde dancer in a red bikini. The men are mainly white, although Hispanic customers are also common. While most are casually dressed, some are in blue-collar work clothes and others in collar-loosened suits. Dancers, or "girls" as they are universally called in the industry, are everywhere. Marie says that because it's still early, there's an overlap right now of the early-evening and late shift girls. About thirty dancers roam the club, sitting with men at the tables, doing individual lap dances, taking turns performing three-song sets on the main stage, or hanging out with each other when there is no money to be made.

Almost immediately after our drinks arrive, Marie's turn in the dance rotation comes up. "Next on stage is the very sexy Foxy," booms the DJ, using Marie's stage name. The previous dancer, Maxine, a tall and muscular black woman, puts her silver thong back on and gets ready to collect her tips. Although set-ups vary from club to club depending largely on the legal restrictions of the county, there are generally three ways for a dancer to earn her money: the private champagne or V.I.P. rooms (where something like two hundred dollars buys you a half hour alone with your choice of dancer for conversation and dance; she pockets one hundred and fifty dollars – not that she has a pocket), the table or lap dance (often twenty dollars a song), and the tip rail. At Mr. Lucky's, the tip rail is an actual brass rail that runs all the way around the bottom of the square stage, except for a small break at the back where steps lead down to the floor. This brass rail separates the dancer from the customers who sit five or six to a side at the narrow counter ringing all four sides of the stage, which measures about eight feet along each side. Sitting at the tip rail – also fondly called pervert row or gyno row, the dancers later inform me – allows patrons a close-up view of the women onstage. As each dancer finishes her set, she puts her G-string or thong back on and then steps down into the aisle between the stage and the tip rail to gather her tips, generally a one-dollar bill from each patron sitting at the rail.

"Sorry, I've got to go," says Marie, getting up and adjusting the line of her thong and décolletage. As she mounts the stage steps, the thought pops into my head, "Could I do this? Would I want to? What would it be like?" The prospect doesn't seem to entice me much. I think I don't have enough of the exhibitionist in me to make it appealing. I'm also feeling rather matronly these days and conscious that my breasts, after two years of nursing, just aren't as perky as they used to be. The music begins, a rap number that seems a rather challenging accompaniment to an erotic dance, but Marie swings right into it. She had explained to me earlier that they always start the set with a fast song before winding down to the all-nude slow last song. "Dance" is perhaps not quite the right word for what the women do onstage. Marie struts and sashays onto the stage. She is swaying her hips, her breasts thrust forward and her buttocks out, her back arched by the towering heels she wears. As she works the stage from one corner to the other, she strokes her body suggestively, fingers splayed and lingering on breasts, hips, and lower belly. Then with one hand, she grabs hold of the bronze pole toward the front of the stage and swings around it, at first keeping her feet on the floor but then jumping up lightly to wrap her knee and ankle around the pole and spinning fast. The move makes her hair fly out behind her. She is smiling, making eye contact with the dozen or so men sitting around the stage, and looks great.

About a minute into the first song, she takes off her top. I admit I was expecting some tease here, a slow disrobing that would highlight the eroticism of the act, but Marie just grabs the peasant blouse by the hem, lifts it over her head, and tosses it to the back of the stage. As the night goes on, I see that this is how all the dancers perform the actual stripping of their work; clothes are shed in seconds flat. The only special attention put into the act of removing costumes is in ensuring that one doesn't trip and fall while doing so, and indeed, it's no easy task to slither out of a thong or hot pants while in stripper shoes. "Striptease" dancers, it seems, have become simply strippers, although I will later find out that the tease element is being revived in the "New Burlesque" movement in places like New York, New Orleans, and San Francisco.

The first song blends into the second, and Marie continues to dance in just her thong now, curving her body suggestively to the music, playing with her hair, using the pole to spin and pose. At one point, she stands with her back to the pole, reaches above and behind her to grip it with both hands, and then lowers herself slowly to the ground with her knees splayed outward. She squats, crotch open toward the audience on one side of the stage, and then thrusts her pelvis forward as she slowly pulls herself back up to her feet. She repeats the move facing the other side of the stage just as the third song, the slow one, starts. The DJ plays for her Phil Collins's "In the Air Tonight," an atmospheric and moody song that she uses to full advantage. Instead of rising back to her feet, she lets go of the pole and falls forward onto her hands and knees. She crawls seductively to the center of the stage, rocks forward to arch her back and then slowly rolls over onto the floor. Her legs, looking enormously long with the heels, rise straight in the air. She crosses her ankles in a teasingly demure move before lifting her pelvis and slipping off the thong, which she adds to the heap of her blouse.

Naked now, she scissors her legs open and shut as she again arches her back and stretches her arms behind her head. It strikes me that she looks like a woman lost in a fantasy of making love. Her hands mimic those of a lover caressing her body; her slow writhing suggests this invisible presence of an imagined partner. She appears sure of herself, very in control as she blends one languorous move seamlessly into another, but at the same time she looks abandoned and very, very sexy. The song ends, and Marie rises to her feet. We clap for her, as is the norm at the end of each dancer's set, and I wonder just what I'm applauding: her art? her athleticism? her eroticism? her gracious sharing of nudity and beauty? Is this a "legitimate" dance performance or is it an illicit sexual pantomime? Is it both, or neither? Just what has happened?

Marie slips back into her neon orange thong and makes way for the next dancer coming onstage. Later, she'll detail for me the art of collecting tips: "After we finish dancing, we step off the stage into the aisle and walk around the stage to greet each customer individually. Here is where we make the link from stage to money." This part of a dancer's work is important even though she doesn't earn much money from it, probably no more than twenty dollars a set, because by collecting tips she makes contacts with patrons that will ideally lead to private dances later in the evening. "When I reach a customer," Marie continues, "I stand in front of him and dance for a few seconds. Then I lean forward to collect my tip. Tips are taken several ways. I can lift the side strap of the bikini for the customer to slide a folded bill in and make this demure by turning sideways or very revealing by pulling the front of the bikini forward to let him get a glimpse of my pubic area. I can turn my back to him and lift the side strap to let him tip me from behind (good for ass men). Or, I can take the tip with my breasts." She explains to me that this takes considerable finesse if you don't want to get licked or bitten, as does happen occasionally to the unwary dancer. The technique requires you to hold your own breasts by the nipple (so the guy can't touch them), then lean forward so the tip touches your breastbone, and push the breasts toward each other to "grab" the bill. She describes this as "probably the most popular way to give tips among our customers; they place it with their hands, put it in their mouths, or just stick their noses forward and hand you the tip afterwards."

I'm sitting at our table toward the back of the club, watching Marie work the tip rail. I've never seen this breast-tipping technique before, which I later learn that the dancers call the "titty rub." My initial reaction is one of recoil. Here is one of my best friends sticking her breasts in the face of a stranger as both of them laugh! But then I wonder, am I just being a prude? Is this a playful celebration of sexuality badly needed in uptight and hypocritical America, where primetime TV shows like *Sex in the City*, *Desperate Housewives*, and *Seinfeld* reruns dramatize casual sex as fun, but where you can't advertise condoms? Do we need this outlet? Does it encourage good-humored appreciation for female beauty? Is it just a healthy form of sex education? I become aware of the patter of DJ Bill, who not only plays the music and introduces the dancers, but also adds comments to rev up the crowd. Right now he's doing his job, encouraging the men at the tip rail to hand over dollar bills to Marie. For weeks after, one comment that he makes stays with me: "Get those titties in your face," he says, "and life is good."

"That's our girl," says Jeff enthusiastically, bringing me out of my reverie. He surprises me then by adding, "Let's go tip her." I must admit, the thought hadn't occurred to me. He's been sitting at the table with Anita and me, watching Marie. He is relaxed, smiling and chatting and clearly enjoying himself. I don't know him well as I only met him yesterday, but he and Marie have been together for about two years now and she's never voiced a complaint about him. He is a successful local business owner with something of a teddy-bear physique: lots of wavy brown hair and just a little on the short and pudgy side. Jeff has so far defeated all the stereotypes that I arrived with about a man who dates a stripper. He is unassuming and funny, affectionate and respectful with Marie, a warm and easy-going host who cooks for us daily. The two of them clearly bask in each other's company. Jeff now looks proud of Marie, appreciative of her art, and not at all bothered by the fact that his girlfriend is standing near-naked in front of strangers and flirting with them – or pretending to – for money. I'm glad he sets the tone, because I don't quite know how to respond to all this.

We gather one-dollar bills and head down to the stage toward a row of three empty seats at the tip rail. When she gets to us, Marie greets us laughingly. Anita is first, and Marie strikes a cheeky pose turned to her side so that Anita can slide a bill under her thong strap. Jeff gets the "ass man" treatment. Marie smirks at him teasingly over her shoulder as she wiggles her bottom at him. He tucks his tip into her thong and gets a kiss on his cheek in thanks. Then it's my turn. I'm holding my money out, feeling rather off balance in an Alice-in-Wonderland sort of way. But I'm in the hands of a professional. Laughing again, Marie reaches out with both hands to pull my head between her breasts. She holds me there for a second, using her forearms to press my face into her cleavage, and gives me a little shake. I have a fleeting impression of warmth and softness. She then releases me, plucks the dollar from my hand, and turns to greet her next customer.

And that's how I got my titty rub.

"Demeaning or Empowering?" An Ethical Inquiry into the Meaning of Stripping

The answer to the question of whether stripping is "demeaning" or "empowering" will obviously differ for each dancer, often on a night-by-night basis, depending on her reasons for entering the industry and her experiences in it. Even if we understand these two terms as opposite ends on a continuum of evaluation, such an inquiry would still miss the complex, ambiguous, and often contradictory realities of women's work and lives as dancers. "Demeaning or empowering" is, like any dualistic question about a multifaceted area of human experience, impossible to answer and in fact misleading as posed, although it's a common enough question on the talk-show circuit. While I don't believe that stripping can be labeled in a black-and-white fashion as either necessarily degrading or as potentially liberating, I am nevertheless interested in what can be said about the industry as a whole and about how it shapes trends in our larger society. My questions in this book are thus more along these lines: what are the wider societal conditions that give the act of stripping meaning? What are the cultural, economic, and political forces that shape the experience of exotic dance, such that it comes to mean whatever it is taken to mean, by whomever – the dancers, the club patrons, and people in general? And on this last point, what is the significance of the fact that stripping has increasingly made such major incursions into society, such that, in a sense, we all now inhabit a "striptease culture"?

So why did Marie become a stripper, and I a university professor? Is there anything wrong with her choice of profession, anything to be regretted about her not finishing her degree and getting a job to teach college students? We make about the same salary (only because she works part-time and isn't a top-earner – if she were, she'd earn two to three times what I do). I have better benefits, but she has more flexibility in her schedule. I can continue all my working life as a professor whereas few women dance past their twenties or early thirties; however, this inevitability of career change for dancers may simply mirror the typical American pattern of the seven or so jobs held over a lifetime by the average worker. Marie may suffer a certain amount of social censure from working as a stripper, since the job is not one that's universally accepted as legitimate. A lot of people look down on strippers and see them as little different than hookers who ply their trade in a club instead of walking the streets. My profession, in contrast, is generally accorded fairly high value by society. On the other hand, I've been in social situations with Marie – dinner parties with fashionable thirty-somethings – where her mention that she's an exotic dancer galvanizes the group's interest and renders her the talk of the party. The disclosure that I teach college undergrads, I assure you, produces no such reaction.

This dual response of censure and titillated curiosity to the profession of stripper stems from changing social attitudes among the general public as exotic dance becomes increasingly mainstream. In the 1990s, at least three major motion pictures about stripping appeared: *Striptease*, *Showgirls*, and *Exotica*, not to mention the surprise hit about male stripping now turned into a touring theatrical production, *The Full Monty*. HBO has screened the popular series *G-String Divas* about the lives of dancers, and stripper aerobics classes have popped up in workout gyms across America. Stripper clothes and shoes, once hard to come by and available only through specialized stores, mail-order catalogues, or "costume ladies" who visited the clubs, are now much more readily accessible. Indeed, with a Victoria's Secret selling stripper-style lingerie in seemingly every suburban mall and with the "stripper look" ubiquitous among rock stars, Hollywood starlets, in music videos, and on fashion runways, one can ask who doesn't look like a stripper these days? Barbie is even now for sale dressed in sexy lingerie outfits. As the ex-dancer Lily Burana puts it in *Strip City* about her farewell tour across America: "In the past decade the stripper seems to have gone from a social outcast to a thonged 'whatever.'"[1]

This change is probably due not only to the increased presence of the stripper image in popular culture, but also to a general increased "sexualization" of contemporary culture itself. Television is airing some of its raunchiest seasons ever as network programming tries to compete with cable channels, and they both use sex to lure jaded viewers. In regards to sex, the cultural shock meter has been going steadily down. Media sociologist Brian McNair refers to this phenomenon as "striptease culture" in a book by the same name in which he argues that sexual imagery now pervades all aspects of capitalist society. Not only television, but also movies, pop music, contemporary art, advertising, health education and fundraising campaigns, "grrl power," and porno-chic fashion sensibilities all bear witness to this sexualization. The development is a positive one in McNair's estimation, and he takes the high visibility of sexuality as evidence for the advance of feminism, gay rights, and post-war liberalism, and as an important contributor to public health in an age of AIDS.

The role of the stripping industry in this general sexualization of society is, I soon learned, hardly a small one. There are nearly four thousand strip clubs in the United States collectively taking in an estimated fifteen billion dollars annually. According to various estimates, this number of clubs has increased between 30 and 100 percent from the late 1980s: business, in other words, is booming. In fact, according to *U.S. News and World Report*, "Americans now spend more money at strip clubs than at Broadway, off-Broadway, regional, and non-profit theatres; at the opera, the ballet, and jazz and classical music performances – combined." Exotic dance is, in other words, one of the major forms of paid performance in the United States today. The clubs are staffed by an estimated 250,000 women working as exotic dancers. The dancers, who are mainly in their twenties but range up into their forties, come from all walks of life and ethnicities. Similarly, the places they work run the gamut from big-city downtown "gentleman's clubs," to rural establishments frequented by locals, to a whole series of mid-level clubs sprinkled throughout the endless sprawl of urban America.[2]

Books about stripping abound now also. In just the last few years, more than a half dozen academic and trade books have suddenly come out on exotic dance, whereas before relatively little was written about the field. These recent books include articulate strippers' memoirs reflecting on the industry, such as Elisabeth Eaves' *Bare: On Women, Dancing, Sex, and Power* (2002) and Lily Burana's *Strip City* (2001), as well as the anthology *Flesh For Fantasy: Producing and Consuming Exotic Dance* (2006), edited by three university professors who are all former dancers. At least two graduate students researched their Ph.D. dissertations by working in clubs and then turned their theses into books. Katherine Frank wrote *G-Strings and Sympathy: Strip Club Regulars and Male Desire* (2002) based on a Ph.D. dissertation in cultural anthropology at Duke University and was a dancer herself for six years. Chris Bruckert worked as a dancer and club bartender while researching a dissertation in criminology that became *Taking It Off, Putting It On:*

Women in the Strip Trade (2002). And Katherine Liepe-Levinson's *Strip Show: Performances of Gender and Desire* (2002) comes from dissertation research in theater and performance studies, although she didn't work in the clubs themselves. Sociologist Bernadette Barton has also published *Stripped: Inside the Lives of Exotic Dancers* (2006), based on extensive club observation and dancer interviews. Add to these accounts theater professor Rachel Shteir's *Striptease: The Untold History of the Girlie Show* (2004) and David Scott's earlier *Behind the G-String: An Exploration of the Stripper's Image, Her Person, and Her Meaning* (1996), which to my knowledge is the first book-length academic analysis of contemporary stripping.

My interest, then, in investigating the phenomenon of stripping seemed to match several intertwined cultural trends toward more growth in the industry, more reflection about it in popular and academic literature, and more incursions of striptease culture into everyday life. When my friend got into the world of stripping I followed her – not as a stripper, but first as a concerned friend and then more and more as an observer and analyst. I read the literature and found that there were questions I wanted answered that I didn't find fully explored in these recent books.

For instance, my background as a university professor trained in religious studies equips me to look at the role of religion in culture. This realm of religion is often the realm in which people ask questions, or make assumptions, about values, ethics, and meaning. Once I started thinking about the stripping industry, my training predisposed me to ask such questions about values, ethics, and meaning in the world of stripping. Specifically, how are value systems constructed and communicated in this realm? What do the popularity of stripping and the life stories of exotic dancers tell us about how women are valued in modern America, especially women's bodies and their sexuality? What emerges when we submit these values to a process of ethical scrutiny? To what degree is stripping a way for women to gain and exercise power, and in what ways is it an unethical realm in which women are used and ironically stripped of their power? More generally, what does it *mean* to be a stripper? Clearly, you take your clothes off and dance – suggestively, erotically, teasingly – for an audience, who pays you money. But what is the deeper, symbolic, or cultural meaning of these actions: for the dancer and for the (mostly) male patrons?

As I first embarked on my venture into the world of stripping, probably the most basic question I started out with was this: *Can a woman freely choose sex work?* By "sex work," I mean the work of a prostitute, adult-film actor, phone-sex operator, peep-show performer, or – as in the segment of the industry that I examine – that of an exotic dancer. The worker offers a sexual service and is paid in return by the customer. Typically, but not always, this worker is a woman, and the client is a man. In other words, I wondered, can a woman make this decision not for all of the standard, stereotypical reasons that people presume are what motivates a stripper – low self-esteem, drug habit or alcohol addiction, promiscuity, history of sexual abuse – but because after weighing the benefits and drawbacks, she decides – like any other employee in any other industry – that stripping is a good job for her? Can she say, "Hey, I could be an office worker or a lawyer or a restaurant manager or a college professor or an engineer" – all actual career options of dancers I've spoken with – "but instead for now I want to work as a dancer"? *Can* stripping be in a woman's best interests? Not only her immediate financial interest, but can stripping be good for her emotionally, physically, sexually, spiritually, socially, intellectually – and not only now, but let's say even thirty years down the road in retrospect? Is there such a thing, to adapt the title of Xaviera Hollander's best-selling 1972 autobiography, as "the happy stripper," or is this just another tired stereotype and convenient male fiction?

These were my first questions, although as I proceeded with the research I soon came to see their limits. Is there anyone who "freely chooses" his or her profession? Was free choice involved in my decision to become a professor? My father teaches in a university, and I am not sure that it ever occurred to me to *not* earn multiple degrees in higher education. Is being a lawyer or a soldier or a cashier or a downhill-ski racer in any woman or man's "best interests"? In some ways yes, in others no; it's hard to tell, and it really just all depends. The messiness of the answer indicates the inadequacy of the questions, and so I tried to improve my queries as the study unfolded. I began to frame the inquiry differently: What are the conditions – material, cultural, and social – that shape a person's decision to do sex work? How does a woman understand this work and what does it come to mean for her? And what meanings does it take on in the wider culture?

All these, then, are the questions that set me off on a journey out of the ivory tower of academia and into the field – into the strip clubs – to find out.

Stripping, Sexism, and Consumerism

After Marie dances, Jeanette comes off the stage next. She's a beautiful Philippine woman, slim and quite petite but muscular, with dusky skin, highcheek bones, and long black hair falling down her back. As she makes the circuit to collect her tips, she smiles and laughs a lot and appears very sweet. In a later interview, however, Jeanette insists, "I don't feel bad about taking their last dollar, because you know it doesn't matter how nice they are, if you were outside the club, they'd rape you. They'd rape you in a second." She is dead serious, shaking her finger, her voice intent and angry. But at the moment, she is holding a man's head between her naked breasts, face tilted back and laughing like she loves it, the very picture of a happy woman. Juxtaposing these images of Jeanette leads me to ask: is there a problem here? The two most common objections to stripping are that it degrades human sexuality and intimacy by turning them into commercial transactions and that it objectifies women in a sexist and demeaning way. These critiques invoke the twin evils of consumerism and misogyny, or of capitalism and patriarchy. While the entire book explores this critique in one way or another, the rest of this first chapter opens up these two issues to begin digging deeper into the meaning of stripping for the women who do it and for the society in which it flourishes.

On this point, the moment of the "titty rub" becomes a test case for me. Many people would say that some of the other things strippers do – friction dances, for instance, where they rub against customers' laps – are "worse," but for me, it is this moment that violates the most taboos. I think it's partly because I had only recently stopped breast-feeding my child, an experience I couldn't help but recall while watching. What the exotic dancer does with a customer in quick playful parody, I had done in earnest for many long months, nestling my baby's head to my breast. "Get those titties in your face, and life is good" is the mantra of the breast-feeding infant. Does the titty rub fondly recall that experience or grossly devalue it, and devalue also the experience of sexual intimacy between two lovers?

And if there is a problem here, is the problem so much patriarchy or is it more consumerism? Is the problem sexism or is it commodification? We live in an advertising culture where communications scholars tell us we are now bombarded by 3,600 "commercial impressions" a day, that is 3,600 daily appeals to us as people with money to spend.[3] These appeals come in such forms as TV, radio, and print commercials; billboards; storefront signs; and even corporate logos on clothing. In the strip club, a woman's naked or semi-naked body counts as one such commercial impression. When I see a woman rubbing her breasts on either side of a man's face – a stranger's face or even the face of a regular customer – for *one dollar*, I really have to wonder whether that's making a commodity out of something that shouldn't be. Are there some things that just shouldn't be sold?

Elisabeth Eaves, for example, an ex-dancer at the Lusty Lady peep show in Seattle who wrote the memoir *Bare: On Women, Dancing, Sex, and Power*, recounts a story about a friend who comments that he likes the idea of women dancing around naked, but that he doesn't want to have to pay for it. She says that her first response was disdainful: "Of course you don't want to pay, you want it for free." But she then criticizes her own reaction as a problematic one typical of a sex worker: "I had accepted a lesson that I wished I hadn't – namely that a woman's appearance should have a price tag." In the end, she concludes that "all sexuality for profit was insidious" and that she "didn't want to live a world where women's bodies, images, or characters were treated as something to buy." And so she quit.[4]

The objection to stripping here is that it cheapens or even deadens a precious part of oneself. Human sexuality is natural and healthy, the argument goes, and indeed presents exquisite pleasures, but these pleasures are best enjoyed in private, ideally in an intimate and loving relationship with a partner. The stripper flouts this norm by publicly selling the fantasy of her sexual availability and desire for the customer (although in her personal life, she may well be married or with a steady partner, whether male or female). Through the profession's commodification of sexuality – and of women's sexuality in particular – is stripping thus sexist and immoral, or simply demeaning: to the woman, to the man, to human sexuality itself? Does selling access to your breasts, to your body, to your sexuality, denigrate this central aspect of our humanity? Is stripping an inappropriate public and commercial display which devalues and belittles the intimacy that is more properly reserved for private and noncommercial relationships?

Most of the dancers I've talked to say no, not at all. They say stripping is playful, it's fantasy, it's power, it's getting back at men, it's having fun with men, it's just a job like any other job. Marie says that the titty rub in particular is where she has fun with her customers. If he wears glasses, she tells him "Now you see the world through breast-colored glasses!" If he's bald, she rubs his head with her breasts. If a man and woman are seated together at the tip rail, as occasionally happens, she'll laughingly do a titty rub on the woman, as a joke, to relax her. Indeed, the titty rub, as opposed to a lap dance, seems always done in laughter on the part of both dancer and patron. It's a deliberately silly and fun moment shared between the two.

So maybe I'm missing the point. Maybe we're all selling something most of the time. Men have always been allowed greater sexual freedom and experimentation than women. Am I simply surprised here at women's usurpation of traditional male freedoms, at women daring to say "No, I won't reserve my breasts and body for the exclusive enjoyment of my partner or baby; I'll use them as I damn well please for my own amusement and enrichment, both financial and emotional"? Am I just repeating the same oppressive bourgeois morality over which strippers and other sex workers protest by joining outfits such as COYOTE ("Call Off Your Old Tired Ethics") or the Exotic Dancers Alliance (with separate organizations in San Francisco and Toronto), all sex-workers' rights groups that seek to improve working conditions and increase public acceptance of sex work (as discussed in Chapter 6)?

And when we ask whether stripping is demeaning by turning beauty and sexuality into commodities or whether it is sexist in its treatment of women, we have to ask "compared to what?" We're all judged by our looks all the time, men as well as women. According to recent research, the pay gap between women and men managers actually *widened* in the 1990s.[5] Many women are stuck in dead-end, "pink-collar" service jobs. Sexual harassment happens in all workplaces, not just in a strip club. Sexual violence is commonplace: one out of every four women in America will be sexually assaulted at some point in her life.[6] Sexual objectification happens everywhere. There may not be a woman in America who hasn't had the experience of walking down a street and having a car full of men drive by yelling catcalls or obscenities at her. It happened to me, not for the first time, just a few months ago here in Tuscaloosa.

Given all of that, is stripping in any sense worse? Does it make the situation for women in America any worse? Is stripping so different from being a fashion model, or a pop singer, or a dancer/back-up singer in a music video, or a flight attendant, or a cocktail waitress? Christina Aguilera, for example, left no doubt about the association with her 2002 album *Stripped* and its hit single "Dirrty." Is exotic dance even so different from being a university professor? My career as a teacher reduces the life of the mind to a market commodity, and no one is complaining about that. My work is objectified and commodified by yearly "Faculty Activity Reports," filled out by my superiors, that quantify my value on a scale of 1 to 6. There are ways in which my teaching is devalued by the academy's pressure to publish. And if I think strippers are engaged in a demeaning commodification, am I not simply further commodifying them by seeking to write and sell a book about them? Do professors objectify and use their research subjects, similar to the way in which men objectify dancers in a club, but without having the courtesy to pay them twenty dollars a song for it?

Barbarella's and the Westminster Kennel Club Dog Show

A couple of months later, I'm in Ottawa. I had arrived back just a few days earlier. My family and I are here to spend the summer in the area. Before we head up to the cottage we've rented, I go with some friends – including a male friend – to a downtown club called Barbarella's Diamonds. Barbarella's bills itself as "Ottawa's Finest V.I.P. Cabaret." Marie is working here for the summer, again under the stage name Foxy, and is dancing this evening. Later this week, I'll interview Mia, one of the other dancers who works with her at the club.

Marie decided to come to Ottawa for the summer since West Palm Beach is now in its slow off-season. Business is better in Ottawa, and she also wanted to spend time with her father, divorced from her mother and living in a townhouse in our old neighborhood in Ottawa. He's invited her to share the house with him for the summer. She has told him that she is working as a stripper and is gratified that he hasn't said anything critical to her about her choice of occupation. On the other hand, he hasn't said anything positive either. She says she'd like to talk with him about her work, but has the impression that he is too uncomfortable with the topic for her to risk broaching it. Her work is the proverbial pink elephant in the living room – thonged and betasseled – that neither of them mentions.

Despite that, she's enjoying working in Ottawa. She's making about three hundred dollars per night here, as opposed to the hundred dollars she was averaging in the summer last year in West Palm. True to Canadian stereotype, she reports that the men are more polite as well, not as aggressive or obnoxious as her American customers. Too often in the U.S. she would hear from a customer, "You're not like the average stripper; you're actually smart and interesting." After this back-handed compliment, the man more often than not then wouldn't buy dances from her. DJ Bill in Florida had told her that she needed to learn to act dumb. In Ottawa, however, she finds she can talk with the patrons and they still want dances. The Canadian men also seem to better appreciate her body type, with her broad shoulders and pretty but average looks. In Florida, she says, the men tended to go for the girls with the big breast implants and exaggerated tiny waists, or with the really muscular look. Here, the guys whistle when she walks on stage and pay her compliments about how she's a "real woman, with a real body."

Tonight at Barbarella's Diamonds we're with Anita as well. My husband Ted didn't want to come to the club with us. He's not comfortable with the stripping industry and, as it turns out, never goes with me to any of the clubs that I visit. He's very supportive of my project, but says that he doesn't want to support the industry itself, which he finds problematic. I'm the only woman that he wants to see naked, he sweetly informs me, and really, how can I argue with that? So we recruit an old friend to act as our male escort for the evening. Victor is a tall, sandy-haired artist recently back from Europe and soon heading out to Vancouver to work on film crews. He went to high school with us all, and as Marie takes a break and joins us at our table at the club, it is a bit of a high school reunion.

Despite the V.I.P. billing, Barbarella's isn't that fancy a place. It's rather like a mid-range sports bar constantly playing rock music that just happens to feature naked women dancing on a stage. You enter into a squarish room, with the stage straight ahead. A bar counter and barstools surround the stage on three sides, with a dozen tables and chairs scattered around the rest of the floor. A vinyl banquette lines the far right and left walls of the main room, and a black curtain hangs in the middle of the left wall, draping the entrance to the semi-private champagne rooms. A large-screen TV is built into the wall behind the stage, and two smaller TVs hang from the ceiling in the corners of the left wall. On two of these TVs, baseball is playing, but on the one above our heads TSN is covering the Westminster Kennel Club Dog Show, live from Madison Square Garden in New York City. As we sit and order drinks, the dog show adds a surreal backdrop to the spectacle of the strip club, and I crane my neck back and forth to watch both.

The sound on the TV isn't turned on, and I know nothing about dog shows and not that much about dogs, so I have to piece together a lot of what is happening on the screen. A caption appears to indicate that the short, massive-chested dog I'm looking at is a leatherneck bull mastiff. Its handler is similarly short and broad. She is an older blond woman, dressed in a floor-length black evening gown with a full chiffon skirt. She runs with the bull mastiff on a leash around the floor of the event area, I assume to demonstrate the dog's paces and style. She and the other handlers also arrange their dogs in spread-legged stances and then reward them for maintaining the stance with tidbits of food that the handlers seem to keep stashed in the pockets of their evening wear. As the dogs pose, the judges run their hands over the dogs' bodies and into their mouths, evaluating, I presume, condition of the teeth, muscle tone, depth of the chest, quality of the coat, and obedience of the dog. This biddableness of temperament is clearly key, as the dog must permit itself to be thus examined and stroked, not in affection, but in brisk judgment and by a stranger in front of what must have been an audience of thousands. There was also a tall poodle, or maybe it was an Afghan, that I swear had its hair coiffed in Rastafarian dreadlocks. It posed especially tranquilly for the judges and the cameras.

Meanwhile, the show of the strip club continues to unfold around me. About twenty young women, including Marie/Foxy, move about the club in slinky stripper outfits on five- and six-inch heels. They are laughing and talking with the customers and with each other, arranging table dances or time in a champagne room, and taking their turns dancing on stage: first to two faster songs where they peel off the top of their outfits to expose their breasts, and finally to a slow song during which they take off all their clothes – except for the shoes, never the shoes – and dance naked onstage to the music.

Stripping and Feminism

Many people have a problem with stripping. People in general frequently view the whole stripping industry with suspicion, as unsavory, bad for communities, and implicated in a generally seedy lifestyle. Some feminists tend to strike an alliance on this point with moralists from the religious right and from the ranks of social conservatives: both such feminists and moralists alike generally find the profession of exotic dancer to be problematic, although for different reasons. As David Scott notes in *Behind the G-String*, the moralist sees the stripper's presentation of "unbridled eroticism" as posing the danger of undermining both individual and social morality.[7] Feminists, on the other hand, are concerned that stripping exposes vulnerable young women to the dangers of drug and alcohol addiction, assault, organized crime, poor labor conditions, and coercion into prostitution. The composite picture of all these perceptions is a stereotype that dancers often complain is falsely applied to them: strippers are prostitutes and drug-addicts who are exploited and degraded by men and who are either too stupid or too low in self-esteem to recognize and escape their exploitation. Even barring such problems, many feminists' concern is that stripping simply represents the appropriation of female sexuality for men's gratification and that it demeans women. Thus, the standard feminist response to stripping – as well as to other forms of sex work and to pornography in general – is to condemn the stripping industry as yet another sign that we live in a patriarchal society, wherein women are still viewed and valued as sex objects for male pleasure. Even if some women can turn this situation to their immediate advantage by capitalizing on their stripper appeal, the existence of the industry itself still harms women overall by contributing to societal expectations that women should be young, thin, busty, groomed, ever-eager for a man's attention, and wanting nothing more than to writhe naked on his lap.

Susan Griffin, for example, whose passionate and poetic book *Woman and Nature* came to mind as I sat in Barbarella's, has a chapter called "The Show Horse" about how society contributes to woman's voicelessness and powerlessness by assigning her the role of well-trained and well-groomed gratifier of her master's desire. The Show Horse – or the show dog – is the woman who finds her pleasure in her master's visual and physical pleasure in "riding her" and showing her off. Her power derives solely from the extent to which she pleases her master. In Griffin's analysis, this dynamic is part of how patriarchal culture treats women as less fully human than men. Not socialized or recognized as full subjects with will and agency of their own, women are broken in to patriarchy like a horse. They are trained to see themselves through the eyes of men and to devote themselves to fulfilling men's sexual fantasies. Griffin's analysis fits perfectly here as an analysis of my experience at Barbarella's and as a condemnation of striptease culture in general.

Yet at the same time, that moment in Barbarella's makes me think too about the contemporary burlesque performer Suzanne Ramsey and her rollicking song "Pony Girl." Ramsey is a talented pianist, comedic singer/songwriter, and – in her better known persona as Miss Kitten on the Keys – mistress of ceremony for the national neo-burlesque convention Tease-O-Rama (discussed in more detail in Chapter 4). Kitten on the Key's performance style is a combination of wide-eyed cheesy innocence ("Golly, wasn't she just so beautiful and elegant?") and the raunchiest, most politically-incorrect piano lounge music that one can imagine. "Pony Girl," for example, is a wild romp that embraces the groomed submissiveness of Griffin's analysis while parodying it with over the top, tongue-in-cheek excess: "I'm your pony girl in training/ A dainty filly it is true," Kitten sings, "Rigid mane and silky tail/ And I'm smarter than Lassie too!" (a claim she punctuates with a perky "Ruff!"). "My hoofies go clip-clop/ Your riding crop gets me HOT!" Kitten mocks the patriarchal model while gently mocking also the well-meaning feminist critique of it: she can choose to be the Pony Girl but she is also the creative agent who makes the Show Horse into an object lesson in how to dismantle the master's house with the master's tools (to turn around Audre Lorde's famous phrase). In other words, if what we're offered by the Ringmaster is the role of the Show Horse, why not take that role and use it to poke fun at the master and at the Show of Patriarchy itself?[8]

Translating Kitten's chirpy submission-domination erotica into feminist exposition might render a text something like this: "You tell us that we have to be the Show Horse? I'll do you one better, stress the infantalization even more, and become Pony Girl! I'll take your rules and roles and inhabit them with such parodic excess that anyone with half a brain and a sense of humor will be able to see the Show of Compliant Femininity for what it really is – just an act, an ideology that we can be conditioned to believe is our true nature as women, but one that is really no more than a fantasy creation. This ideology of submissive femininity is certainly oppressive, but only when one is forced to live it for real and for always. If you don't have to take it seriously, you can actually have a hoot playing with it!" If the Show Horse reduces women to less than complete subjects who are trained to voicelessness, then the Pony Girl has figured out the game and now turns it on its head: she adopts the role in full consciousness, as feisty subject and creative agent with a voice that now soars, snorts, and chirps. When Kitten performed this and other songs at Tease-O-Rama 2005 in San Francisco, the audience lapped it up with roars of approval, laughter, and extended applause. "Feed me hay and alfalfa/ Apples lumps of sugar too/ I'll be your pony girl forever/ Never put me in the zoo!" Griffin is right, but Kitten is on to something too.

Here, then, is another type of feminist response. From this other perspective, strippers are simply smart women cashing in on what patriarchy most values in a woman and, moreover, having fun doing it. This response comes from "sex-positive" or "sex-radical" feminists who often also defend pornography and prostitution as at least potentially empowering and legitimate, under the right circumstances, for the women who choose these professions. Feminists who adopt this perspective view sexuality as one of the great and pleasurable realms of a woman's power – if properly wielded. Two fairly recent feminist anthologies are examples of this genre: Jill Nagle's *Whores and Other Feminists* (1997) and Frédérique Delacoste and Priscilla Alexander's second edition of *Sex Work: Writings by Women in the Sex Industry* (1998). Stripping is clearly problematic in at least one way, these sex-positive feminists agree: it lacks social and professional support. Accordingly, they seek to improve job conditions for strippers through unionization, lobbying efforts, and the sex-workers' rights organizations that I will examine more thoroughly in Chapter 6. On this front, they are happy to see that stripping is now more socially accepted than even ten years ago.

Sex-positive feminists make the argument that if the name of the game is patriarchy, then one way to win the game is to use that which patriarchy most values in a woman – namely her youth and beauty – to make as much money as possible off the men who come into the clubs. If we live in a society that places such high value on women's physical appearance, are strippers simply very clever at making the system work for themselves? Have they figured out how to beat patriarchy at its own game? Exotic dancers can manage to achieve economic freedom in a society that still pays women only about eighty cents on the dollar compared to pay for men's labor. *For a woman without higher education, exotic dancing is the single most lucrative legal profession open to her.* Although money is by no means everything, this is not an insignificant fact. Speaking as a woman who has had fifteen years of higher education, I doubt I'll ever earn more in one year than a top-earning, high school drop-out stripper, although I may well earn more over a lifetime, since few dancers continue into their late thirties. Yet even this lifetime-earning potential may be in some cases similar, since I've talked to a fair number of strippers who go on to finish college degrees, become working professionals or businesswomen, or marry middle-class men. Are strippers then simply women who dare to reject patriarchal restrictions on their sexuality and economic worth? Many dancers with whom I've talked are indeed generally happy with what they're doing – as much as most people are about their jobs – and sex-positive feminism is one theoretical framework that affirms their choice of profession.

When I began the research for this book, I had this twofold focus: first, on an ethical and values-based inquiry into the meaning of stripping and second, on bringing a feminist perspective to that inquiry. I have long been committed to such a feminist perspective, by which I mean that I share the belief that we live in a society still unfairly shaped by patriarchy. A woman's value more than that of a man's *is* measured in terms of her youth and beauty; greater economic opportunities *are* generally available to men than to women; and most political and economic positions of power *are* still held by men. Furthermore, I agree with the basic claim made by researchers in the field of gender studies that women's stories have been unfairly excluded from much of written history. Thus, I am convinced that the fullest interpretation of exotic dance must involve talking with dancers and paying careful attention to their own stories. In this sense, I seek to give voice to women's experience, to "hear them into speech." It is for this reason that I decided early on to conduct in-depth interviews with exotic dancers.

But on the specific question of what to make of stripping, as I've noted, feminism can point in either direction, or in both directions at once. Although I started my venture into the world of exotic dancing committed to neither form of feminist response, the more interviews I did and the more I read, the more sympathetic I became to the sex-positive feminist viewpoint.

I use this viewpoint to explore the extent to which dancers are subverting and resisting patriarchal norms, perhaps even at the same time as they are replicating them. One of my central curiosities is the degree to which stripping can be empowering – economically, emotionally, sexually, spiritually – for the women involved, or can be perceived by them and others as empowering. Another, perhaps more subtle, way to put the question asks: what is it about the current cultural milieu, the material and social conditions in which we live our lives in contemporary North American pop culture, that makes exotic dance into an acceptable or meaningful choice of profession for so many young women and that makes striptease culture so widespread and popular itself?

I have proceeded on the assumption that the best way to explore all of these questions is, in the first place, by talking with dancers about what they do and why they do it, by listening to their own stories about their work, and by judging its impact on their sense of self. I then pose questions about the deeper or long-term meaning of the dancers' experiences and about the overall effects of striptease culture on the value systems of contemporary popular culture. I present my judgments and I invite readers to make their own, as the dancers' narratives unfold.

What emerges from the stories for me is an ambiguous and complex picture of power, pleasure, agency, and fantasy in the lives of dancers and in the broad realm of pop culture today.

–2–

The Work of a Stripper: Six-inch Heels and Pole Tricks

The Flying Body Spiral

While I am in West Palm Beach with Marie and Jeff, they take Anita and me on a tour of several other area clubs within an hour's drive of their house. By the end of my visit and another return trip the following year, I've interviewed or talked informally with about two dozen dancers, including a handful of dancers' partners, patrons, and club workers, and worked my way through clubs ranging from the upscale to the low down. The lessons about exotic dance continue to unfold.

On my second full day in town, we plan a club crawl and head first that evening to another midrange place named Pearls. Even while we are still in the car, I worry about the ambition of the schedule that we have laid out and wonder whether I can handle it. The experience of the clubs is so new to me that there is a quality of emotional assault to it. The night before, at Mr. Lucky's, I had felt somewhat battered by the end of the evening: edgy, delicate, a little shell-shocked. The ever-present cigarette smoke didn't help either, since I have never learned to smoke. (That is, except for the occasional cigar enjoyed in the company of two dear women friends as we were all finishing our dissertations during that period when Demi Moore graced the cover of *Cigar Aficionado* magazine. At the time, it seemed any legal act that helped one to finish a Ph.D. was acceptable, and to be encouraged. My father even started buying me cigars.) It took me hours after leaving the club last night to unwind enough to get to sleep. Jeff and Anita felt the same way and went out dancing to dispel some energy while Marie finished up her shift, but I was too drained for what just seemed like more noise, smoke, and glitter. Instead, I tried to relax by watching a video from Marie's collection back at their house. I put on *Strictly Ballroom*, a gypsy-girl-meets-Australian-boy, ugly-duckling-to-swan film about finding love on the ballroom floor. I think I was hoping that the mythic narrative of the love story – naive innocence blooms into passion and happily ever after; true love conquers all, including cultural difference, interfering parents, and klutzy feet – would balance the counternarrative of the strip club: innocence long fled, passion a commodity to be bought, love an illusion. I am not saying that these tropes constitute the whole narrative of the strip club, or even that there's anything wrong with such a narrative, but it had been a long night and I had a lot to process.

When we arrive at Pearls in a nondescript commercial neighborhood not far off the highway, I gird my loins – so to speak – and we head inside. The club's layout is a large rectangular room. The middle of the floor is taken up by the smaller rectangle of the raised stage, with a short catwalk leading to a backstage door at the rear of the club from which the dancers emerge. The DJ's control booth is tucked up next to the catwalk, and he introduces the dancers and orchestrates the crowd response throughout the evening. Four poles line the stage, more than at any other club I visit. A long bar lines the front wall, and two semi-private alcoves are tucked into the corners of the room. In one of these champagne rooms, we can see a dancer half straddling and lying on top of a man reclined on a couch. He languidly strokes her back as they barely change positions for almost an hour. Marie tells me that such an interaction would not be permitted at Mr. Lucky's. While Pearls is more lenient in this regard, Marie also explains that despite the private room license here, the club has a policy of no contact while tipping dancers at the stage. I won't be getting any titty rubs tonight.

This variation in set-up is one thing that I am learning about the clubs: they tend to have different policies regarding the extent of physical contact permitted between patrons and dancers, as well as the degree of nudity exhibited by the women. Some clubs are topless only, while others offer full nudity (as in the iconic blinking neon proclamation "Live Nude Girls!"). Strippers sometimes have to dance on a stool and maintain a prescribed distance from a patron at all times; some nude clubs allow a lap dance but require a dancer to put her thong back on to perform it. The customer may be allowed to touch the dancer's shoulder or arm but not her leg or breast, unless he pays more for such privileges in the V.I.P. room. Some places allow a "nude friction dance" – the Holy Grail of extreme lap dances in which a woman will grind naked on her customer's lap – whereas in other places this service is prohibited as akin to prostitution.

Some of these rules are set by local city and county governments or state regulations, some are related to the club's liquor license (full-contact nudity and alcohol are often a prohibited combination), and some are determined by the club's own management. The individual dancers can also set their own standards of what they will and will not do and whether under certain conditions (for a favored regular and enough money) they are willing to bend the rules. Clubs vary as well on how strictly they police the women to enforce these codes of behavior. Some employ bouncers, DJs, and security cameras to monitor closely clients' interactions with the dancers, and pride themselves on running a "clean" or "high-class" establishment; other places are known as "dirty" clubs where anything goes and where nothing short of a police raid will uphold the law. All of these variations can create understandable confusion for a patron. Marie says that the best of them will just straightforwardly ask one of the dancers when they arrive at a new club what the rules are and will then respect those parameters without trying to get around them with extra cash or by sneaking an unauthorized grab. These differences in what is permitted and the occasional possibility of negotiating private under-the-table arrangements also create competition among the women in the club: if one of them will break the rules in the privacy of a champagne room or a dark corner, such defiance can take customers away from others more inclined to compliance.

At Pearls, I spend five dollars for a ginger ale as our group settles into one of the round tables scattered around the floor on all sides of the main stage. To my left on a large flat-screen TV, naked women pleasure each other endlessly in a soft-porn video loop. About twenty five to thirty women – I find it so hard to call them girls, although that is how they universally refer to themselves and to each other – seem to be working at the club tonight, which isn't yet crowded with patrons but is beginning to fill up. More than one dancer is usually onstage at a time, with each covering a different part of the long stage. While they display somewhat more diverse body types than those at Mr. Lucky's, they are all still basically young and pretty. The women are mainly white, as is the clientele – all male except for my little group – but more so among the dancers there are a number of Asians, Hispanics, and African-Americans. Some – maybe half? – of the dancers seem to have had implant surgery, with the resultant large and suspiciously round, high-riding breasts, whereas the unenhanced bosoms range from flat-chested to naturally voluptuous. The women themselves vary from skinny (for example, a thin Asian woman with long legs, a boyish chest, and glasses) to somewhat overweight (a chunky white woman, sporting spiky dark hair and black hot pants, who does a great dance to a fast hip hop number).

We spend some time watching the stage shows and politely fending off the occasional dancers who approach our table to ask if we would like private dances. I start to appreciate how the women vary in their stage routines and self-presentation. Some focus on pole work and are very athletic and gymnastic. Some make a lot of eye contact and are clearly working the audience. A number of them interact mainly with each other, laughing and teasing among themselves onstage. Others are dreamy-looking with a mysterious little smile and an inward-focused sensuous style. And there are dancers who simply seem bored and who don't do much at all.

One, whom the DJ introduces as Candy, is a very slim and pale woman with improbably large breasts and waist-long white-blond hair that must have been a wig. She wears a pleated cheerleader miniskirt and specializes in skipping around the pole and swinging her straight hair out in a circle like a young girl. Watching Candy, I feel my unease with her pubescent spectacle and I think of the writing of sex worker and theorist Carol Queen in *Real Live Nude Girl: Chronicles of Sex-Positive Culture*, where she writes about the appeal of this "little girl" persona for certain men whose fantasies incline in that direction. Does a sex worker who acts out that character, whether she be dancer or prostitute, lessen the chance of real crimes of pedophilia by such men or does she instead encourage their fantasy to grow and increase the likelihood of their acting it out in real life? I know of no definitive research on this question, but anecdotal accounts such as Queen's favor weaving this fantasy with clients despite the "tightrope of opprobrium" involved. Similarly, Elisabeth Eaves, in her stripper memoir *Bare*, quotes a colleague who specializes in such work: "I am hopeful that it's a safe redirecting. I am not one hundred percent confident."[1] I myself remain unsure as well.

A new dancer comes out on stage, a straightforwardly pretty young woman in a long black gown with a thigh-high slit and spaghetti straps. She performs with a little silver purse slung over her shoulder. It strikes me as an awkward accessory that annoyingly bangs into her side as she twists, but a girl needs somewhere to put her tips and not all favor the garter. The DJ introduces her as Sarah and induces a round of applause. When she turns around, I suddenly see that a tag is hanging out the back of her dress. I feel a clutch of embarrassment for her and to be seeing her. Amidst the sea of nudity in the place and even though she is still fully clothed, Sarah seems the more naked one as we are made privy to something that is supposed to stay hidden. That simple tag somehow exposes her more and makes her more vulnerable than do all the club's G-strings and splayed legs. It makes me feel motherly; I want to go up and unobtrusively tuck it in for her and pat her on the shoulder.

Another dancer named Mindy also evokes a response of poignancy, although Marie says that I am overreacting. Mindy marches across the stage with no wiggle or sashay. She fiddles with her hair constantly, not in the erotic stroking or fluffing manner of many of the dancers, but to check if her clubbed-back ponytail is in place and to repetitively tuck a stray strand behind her ear. Her hips are slim, her derriere flat, and her breasts nearly non-existent. Instead of the universally towering stripper footwear, she wears regular street shoes with short heels in which she paces quickly back and forth. She doesn't appear nervous, but simply as if she doesn't quite get it and doesn't want to or can't play the game. She seems more like a model for a *Comme des Garçons* fashion show or a solider drilling on the parade ground than like a stripper. She doesn't smile or make much eye contact either, and I can't imagine that she is a big earner. I feel sorry for her that she seems so out of place, but Marie suggests that I'm reading it all wrong and that Mindy's stage presence merely illustrates the diversity of body types and styles found among strippers.

As the club scene spins out around us, it's the pole work that more and more comes to fascinate me. "Pole work," I learn, is the industry term for a dancer's use in stage routines of the upright metal poles – chrome, brass, stainless steel, or enamel, usually two inches in diameter, and bolted into the floor and the ceiling. Pole work is a specialty. Not all dancers do it. While I never visit a club that doesn't have a pole, not all clubs feature true pole work. All dancers will at the very least sometimes put a hand up to the pole as they move from one side of the stage to another, using it to steady themselves or to lean out and swing their hair, and many will also use the pole to anchor themselves as they slide down to the floor or as they bend over, either frontward or backward. Only some, however, are true mistresses of the pole. Developing a full repertoire of pole tricks requires months, if not years, of practice. Such practice used to be hard to come by: dancers had to negotiate to come into their club before it opened in order to try out new moves, or they would simply practice during their shifts. There were a few, but not many, how-to videos available by mail order. Now, however, with the recent advent of stripper aerobic studios and pole-dance classes, as well as the current ease of home pole installation, anyone can get instruction on how to fly and twirl. Sheila Kelley is a Hollywood actress and author who has opened stripping and pole dancing exercise studios in Los Angeles, San Francisco, and New York. She promises that the freedom and power of pole work makes one feel like "a sexual goddess, a kid, and a superhero all at once."[2] That's quite a promise, and sitting at Pearls, I begin to see the appeal.

About half a dozen of the dancers here do really great pole work. They leap into the air, grab the pole with one or two hands, and spin around it fast. Sometimes they corkscrew down to the ground close to the pole; sometimes they keep their bodies flung out. Legs can be bent, outstretched, or hooked around the pole. The spin can be forward or backward. The women climb the pole to the top and slither down, either right-side up or even head first with no-hands. They do complicated swinging flip moves that I later learn are named "Descending Angel," "Firefly," "Pole Cat," and "Snake Dive." Wow, I think, now this – theoretically – I would like to learn. Marie tells me that it takes a great deal of upper-body strength, of which I sadly have none, and a lot of coordination and practice as well. She herself does some of the simpler twirls and bends, but hasn't had the time or inclination to move on to the next level. Pole tricks don't necessarily earn one higher income; they are eye-catching for the audience and can be a way for the dancers to differentiate themselves from other co-workers, but the musculature involved can also be intimidating to a guy who is simply trying to decide on which girl he should spend his twenty bucks. The dancers who specialize in pole work do so, it seems, for the sheer pleasure of it, for the professional competence of mastering a skill, and for the thrill of flying. These pole tricks fast become my favorite part of the dancers' stage shows. In any other context, the athleticism, grace, and daring of these moves would qualify them for Olympic event status. If you can go for the gold in synchronized swimming and rhythmic gymnastics, why not in pole work?

Halfway through our stay at Pearls, a dancer near our end of the stage executes a great trick, a wild upside-down flying body spiral with her legs hooked around the pole. This woman, whose stage name I never catch, does some of the best pole work I witness in my research. She is a somewhat older blonde, maybe a little heavier than the others, and has likely had a couple of kids (I think, conscious of my own soft middle), but she is attractive and certainly an athletic dancer. Her costume is a sparkly silver top and miniskirt. A group of six older men who appear to be in their sixties clap for her and whoop appreciatively. They are sitting together at a table in a banquette alcove at the back of the club, one row away from the stage. When the dancer gets down from the pole, she playfully goes over to the side of the stage and beckons to the men, pointing at the garter on her thigh over which she has folded her tips for the night. Her message is clear: if you like the show, come tip me a dollar. Such tipping is standard practice in a club, especially for anyone sitting at the stage. But the men won't get up to tip her, at first laughing and waving her off as if they're declining in an almost self-deprecating way her offer for personal attention. They don't seem to quite grasp the point, that she expects anyone appreciating her show to come and tip her. Perhaps they haven't been to a strip club before and aren't familiar with its etiquette, although I think it's more likely that they simply have a sense of entitlement to a free show. The dancer becomes less playful and more insistent – "Hey, aren't you going to come over and tip me?" – and the moment becomes increasingly awkward as the men continue to refuse to get up and give her money. Finally, in solidarity, Marie walks over from our table and hands her a dollar. The dancer thanks Marie with a smile and then turns back to call out to the men, "See, the women know how to act," but even then they couldn't be shamed into tipping her a dollar.

When she gets off stage five or ten minutes later, now covered up in a matching silver minidress, she walks up to their table. I can't hear what they say, but everyone at the table – including her – is smiling so she doesn't seem to be calling them "cheap mother-fuckers," which Marie informs is the standard stripper putdown for deadbeat tippers. She may have asked them which girl they did find interesting and thus tip-worthy, because she soon brings over Candy, the cheerleader girl. But the men send Candy away too and then they themselves leave soon afterward. They seemed to just want to sit there and have a drink and watch the dancers, but from the women's point of view, since the dancers are not paid by the club and their income consists solely of tips and private dance arrangements with customers, if you're in a club you should be tipping. Otherwise you're trying to get something for free and you should just go try your luck in a regular bar.

The Body Work of Stripping

This moment is a good one for untangling the physical and emotional work that together make up the job of stripping. You need to learn your pole tricks, or at least to develop your look and dance routines, but you also need to learn to deal with customers, including boorish or difficult ones. While the most obvious part of this profession may be the physical component, it is probably the mental and psychological aspects of the job that are ultimately the more demanding.

First off, however, the task of the stripper is to look good, to take off her clothes, and to dance, either on the main stage or individually for customers. Much of this job, then, entails body work. It is about the dancer's body and her use and management of it. Indeed, the sex-positive defense of all forms of sex work revolves around the claim that an individual has the right to determine how she uses her own body to make a living. The same argument is made as in the feminist defense for abortion: "This is my body and I can do with it as I please." If an adult woman and client consensually agree to the exchange of money for dance (in the case of strippers) or sex (in the case of prostitutes), on what legitimate basis does society tell that woman that she may not use her body in that way? While experiences in other clubs will later lead me to dig deeper into these arguments in Chapter 6, I first want to spend more time examining this bodily aspect of the dancer's work.

Physically, this is a tough job. Try walking around all night in six-inch platform heels and you'll quickly see why. Back home at Marie's the day after our club crawl, I try on some of her shoes and costumes. I figure that if I am going to write about stripping, since I don't seem to have the exhibitionist will to actually get up on stage, I should at least have some first-hand experience of what it feels like to be decked out in towering heels and slinky little outfits. We find a pair of shoes that fit my feet, which are slightly larger than Marie's. I reject clear heels and platforms with clear plastic straps – too tight across the toes. Gold sandals with buckles that crisscross over the ankles are only slightly better. The pair that fits me best are the cherry-red patent-leather heels: open-toed sandals with a strap across the top of the foot and another that fastens with a buckle at the ankle.

I take my first tottering steps. The shoe has a stiletto heel, six inches high, with a steel rod built into the heel to prevent it from suddenly snapping – every dancer's fear, a disaster that can result in twisted ankles and broken bones in a profession without health insurance, sick leave, or workers' compensation. The circumference of the bottom of the stiletto where it touches the floor is considerably smaller than that of a dime. The front part of the shoe is a platform two inches high, so that the rise between the ball of the foot and the heel is four inches. The shoes turn many girls into six-footers, or more. One dancer whom I interview, a good friend of Marie's named Laura who is 5'9" in her bare feet, says "When I'm in my shoes, I'm an Amazon." Marie helps me figure out how to walk. You can't go heel-toe as you normally would when walking in bare feet or flat shoes. You have to put the toe and heel down at the same time. To make this happen, Marie demonstrates how you have to tighten your bum muscles, tilt your pelvis, and sway your hips. I get my sashay going pretty quickly and decide to keep the shoes on all night, in order to see what it feels like. I last an hour.

I hear many shoe stories in my interviews. The stripper shoe is such an iconic symbol of the exotic dancer that it becomes loaded with all she represents: the oppression of the industry, with echoes of foot-binding ("the shoes of slaves," one of my own professors balefully intones); the element of fantasy, play, and glamorous theatricality; a perceived low-class, vulgar aesthetic; and the possibility of a get-even-with-the-boys empowerment. Indeed, the shoes' platform risers and stiletto heels embody many of the paradoxes of the profession itself: sexism and sexiness, power and vulnerability, glamour and tackiness, pleasure and pain, danger and desire. Marie says that she thinks of a herd of gazelles when the women come out of the dressing room and hit the floor: rendered more delicate by the shoes, but also sleek and musical as they move together. Although such footwear is highly impractical – bordering on insanely hazardous – to wear as a street shoe, in the last ten years the rise of striptease and raunch culture has meant that some intrepid girls outside the profession do now navigate their way to nightclubs and parties in these shoes. This practice inspires the scorn of real strippers, who call it "sluttish" and downright stupid and who insist that they wouldn't be caught dead outside the club in their work shoes. In some ways, I think their concern is territorial: it's these shoes that make you a stripper. You almost never take them off; in an all-nude club, they alone of your toilette stay on all night. If girls wear them outside the club, what will the dancers' uniform become inside the club? When your heels are already six-inches high and you are near-nude most of the night, there's not really anywhere left to go.

While I had expected more ambivalence and resentment toward the heels, given how uncomfortable they seemed to me to wear all night long, most of the dancers with whom I talk are surprisingly positive about their shoes. I come to see that I'm simply not a high-heel sort of gal; the only ones I own are an unsexy two-inch pair with a chunky heel, which I now realize don't count at all. The appeal mystifies me; a woman in very high stilettos looks to me hobbled, not sexy. But the dancers seem to get used to the shoes quickly, learn how to walk in them, and then embrace them as an integral and valuable part of being the stripper. Andrea, an athletic little fireball dancer with curly brown hair who works at Mr. Lucky's with Marie, tells me that for her first shift she wore leather boots that she had bought at a $9.99 shoe store. They had heels higher than she had ever before worn in her life, and afterward her legs hurt so much that she could barely walk for four days. Now, she is one of Mr. Lucky's top earners and insists to me, "I wouldn't trade what I do right now for anything in the whole entire world." I ask Laura about the shoes when she tells me about how they turn her into an Amazon: "But aren't they painful?" "No," she replies, "the shoes were never painful for me. They are hard to find, because I have big feet," she laughs, "but they're kind of fun, actually." She does add that "whoever came up with the heel thing should probably be shot," but when I then ask her if she would prefer to wear lower heels, she replies, "No, I don't think so, because I think they're sexy. I think high heels are very sexy."

Almost without exception, the dancers describe the shoes in this way, as "sexy," so I try to figure out what sexy means here. Chrissie helps me the most on this point. She is an ex-dancer whom I interview in my office back in Tuscaloosa, where she has recently enrolled at the University of Alabama as an undergraduate to finish a degree interrupted by several years of cocktail waitressing and dancing in Florida and Mississippi strip clubs. She's now paying her way through college by working as a finance and insurance auditor in a car lot. Chrissie talks to me for hours about the industry and ends up visiting as a guest speaker in my gender studies class as well. When I ask her if she misses her work as an exotic dancer, she wails, "I miss the shoes!" She assures me that heels are "essential" in the stripping business, minimum three inches, but five to six is better: "If bars allow less than three inches, they're stupid." What the shoes do, she patiently explains to me, is change the entire way your body looks and moves. "You'd be surprised what it does for your posture for one. When you get in the heels, you have to lean back because the toes are so far down that you would fall over otherwise, so it straightens your posture up automatically. There is no slumping when you're in heels. You have to bring your shoulders back and then that puts your chest out. So of course just by standing up straight you're going to portray more confidence and more sexiness."

And the effect doesn't end there. Chrissie stands up on her tiptoes in my office to illustrate for me how as you lean back, your pelvis goes forward. When you move, you lead with your hips in a buttock-swaying catwalk. Moreover, Chrissie explains, "it thins your body out. If you're a little chunky and you want to get rid of some weight visually, put on some spike heels. It's going to make your legs look longer which is also going to slim up the rest of your body from your toes to your head." As your leg elongates, your calf is rounded, producing more definition and curve. But it's the final point that is perhaps the most important: the shoes make you *tall*. "Height is sexy," Chrissie declares. "You see a woman in a pair of five and a half inch heels, and she's very tall and long and her legs look really long and everything and you're like, 'Mmmm, okay.'" She's purring, wiggling on my office seat in her animation on this point. She happens to be lesbian and clearly shares the view that I, in my oldschool-feminist-bourgeois-heterosexual naïveté, had thought was a man's: that these shoes make a woman more sexually desirable to the viewer. Her partner Faye, a master's student at the university whom I also get to know, agrees as well. Faye confesses that she "can't wear high heels at all" – to which Chrissie cracks up laughing, "She can't!" – but when I ask her if they appeal to her as sexy, her eyes go round and she nods vigorously, "Oh, yeah!"

It's when the topic of height comes up that I finally start to get it. The dancers talk about the shoes as sexy because they arc your body into a sleek elongated curve and give you a hip-rocking prance of a walk, but they talk about the shoes as conferring power because they make you *tall*: as tall as or taller than the men. Once, when I am presenting my research at an academic conference in Atlanta, a young woman comes up to me after my talk to tell me that she's been working as a stripper. Jessica has double undergraduate degrees in English and religious studies and is now starting a master's program at a leading state university in the South. I take her out to lunch, and one of the things we end up talking about is the shoes. Her physique is particularly fine-boned; she is a slim and classically pretty petite young woman. "I loved, *loved*, being taller than everyone else, especially the men," she confesses. "I felt *very* empowered." She is animated and emphatic on this point: she adores how tall the shoes make her feel. The experience of looking down on people from a position of height is one that is totally new to her and strikes her as quite marvelous. "There is something about turning stereotypes upside down that just makes me feel alive," she says. "Here I was, technically shorter than almost all of the men, an object for them, yet I stood much taller than them and felt like I could intimidate them." Other dancers echo Jessica's sentiments, using the same phrase that Laura had earlier. Mia, a dancer from Ottawa, tells me at one point, "God yes! I love the shoes. I feel like an Amazon when I go to work! I'm so tall!"

Height is one salient, and perhaps under-appreciated, aspect of male-female difference. References to the short man's inferiority complex abound, but most women are shorter than most men. What is the effect of this difference on women's psyches and self-esteem, of always on average being the shorter ones? And how do we measure the value, the satisfaction, the feeling of power – fleeting or illusory though it may be – of suddenly being able to look men in the eye, or even to look down on them? Our society rewards height, and, in this age of plastic surgery, it's the one thing about your body that you can't really change. The only option is to strap on a pair of heels. If height is power, and power is sexy, then Chrissie is certainly right that height is sexy. Almost all of the dancers who talk to me about their shoes stress the pleasure and the feeling of power–especially power over men – that they gain by wearing the shoes. It makes any discomfort worth it. It's one of the ways, as a stripper, that you get to lord it over the men.

Of course, the dancers' comments that the shoes make them feel powerful are ironic also, in that the shoes at the same time make them vulnerable. Women do get hurt in them. One night when I am with Marie in the women's washroom at Mr. Lucky's interviewing a group of dancers on break from the club, we hear a thumping, tumbling noise that turns out to be Sable tripping down the stairs from the dressing room upstairs. She picks herself up and luckily isn't hurt, but I hear other stories of women who twist ankles or suffer bone fractures and are sidelined for weeks. The only dancer I ever meet who admits to disliking the shoes is a very no-nonsense Canadian working under the stage name Fire who has been spending winters in Florida to pay for a house she's having built back in Halifax. When I ask her how she feels about the shoes, she spits out, "Hate 'em. I'm always about to trip." When I probe further into whether they might nevertheless make her feel powerful, she repeats her point, "No, they just make me feel like I'm going to fall on my butt on the floor!" All the dancers are aware of the need for caution: Chrissie says she "refused to take in an alcoholic beverage for weeks, until I was completely comfortable with being on stage and in my shoes without falling." She claims that tripping was her only fear when she started dancing; she wasn't nervous about getting nude, but about tumbling to the floor while doing it. "In that profession, if you sprain an ankle, you throw out a knee, that's it. You're out until you heal. There's no health insurance, there's no paid vacation, there's no sick leave, and I couldn't afford to be off." In fact, one of the reasons she's not dancing anymore is a degenerative knee problem that was exacerbated by her dancing: "the stress on the knees, the stress on the back, the hands, the pole work. It's just really really hard on the body," she sighs.

Along with the shoes, Marie had also brought out a couple of duffel bags stuffed with her stripper outfits. I try some on while still in my heels, going for a range of different looks to see how I feel. There is a pair of pale blue teeny shorts made out of a stretch cotton knit that I wedge myself into (stretch fabrics are big in stripper clothes). The shorts have a matching top sewn from a see-through mesh material somewhat like mosquito netting. The outfit is decorated in little blue and white flowers that Marie assures me will glow in the dark. There is also a floaty see-through chiffon robe in an aqua floral print. It has long sleeves, ties at the breasts, and then falls open to the ankles. It's meant to be worn with a thong, also called a T-bar and not to be confused with a G-string, the latter being a simple triangle of fabric over the pubic area with a string that nestles between the cheeks of one's bottom. At the first club where Marie worked in the Midwest, G-strings were prohibited, since the law there required one inch of fabric across the back of all underwear. (The big joke, of course, was about the state agents who came in to measure.)

Next on is a long gown, ankle-length but slit up to the thigh, in lime-green stretch velour. I feel most comfortable with this amount of coverage and can almost imagine wearing this dress somewhere (although where, in Tuscaloosa, I'm not quite sure). It has a halter top that ties behind the neck. Marie explains that these halter styles are very popular because all you have to do to strip out of such an outfit is bend forward and pull the strings over your head while they are still tied together. This disrobing allows you to flip your hair back – always a nice move – and reveal your breasts all in one fell swoop. Although I never quite get what the hurry is, I realize again that the premium in this industry is on high-speed undressing, and not on a slow-burn tease. It is for this reason, Marie explains, that dancers rarely wear bras: they take too long to remove and don't flatter the woman reaching behind herself to fiddle with the clasp. A couple of compromises on the no-bra rule are a black sequined tube top that I try on and that fastens at the front with Velcro – again, to rip it off fast – and a biker-look bikini top with tiny triangles of leather outlined in silver chain. The biker bikini is not a good look on me since any sort of rapid movement seems to make my breasts fall out. Many of the outfits are actually intended to expose the breasts, such as the red spandex minidress I wiggle into last that features a spider-web top of cut-outs and tiny circles barely big enough to cover my aureoles. It comes with a matching red garter and lacy stay-up stockings with frills around the top.

So how do I feel? Naughty? Sexy? Well, sort of, although without having done up my hair or makeup and with my glasses on, the look doesn't really work. These are clothes that are meant to be worn at night and in dim lighting; the full Florida sunlight flatters neither the costumes themselves nor them on my no-longer-spring-chicken self. "Is this top crooked," I ask, cocking my head, "or is it my breasts?" I start to be critical of my body, aware that it is that of a 36-year-old mom, still fairly slim but with soft belly and breasts that are certainly not as large and firm as those of the surgically-enhanced dancers. I am, however, definitely on my way to looking thoroughly tarted up, and I must admit that there is a certain fantasy pleasure to that. It is the pleasure of make-believe and pretend, where one can act out the costumed role of hooker, or buxom barmaid, or madam, or dominatrix, or girl-next-door, or sex kitten. It's like a masquerade ball or Halloween dress-up party in which we get to play with a part of our sexuality, to loosen up the reins on an aspect of self usually constrained into narrower socially sanctioned outlets. This tarting up is a way to connect with a certain form of sexual power as a woman – a form that is rawer, edgier, more raucous, less decorous, less restrained – to tap into this power, to trace out its shape and extent, and to experiment with the feel of wielding it like a whip. It is a pleasure that appeals to both costume party and real-life stripper alike.

Along with these clothes goes a full and constant grooming routine for the dancers: shaving of legs, underarms, and pubic area; makeup; hair; manicures and pedicures. (Some clubs check your nails and won't let you on the floor if your polish is chipped.) Instead of finding such a practice oppressive and overly time-consuming, most of the dancers that I speak with seem to enjoy it. I think again of Andrea, the little fireball dancer with the $9.99 boots. When I had interviewed her, she was on her way to the mall, a place where she tells me it's very easy to "blow five hundred dollars." Part of why she likes being a stripper, she freely admits, is the chance to buy and dress up in all the outfits. "I've always been a prissy little bitch," she explains. Despite her words, she doesn't fit a prissy airhead stereotype. She is assertive, strong-opinioned, and athletic, renowned as the best pole dancer at Mr. Lucky's, and with smallish natural breasts. Having grown up in New Jersey as a Jehovah's Witness, going to church three times a week, she tells me that she developed early on the ambition to become an exotic dancer: "Some girls wanted to be princesses, some girls wanted to work at the mall, and I wanted to be a stripper." It's not just rebellion, she is quick to assure me, and she's really rather shy about her body, but she loves the glamour of the dress-up routines and then the attention she gets when she performs decked out in full stripper regalia.

Mia is another dancer similarly drawn to the dolled-up vampiness of the profession. I meet her in Canada, at Barbarella's Diamonds. She has only started dancing a few months ago, after tiring of the low-paying office job she landed with her undergraduate degree in criminology and psychology from Ottawa's Carleton University. At the strip club, not only was she making at least four times more money, but she said she was having a ball and loving the hyper-feminized theatricality of the place: "I like putting on costumes, it's great, the feathers and the sequins, oh my God … Sometimes I dress up and I feel like a diva! It's like 'Look at me!'" The night that I see her dance at Barbarella's, she is outfitted in black vinyl mid-shin boots, a see-through black lace dress, and dramatic horn-rimmed glasses that set off her short dark red hair. She moves gingerly on stage, as a tattoo artist had just etched a bird across her stomach the night before. (It's her second tattoo – the other being the Chinese characters for serenity, courage, and wisdom on her back – and it goes along with a ring in her navel and another in her outer labia.) When I ask her about the work involved in maintaining the soigné dancer look, she assures me that she has "always been very into grooming, makeup has always been a huge thing in my life. I don't groom myself any more than I used to. I always used to shave my pubic hair, except for a little patch; I don't like body hair." Like Andrea and other dancers that I talk with, Mia loves the costumes, loves doing up her face in glamour or fantasy makeup. She loves getting paid, in effect, to tend her nails and hair and makeup and clothes and then show it all off in the party atmosphere of the club.

As we start to pack up her shoes and costumes, Marie shows me the box full of nail polish that she has acquired as a dancer, and because I'm in West Palm Beach and it's warm and it somehow seems the thing to do, I paint my toenails fuchsia that afternoon, something I haven't done since I was maybe thirteen years old. Here's my big confession: I enjoy the flash of bright color so much that I acquire a few bottles of my own and have been sporting painted toes ever since. As we talk about typical dancer grooming routines, Marie argues that the "choice to be girly has to be acceptable to feminists. It's sour grapes to demand choice for women and then not like what some of us choose." She too never used to wear heels or makeup or nail polish, but now finds herself sporting them even off the job, "just to be sexy." She continues, "There's a lot of playfulness in it. All I ever perceived of it was the hassle, but now that I have to go through the hassle for work, I've found that on the other end, wow, this is actually fun, like playing a role. I get a lot more enjoyment now out of playing with these aspects of femininity." This element of *play* is important. It highlights the extent to which the stripper's body work is a creative, fantasy, dress-up game, over which she generally has a fair amount of control. From this perspective, what's not to like? You get glitter, color, and glamour. True, the fashion sensibility is all rather trashy, but this too is part of the fun: tongue-in-cheek camp, as opposed to any pretension at *couture*.

In a way, stripping offers the perfect justification for spending your time and money on the grooming that is both generally expected of women in our society yet also just as easily mocked. Sexualized femininity is somewhat of a requirement in women's self-presentation – not just for strippers in the club, but for all women on and off the job everywhere – and yet too much can earn you censure. As a woman, you are supposed to care about how you look and to take the time to "look nice." In other words, if you don't dress and groom and act to a certain feminine standard, you will likely be penalized in various ways – someone else may get the job or be promoted or make the sale or attract the attention or get the guy – but if you focus on such primping too much, you can be disciplined as well (labeled the superficial airhead forever shopping, doing her nails, and reading *Cosmo*). Strippers have to – but also *get* to – engage in this endless body work. I suspect that many of them are drawn to dancing in the first place partly for the chance it offers to engage guilt-free and full-time in these rituals of femininity. I think of the sultry and ultracurvaceous animated Jessica Rabbit in the 1988 feature film *Who Framed Roger Rabbit?* and her immortal line, "I'm not bad. I'm just drawn that way." The dancers even get to claim manicures and breast implants as professional business expenses for income-tax purposes (although many work too far under the table to be quite so organized).

Once dressed in their towering heels, their sequined thongs and mesh tops, the dancers work shifts – usually divided into lunch, evening, and a mid-shift between the two – that last from six to eight hours. The number of shifts they choose to work is generally up to them and can be tailored to vacation schedules, childcare, and other varying needs. Some dancers are content with part-time work of two shifts a week; others routinely schedule themselves for four or five nights every week. The typical shift consists of dancing sets on stage in rotation with the other dancers, going up to customers to solicit dances and often sitting with them at their tables to talk, performing individual table or lap dances, and aiming for as much time as possible in the lucrative V.I.P. rooms, either with established customers or in an attempt to develop such regular contacts. The goal of every dancer is to have a stable of well-known patrons who come in at scheduled times and who can be relied upon to spend one or two hundred dollars or more per visit. Ideally, she would have such patrons scheduled every night of the week that she works – the retiree as her early-bird special on Tuesdays, the downtown lawyer on Wednesdays, the out-of-town businessman every other Friday – but few dancers are quite this successful.

The regular dancers at a club – the house girls – also sometimes share the stage with a feature dancer, who comes into the club for just a week. A feature is paid a flat fee of two to five thousand dollars by the club to perform about three stage shows a night, from Tuesday or Wednesday through Saturday, as well as to sell autographed posters and offer private dances to the patrons. Not all clubs bring in feature headliners, who are usually minor porn stars, centerfolds, or experienced exotic dancers. They often come with titles, like Miss Nude Miami, or Best Chest in the 2005 Miss Wisconsin contest, or Best Legs. Being a feature can be a hard life for them, since they travel constantly and have to raise the bar from what the regular dancers proffer – already a generous offering of crotch, grind, and bosom. Feature dancers' heels are usually higher, their costumes fancier, their performances more sexually hardcore. They typically have some kind of gimmick, like the burlesque queens of old but involving a lot more flesh than Gypsy Rose Lee ever flashed. They may set up a kiddie pool or giant champagne cup onstage and do a water show, or stroke themselves with a brush and body paint, or lay down a towel and dribble lotion over their body, or play with dildos, or do a fire show or snake show.

Outside the club, the work doesn't stop for dancers. The upkeep for the professional stripper involves a considerable commitment of time and money: trips to the hair stylist and the manicurist, home shaving routines, and of course costume shopping and planning. Chrissie tells me that "People don't realize how much money it takes to be a dancer. They're like, 'God, but you make so much money!' But they don't know how much it takes to *be* a dancer." Citing just one of the expenses, she complains that "Dancer clothes are the most expensive and least durable on the market. There's not another article of clothing that will cost you more and last you less time than dancer clothes." Some of the white girls also tan regularly at salons, despite the health risk involved. (Then again, so do many of my students: tanning salons are more numerous – by far – than bookstores around our Tuscaloosa campus.) They tan naked, to avoid lines, except perhaps for a Playboy bunny head decal that they strategically locate on a shoulder or hip so as to leave a white patch to glow under the club lights.

Finally, many of the dancers work out or pursue other strategies of diet and exercise to stay trim. Marie tells me that the top-earners at Mr. Lucky's are the ones who make daily trips to the gym and who treat such a fitness routine as simply part of their job. Not only are they slimmer and thus more conventionally attractive to the men, but they dance with more energy and suppleness and can maintain this high energy level over the course of a shift in order to keep the tips flowing. An evening of lap dances requires strong thigh muscles; if you're out of shape, you quickly feel the burn. While there is somewhat more body diversity in the clubs than I had expected, if you want to be a stripper, you basically have to be fairly slim. Few dancers are successful if carrying around more than twenty or twenty-five extra pounds. The club management will say something to you or you simply won't earn dances from the customers. Indeed, gaining such weight is usually a sign that a dancer is falling into trouble with drinking or drugs or a spiraling feedback loop of loss of self-confidence and loss of income.

The dancers, then, are under significant pressure to stay thin and to look good. In an age of fast food and obesity, such pressure is in some ways beneficial, but also easily mounts to toxic levels. Stripping *can* be a physically active job that allows a woman to indulge a love of dance. Marie, for example, lost fifteen pounds of excess fat in her first six months dancing and noticed a big improvement in her muscle tone, stamina, and energy level. One of her Florida co-workers tells me that the job is how she stays in shape: "Dancing keeps me aware of my body, so that I don't get sloppy about taking care of myself." But on the other hand, the demands inherent in the body work of the profession can be quite dangerous to dancers' health and self-esteem. Clubs vary in how strictly they enforce norms regarding dancers' weight; in some, not just your figure but also your costume, makeup, hair, and nails are all subject to daily scrutiny and judgment. Johanna, a former dancer who had worked at a high-level club in San Francisco, told me that management at her club "had these cards, and could write whatever they wanted on the card each day, like her costume was ugly, she looked fat today." Dancers felt very stressed in such an environment, particularly as there were no clear guidelines regarding appearance ("You're just supposed to look hot") and as criticism often seemed arbitrarily applied. Even today, when Johanna drives by the club she still feels "this heightened sense of anxiety."

Another woman tells me a story that further illustrates these dangers to health and self-esteem. Hallie is a 26-year-old engineer who stripped to put herself through an expensive college program in Atlanta and who is now temporarily dancing again after her firm downsized and she was laid off. She is smart and trim, and has her life well together: she makes payments on a condo, owns her car outright, has a job-search plan, and boasts twenty thousand dollars in savings. Hallie is one of the most successful strippers whom I meet. In terms of using the profession to fuel longer-term educational and career goals, she is the poster child of sex-positive feminist stripping. Her friend, however, isn't doing as well. About six months previously, the manager of the club in Atlanta where they both work had announced that they were going to institute "appearance evaluations." Girls who were gaining too much weight or looking "sloppy" would be warned and then fired if their appearance didn't improve. The move coincided with an economic downturn that was resulting in fewer customers and lower profits for the club.

"My friend, she wasn't skinny, but she wasn't fat either," Hallie recounts over lunch at an Atlanta hotel when I am in town for a conference. Management told her that she had to slim down. Unfortunately, she was dealing at the same time with a breakup from a husband heavily into crystal meth who had been burning through their money and against whom she eventually had to get a restraining order. Hallie's friend had previously used crystal meth herself, but had cut way back on her drug use while dancing at the club. Now under pressure from the club to slim down quickly, she returned to drugs specifically to lose weight. "She got down to 108 pounds," Hallie tells me, "and people were coming up to me, 'Make that girl eat!'" She says that drugs are considered among the dancers as "an easy way to drop weight fast. There are girls who get on crystal or coke and stuff and lose a bunch of weight." "I heard of another girl," Hallie continues, "who had gotten off drugs, but then gained too much weight as part of getting clean, so she got back on heroin. And I was like, 'Oh Jesus,'" she says, rolling her eyes. Hallie admits that she nonetheless understands the pressure: "It comes to the point where someone tells you that you can't come to work until you've dropped weight. You don't get disability, you don't get workman's comp, and there's no insurance of any nature. And so obviously now you're like …," Hallie shrugs, grimaces, "So a lot of girls do drugs."

One final point needs mentioning about the body work of exotic dance: it often involves the literal remaking of the body to better match the stripper ideal. Hallie goes on to tell me that 65–70 percent of the dancers at her upscale Atlanta club have had breast implants. My guess from the clubs that I visit is that around half of the dancers I see are surgically enhanced. Become a dancer and there's a good chance that you'll soon be saving your tips for the industry *rite de passage* of the "boob job." Hallie herself is adamantly against the procedure. My question to her about breasts has her shaking her head and immediately sets her off: "When you start changing your body to try to make money and to fit some kind of ideal, you're losing your sense of self. To me, breast implants are horrible: they look horrible, they feel horrible. Girls are like, 'Oh my gosh, they look so real!' I'm like, 'No, they don't. Look at me: this is what real breasts look like.'" She tells me story after story: "This one girl, she's got a trainer, she's buff. She's from Bermuda, she's got these blonde ringlets down to her waist, gorgeous hair, can dance really well. She just didn't have big boobs. And she's getting a boob job! She's determined about getting it, and I'm just like, 'You don't need it. So your boobs are a small B. That's beautiful.'" And also: "This one girl, her stage name was Barbie and she had blonde hair and big boobs. Every other part of her body had had plastic surgery. So, Barbie was a good name, because she's plastic."

Despite the trenchancy of Hallie's critique, many dancers are clearly all for the operation. One day Marie, Jeanette, and some of the other girls are sitting around talking about breasts while upstairs in the club dressing room. (Yes, such sometimes is the conversation of strippers.) Jeanette, with her small and pert breasts, confides that she has occasionally considered getting implants, but the truth is that she does just fine without them and is already the club's top earner. They talk about "Grandpa," a club regular in his late sixties who comes in to sit at the bar one or two nights a week. Last year, he paid for Sabrina's operation, although she now says that she regrets taking his money and finds him obnoxious. Marie declares that she doesn't plan on ever having the surgery and is then amused when Darcy, Jeanette's dance partner, misunderstands her lack of interest and hurries to assure her, "Oh, don't worry honey, you'd look great with implants!" This is the one profession where whatever workplace shame or embarrassed titillation that exists in the rest of the world over breast enlargement is totally absent: co-workers here are all very businesslike as they compare lift, shape, size, cost, and the projected increase in revenue from one's investment in the physical plant.

Such conversations help convince Marie's good friend and co-worker Laura, and when I interview Laura one afternoon back at Marie and Jeff's house, she is recuperating from her augmentation surgery performed just three days earlier. Laura is 23 years old and has been dancing for two and a half years. Her straight dark blonde hair falls down her back and frames a big Julia Roberts smile. She's originally from a small town in Wisconsin and is very sweet and still a little unsophisticated, despite having followed Marie over a year ago now, down from the Midwest where they had worked at the same club, to West Palm Beach. As she settles onto Marie's couch for our interview, she takes off her top to show me her new breasts (32B to 36C): "Umm, very nice," I offer, nodding. Marie had previously told me that many of the dancers who get their breasts done notice an increase in income, but she attributes these extra tips more to an enhanced self-confidence that projects well with customers than to any direct link with bra size.

Hallie had made a similar point: "They feel like if they get a boob job they're going to make more money. Quite frankly, it just doesn't work out that way. You make more money based on your attitude. I've seen ugly girls make a lot of money because they know how to talk and get along with customers." While the top dancers are all in great shape, they don't all have big breasts. Laura is aware, however, that she suffers from "very low self-esteem," as she puts it. Her case illustrates the point that it takes an unusually high degree of maturity and self-confidence to feel good about oneself and to maintain a positive attitude if one is "ugly" and flat-chested, true not only for strippers but for many young women (and men) in our lookist culture.

Laura's reasons for having the surgery are partly aesthetic and show her acceptance of the cultural bias that bigger really is better: "I just wanted to do it," she tells me. "I think women are beautiful, and I like breasts. I like the way that it looks, and I like the way it looks on me." Even if she herself were to question this "bigger is better" mentality, she cynically sees men as unable to resist its appeal. Her motivation here becomes also financial: "In general, you do make more with larger breasts. It's kind of funny because any man that walks into a bar just about, if you tell him that you're going to get breast augmentation done, he'll tell you 'No, no, you have beautiful breasts; don't get them; they're fake, blah, blah, blah,' but that same guy after you get back from surgery will come and tip you five bucks instead of a dollar." Ultimately, however, her motivation is psychological: "A lot of it has to do with how I feel about myself." Laura explains to me that she'd been thinking about implants for three or four years, since well before she'd started dancing, but had never had the money to do it until now. She understands Marie and Hallie's point, that it's not the breasts themselves but the self-confidence they engender that helps a dancer, yet she can't feel good enough about her unenhanced body to project this blast of confidence on her own. She needs the 36C to generate the attitude of sexiness that pulls in the customers. "I'm really happy about my surgery and as long as they look nice, I'm going to feel a lot better about myself and I'm going to feel sexier. And if I put that out, in my aura, then that's all going to help me." Whether she's a dancer or not, she maintains that the surgery gives a badly needed boost to her self-esteem.

So what if a boob job is the only way you can improve your body image? According to Hallie, if you need breast implants to feel good about yourself, well then, honey, you're in trouble. But, truth be told, some version of this need may indeed be the case for many of us. Our culture clearly places an obsessive emphasis on appearance, not just for strippers and not even just for women. Good looks pay, period. It's the rare person – generally a very rich, smart, and/or successful man – who can get away with totally ignoring how he looks. The rest of us have to groom, and strippers *really* have to groom. The profession of exotic dancer requires that a woman literally *embody* a hypersexualized, hyperfeminized ideal image of the female. The physical part of her job is to make over her own body into as close a match as possible to this ideal. The creation and presentation of this stripper body – shaved, moisturized, perfumed, made-up, coiffed, painted, polished, buffed, clad, shod, and then stripped – takes a huge effort to produce and to maintain. It is an ideal that is clearly not natural, but is a construction and artifact of the culture.

Creating this body is work, hard work, but as the dancers also point out, it can be creative pleasure and sensual play as well. The "trappings" of femininity that are a dancer's stock in trade are, from one perspective, traps indeed, and it is for this reason that the second-wave feminists of the late 1960s and early 1970s threw makeup and heels into "freedom trash cans" to set them on fire (the original "bra burners"). The cultural and industry imperative to mold or trap one's body within the stripper's uniform of femininity can sap a young woman's self-confidence, particularly if she starts out with lower self-esteem, and can lead to body-image issues and feelings of inadequacy. Yet these trappings can be fun to play with as well; they can be a source of power and delight. They come at a cost, but they can pay off to the tune of hundreds of dollars a night, and they can help make one feel exotic, sexy, and – ironically – more self-confident. It all depends on the strength of the sense of self that a dancer starts out with, the goals and boundaries that she brings to her work, the particular environment that she experiences at her club, and the support that she receives both there and outside work.

By now, we see that while the dancers are engaged nonstop in body work, they are clearly doing much more as well. Still seeking answers, I head back into the clubs.

–3–

"A Lot of Guys Just Want to Talk" and (Other) Reality Costs of Stripping

The Emotional Labor of Stripping

Later that same night when Marie, Jeff, Anita, and I were at Pearls watching the pole-dancer drama, another stripper walks up to our table, says hello, and introduces herself as Nikki. She shakes hands with each of us in turn, an unusually businesslike opening gambit that proves hard to ignore. While we had already sent other dancers away that evening, I had been starting to feel guilty that, like the table of older men, we too were just sitting in the club and not tipping (or at least not much); we were being "cheap mother-fuckers" ourselves. I am uncomfortable with paying the dancers for interviews and almost never do so. For good reason, researchers aren't supposed to give money to their subjects, partly because it could well influence what they tell you. Yet sometimes meeting dancers outside the club for an interview proves impossible, and on a busy night, I don't expect them to forgo income opportunities to sit through my questions. While we decline Nikki's offer to dance for us, I make no objection when Jeff pulls bills from his wallet and asks her to sit and talk with us for a while.

Nikki has white-blond bleached hair cut very short and gelled up in a spiky do. She is quite beautiful, with wonderful facial bones and creamy translucent skin. Her long gown is in a patterned black-and-white check, with a halter neckline and thigh-high slit. Bills are folded over a black garter high up on her crossed leg. She speaks excellent English with an eastern European accent as she blows smoke out into the air. When I ask her where she is from originally, she tells us her story (or, at least, *a* story). Hungary is home, she has been in the United States for six years, and worked the first three of them in New York City. She has moved south for the weather and now lives about one hour away from the club, but she works at this particular club because they let her keep her bottoms on. In other words, although this is a nude club, the management doesn't insist that she strip out of her thong. "Topless is fine, though, I don't mind that," she explains, "they do it in Europe." She tells us that she has a five-month old daughter as well, and I try to imagine the logistics involved with the commute and her nighttime work schedule. She manages, she shrugs, and likes the money, likes dancing, and likes getting to meet and talk to lots of different people.

When I tell Nikki that I'm writing a book, she doesn't ask me anything about it. I wonder if she's heard that line before: "Yeah, I'm just in here to research a book about strippers." Perhaps she's wary of it as an excuse to not pay the dancers for their time. She doesn't seem to believe me, in any case, because she's soon asking me which girl I like: "Who *do* you find interesting?" is how she puts it, when we once again decline her offer to perform for us. Or maybe she's just pointing out that there's no reason why I couldn't write a book and buy a few dances from one of the girls at the same time. Part of me briefly wonders whether I *should* get a lap dance, just to experience it as part of my research, but given my lack of desire, the dynamic seems wrong and even disrespectful of the dancers somehow, as if I would be treating them like lab rats to put through their paces. What I do find interesting about Nikki is her claim that many of their patrons come in simply for conversation, because they want companionship. When I ask her more about this dynamic, she assures me that "I spend a lot of every evening like this," she waves her cigarette at our table, "just sitting and talking with people." "And," she adds with a laugh, "this is a lot less expensive than psychiatry!"

I end up hearing some version of this line frequently from different dancers: a lot of guys, it seems, really do just want to talk, especially the regular customers whom the strippers aspire to hook. I come to see quickly that this is a key skill. You can get away with not being a very good dancer – "exotic dance" is, one must admit, a euphemism – but you can't earn maximum income without being able to strike up and sustain conversations with a wide variety of people and interest them in your company. You have to be comfortable with people and able to make them comfortable with you. Nikki certainly possesses this skill; she broke through our barrier with her handshake and soon turned us into chatting, paying customers. Her insight on this point helps me to see that while all of the stripper's body work mounts up to an occupation that is highly demanding physically, the job of the dancer is emotionally intense as well.

A concept developed by sociologist Arlie Hochschild is useful here to help make sense of the emotional and psychological demands of this profession. Hochschild coined the term "emotional labor" to describe the type of work required by certain sales and service professions where interacting with the public in a warm and pleasant way is part of the job requirement. Much of Hochschild's early work was done with flight attendants, but workers in many industries are paid to perform emotional labor. What it involves is the presentation, at all times, to customers and potential patrons alike, of a façade or persona that is kind, polite, caring, and upbeat. The workers must never let on that they may well be bored, cynical, or annoyed by their customers and by the act of service, even when such negative emotions might be clearly appropriate to the situation. "The customer is always right" is one slogan that captures the endless demands of emotional labor.[1]

Strippers, it turns out, labor very hard emotionally. The unnamed dancer at Pearls, for example, was managing emotions and failing to manage them well in her encounter with the reluctant tippers. There are several key forms of emotional labor that the profession requires of the dancers. Ideally, they must hustle all night long to forge individual connections with the men through one sales pitch after another. They must act self-confident in the face of rejection and never take it personally. They must perform desire and interest in men who may in fact repel them. They must be empathetic, good listeners. And they must not give in to anger when harassed by boors. Success entails managing all of these emotional dynamics in order to maximize income and to find satisfaction and success on the job. Failure to perform this emotional labor properly will shred a dancer's self-confidence and leave her angry, bored, depressed, and poor. The problem is, however, that success in performing the labor may well bury the worker's sense of self as it involves, to at least some degree, the production and maintenance of a false self. Such is the dilemma identified by Hochschild.

The first of these emotional demands, and the key to navigating them all, is to create connections with the customers. Since all of the dancer's income derives from individual transactions that she brokers for herself, she must above all be an accomplished saleswoman. To succeed, she has to excel at making pitch after pitch all night long. Marie describes it as having a first-class salesperson's ability to bond quickly with total strangers, to forge a sense of relation or common ground that is, or at least seems to be, genuine. Your goal, ideally, is to make the club patron feel sufficiently at ease with you that the financial transaction simply takes place of its own accord, almost automatically, in the background to a burgeoning sense of relationship and desire. Through the projection of warmth, energy, empathy, and interest, the dancer makes the client want to buy her time and services, or not mind paying for them, because he is comfortable being with her. It's a matter of putting people at ease, of drawing them out, of being self-confident, but never obviously fake in your sentiment. There are different styles or personae that dancers can adopt for this work: high-energy bouncy girl, languid temptress, tough heavy-metal chick, misbehaving party-goer, exotic princess – in the words of Chrissie, you can choose to be either "Miss Pretty" or "Miss Bitch" – but the dancer will do best who can play more than one of these roles and who can intuit a patron's preference and switch from one to another on the spot.

For her part, Marie experiments with different approaches. Sometimes, especially when the club is very busy, she sticks with the standard opener, "Would you like a dance?," but this line can be an easy one to turn down, particularly since many of the men seem actually shy or easily intimidated. For a table with just one man, she might try, "You're looking a little lonely; mind if I join you?" She'll sit and chat for ten minutes, and if the money doesn't appear soon for a drink or a dance, she'll leave, but on good terms. Something may turn up later in the evening, as some guys simply want to take their time in choosing which dancer to spend money on that night. Marie has also asked Jeanette for pointers on pick-up lines. Jeanette tends to work as a pair with Darcy; their gambit recently has been to go up to men together and ask, "Do you want to play with us?" It's a good opening move, as to say "No" seems to cast oneself all at once as rude, boring, and not man enough to handle the challenge. If a customer inquires about the possibility of sex, which happens fairly regularly, Jeanette will answer that you have to go into the champagne room. After he's paid and they're in there, she'll say, "Sex? No sex. I dance sexy!" exaggerating her accent and pretending that she's misunderstood his request. She actually speaks perfect English. In fact, a lot of Jeanette's advice involves lying: "Tell them they're making you hot, that they really excite you." Marie tries, but finds the strategy ridiculous and uncomfortable and decides that she doesn't want to lie.

This issue of honesty is an interesting one. It *is* possible to avoid false or manufactured sentiment in the emotional labor of reeling in paying customers, but the move is a hard one to pull off. Marie once tried an experiment in perfect honesty, drawing on some insights from a personal-growth seminar she'd recently attended with Jeff. If a customer said, "Oh, you just want my money," – a classic guy line – to which a dancer feels she's supposed to reply, "No, honey, I'm really having a great time with you! You're so funny (or hot or smart)," Marie would instead declare with a grin, "Damn straight! How much you got?" The guys would hoot with laughter and pay up. Or if she were asked during a lap dance, "Is this making you hot, too?" – another typical male question – she would shoot back, laughing, "No, of course not, I just want your money!" She would tease customers ("You're a horny old man," said to anyone over 40, or "You just want me sitting here so you can look down my cleavage") and tell them they were full of bullshit. Somewhat surprisingly, she found that they loved it. The strategy was lucrative as well; she made top earnings that week of her experiment, including her career high of eight hundred dollars in one night.

Not lying, or not having to manufacture emotion in Hochschild's terms, felt wonderful, but it also took a lot of energy and proved hard to sustain. She found that she had to be fearless and supremely confident. Great attitude sells in a club, Marie told me she learned, better even than a combination package of big breasts, a beautiful face, and a hot body (whatever that might mean). The person with great attitude is the one who is having fun and enjoying herself, who is relaxed and not self-conscious but instead is full of confidence. Such self-confidence sells, mixed with high-energy enthusiasm and goodwill – preferably genuine – toward the men. To pull this off successfully, however, strikes me as requiring the establishment with each patron of what Jewish writer Martin Buber famously called an "I-Thou" relationship: an authentic relational connection that values and respects the other as a person in his or her own right and not merely as a means to an end (that is, as a source of money). In other words, you can only earn top dollar from telling a guy that he's full of bullshit if the context for the conversation is that of the "I-Thou." He has to trust that you're laughing playfully with him, as well as at yourself, and at the tangles into which the absurdities of the sexual knots us all. While you're no longer lying, this is still hard emotional labor indeed.

The more standard approach, which a lot of dancers adopt as their hook and follow-through, is to feign desire. For many strippers, this is a major part of the emotional labor that they perform in the club. As Jeanette had counseled, they often pretend to share the interest and arousal of the men for whom they dance. The aspect of what Hochschild calls the worker's "managed heart" becomes central here, and in a way that applies much more literally than Hochschild probably had in mind. Once you've hooked a customer, the emotional labor you carry out as a dancer is to weave a fantasy for his consumption that your "heart" or your passions are engaged by him. This is almost always to a great degree a deception or, one could say, a performance, a "managing of the heart" that is one of the requirements of the profession. You dance for him or you sit with him, as if you care. Sometimes, especially with your regular customers, you may indeed like him, but you never like him as much as your performance would indicate – that is, you would not spend so much time so intent upon him, near-naked and in sensuous play, unless he were paying you – and you are almost never aroused by him, despite what he thinks.

Dancers walk a very fine line here. They vary in the degree to which they "fake it," in which the emotion they display to a customer is false and simply put on to clinch the sale. Some, in fact, eschew this strategy of the simulation of desire. Andrea, for example, says that "They either like me or they don't like me. I don't sit there and talk dirty or anything like that. Ugh. I can't say, 'You're so hot.' I can't talk to a person like that." Her approach is very straightforward, with little chitchat and no faked heavy panting or dirty talk: "I can't even look at a person if I'm grinding on their lap; I'll just start laughing. I can't help it. Their faces, I'm just, like, giggling." Andrea's strategy allows her to minimize the emotional labor of the profession, which in this case she characterizes as simply "silly nonsense." She succeeds instead with a very high-energy focus on athletic pole tricks and sexy dance. Not so Jeanette, who is a big fan of the "lie and tell them you're horny" school of stripping. There's a businesslike ruthlessness about her that is clearly responsible for her top-earner status. She tells me that she values and likes the men – "Thank God for them, because they make my job possible!" – but at the same time, she has no qualms with deliberately tricking them and, as I quoted previously, is happy to take their last dollar, claiming they're all rapists at heart.

To be fair, there is an important difference here between a line and a lie. Dancers, like actors, recite lines; they know that what happens in the club isn't real. It's a fantasy; it's play-acting; it's desire for hire; it's a woman dancing naked for you because you give her money. Jeanette and other dancers see their job as creating a fantasy for the guys that simply doesn't happen to be real for them. Only the best of the men will accept that the fantasy is not real yet still enjoy playing and paying for it. With other patrons, you have to pretend that it really is real ("Oh, yeah, you're getting me hot"), or that you wish it could be ("I'm sorry, but I'm afraid management doesn't let us go out with customers"), or that under other circumstances you would make it so ("I have a boyfriend now, and unfortunately he's the jealous type"), in order to keep them in the game. The strategy here is to tell them whatever they'll pay to hear, because it's all just a performance anyway. If the guy isn't smart enough to figure that out, that's his problem. It turns out that you can make a lot of money as a dancer either by genuinely enjoying your customers or just by pretending to. Marie says she really means the thank-you kisses she plants on the cheek of each paying customer; others say that the men are almost universally "assholes" and idiots with whom one simply has to put up to make a living. In the smoke, mirrors, swilled beer, and tequila shots of the club, it seems that most guys can't tell the difference between a real "I-Thou" moment and a faked one. Most of them either don't know or don't care to know if your interest is faked, as long as you're not too obvious about it. A good performance is often as satisfactory as the real thing.

Many of the dancers are ambivalent about this aspect of their job, and the emotional labor they perform in this regard takes its toll. For example, back in the women's washroom, halfway through her shift, Fire, the no-nonsense Canadian, tells me her take on the "Are you hot, too?" question that she had just received from a problematic private dance customer. She's lit up a cigarette and is dragging on it hard, running her hands through her hair and looking like she's ready to pull it out: "Of course, how couldn't I be hot?" she scoffs sarcastically, "I'm rubbing on your dick!" The man's credulity and ego have her rolling her eyes. This isn't what she replied to him, or at least not *how* she replied to him, but the standard stripper script comes out differently when delivered in the woman-space of the change room. Here a truth surfaces that is submerged amid the pounding music and neon murkiness of the club's fantasy, fictions, and play-acting – or what some would simply call lies. Few dancers seem to escape such moments of cynicism, annoyance, and even revulsion against men. Sable – named I assume for her long brown hair and melting dark eyes – pats Fire on the shoulder as she heads back out onto the floor, "Clubs just bring out the worst in guys." Managing this cynicism, not letting it show with the customers, and not letting it damage the dancers' relationships with men outside the club, is an important aspect of the emotional labor around these issues of the performance of desire.

Some of the other dancers, such as Nikki back at Pearls, take a different tack and specialize in conversation. "A lot of people are just lonely," Nikki insists. "They don't necessarily have anyone they can talk to, who will just listen to them, maybe not even their wives or girlfriends." Especially when dancers develop relationships with regular visitors who book blocks of their time hours-long, much of what they will do together is talk as they share a meal or drinks. Such clients sometimes won't even ask their favorites to dance for them. Here the emotional labor entails listening, drawing out a customer, paying attention to his moods, keeping the conversation going, being – or acting – interested in what he's telling you, and providing whatever emotional foil seems most desired: usually an upbeat, funny, sympathetic, and charming persona. For a dancer who is shy or impatient with fools, this talk-work can be hard slogging indeed. Jessica, the petite graduate student who loved how tall the shoes made her, tells me that while it's true a lot of guys just want to talk, and while she really enjoys her workplace conversations and camaraderie with the other girls, "I don't like having to chitchat with the guys, like about their jobs or their family. I just don't care," she shrugs, "not at all." Or as another dancer tells me, "I really don't want to hear his stories. It can be hard, you know? There's only so much you can talk about, then it's like, 'Do you want a dance?'" Many dancers complain that much of what the men have to say is boring or insulting (with Marie having gotten remarks like, "Hey, you're pretty smart for a stripper!") and that the inevitable pick-up lines just become too tiresome.

Some of the strippers, however, like Mia, the dancer whom I interview in Ottawa, just have a great mouth on them and make their reputation – and money – on their wit. Mia loves to talk; she is smart and comical, with a sassy sense of humor and a genuine warmth for people. She and Marie become good friends the summer they work together at Barbarella's Diamonds in Ottawa and I'm charmed by her myself in our interviews. Mia is a party girl who believes that in stripping, she's finally found her calling. "Before, I used to always get in trouble at work for being sarcastic. Now? It entertains people. YES! Finally, people appreciate me." Dancers like Mia excel at this talk-work of stripping's emotional labor, such that it doesn't even feel like labor, but more like liberation. Much of what she does is just sit with customers and joke around with them, although she assures me that she has serious conversations, too.

"One time," she tells me, "I had this guy sitting in pervert row. He said, 'Mia, if I got on stage with a loonie or a toonie, would you take it from me?'" (In Canada, a "loonie" is a one-dollar coin, named for the loon on its face. When the two-dollar coin was introduced soon after by the Mint, it was popularly nicknamed the "toonie." No bills folded over garter belts for the girls up here; they have to go for the evening bag instead.) Mia continues: "I'm laughing, 'A loonie or a toonie? Fuck you, ya cheap son of a bitch.' The guy looks at me and he's like smiling and says, 'Mia, I like you!' I made $125 off that guy. He liked my sarcasm. Any other ordinary job, if I said something like that, I would have gotten fired." She shakes her head slowly, amazed herself at how much you can get away with in a service-profession job when your breasts are bare.

She recounts another story about a favorite client – "the nicest guy" – a software programmer commuting between the United States and Ottawa, who is divorced with two daughters and a salary of about $140,000 a year. "So this guy who's my best customer, once he said, 'You know, Mia, I come in here sometimes just to talk to you, because we think alike,' since I'm very liberal with my thoughts. We talk about everything." But what keeps him coming back, I suspect, is their shared sense of humor. She gives me an example: "He's black, this guy, black as the ace of spades. And he tells black jokes all the time, he calls me 'white bread,' that's just the way we joke around. And one night he asks, 'What do the three Chinese characters on your back say?' and I said, 'John, it says No Niggers Allowed.' He laughed *so* hard, everyone in the club is looking like, 'What's that guy laughing at?' To this day, he'll look at me and just start laughing and I ask him what he's laughing at, 'That day you told me what your tattoo meant.' He's told everybody, all the guys back home what I said, and they all laugh. He thinks it's just the funniest thing. And that's just the kind of relationship we have." While not all dancers can pull off this brand of stripper humor, which admittedly strays toward the fine line of the offensive, her evident goodwill seems to make it work for her, both financially and in terms of her sense of the emotional return on her labor. Mia finds that she makes a good living – two to five hundred a night – and is "having a blast" wise-cracking with the boys.

Not all clients are so receptive to a dancer's efforts, and another aspect of the emotional labor of the profession is that you need to deal with the boors, the industry-labeled "assholes." Marie once had a customer deliberately blow cigar smoke in her face. Andrea had a man spit champagne at her. Jeanette had a client who tried to leave without paying up on owed tips. (She got her money, I was not surprised to learn.) They all have their stories about disrespectful customers, often drunk, who call them ugly or fat or swear at them or snap their thong straps. Laura was collecting her dollar bills at the tip rail one night when one man slapped her butt. "He thought it was funny," she tells me, "but I got really mad. I almost went to hit him, and he started laughing, and I said something crude, and then I got him kicked out of the bar. *That* felt really good," she nods firmly. The dancers all have *many* stories where a guy thinks he can get sex from them and that they're just holding out for a higher price ("How much will it take for you to go home with me?"). When Fire walked away from a man who wanted more and tried to grab at her breasts during a lap dance, he yelled at her, "Send over the dirtiest hootchie in this place!"

This is where the job gets really hard: not just dealing with the endless requests for sex but with what Mia calls the "hardcore degenerate freaks … that want to make you feel like a whore and make you feel like trash, guys that talk really mean to you and are rough." Her examples are chilling: "Do you know how many guys I have had ask if they can stick their finger up my ass?" And, less frequently but worse, are the men "who ask disgusting questions like, 'Do you like it when a guy slaps you in the face after sex?' or 'Do you like it when a guy fucks you hard up the ass?'" Those, she says, are the hardest people to deal with. A version of this client, sometimes more amusing than disgusting, is the man whose sexual tastes run beyond the standard. Fire tells me, "I had a guy once who paid me two hundred dollars to walk around the club in my bare feet, and then he sucked my toes. When I had my shoes back on, he sucked my heels. He loved it. He was sick." While perhaps all he needed were the more sympathetic services of a professional dominatrix, dealing with such requests for many young women is indeed hard emotional labor. Men do get routinely thrown out for abusive behavior – at least in a well-run club – but while a dancer may derive emotional satisfaction from seeing a bully banned from the premises, she still has to cope with his abuse after the fact. The management of feelings of anger, embarrassment, outrage, and hurt can be constant. Were it not for the omnipresence of rape, sexual harassment, and battery throughout the culture, this aspect of the stripper's job might well make the whole seem not worth it. Some may say that a dancer deserves no better for exposing herself to such an environment, but the women shame the men right back with lines like, "I'm a human being; I deserve better than that!" "That's so rude; would you talk to your sister like that?" or "Oh, are you soliciting prostitution? That's illegal, you know."

Finally, all the dancers have to deal with rejection. This is the part of the emotional labor that proves most tiring for Marie in the end. Hustling for dances, even for the top earners, inevitably entails hearing a lot of "No's." Such rejection can sting and is hard not to take personally, which is exactly what you must learn not to do. Marie, before she decided to dance in Ottawa during the off-season, spent a summer in West Palm Beach, when the crowd is much thinner at the club and a lot of the wealth is out of town. She wasn't getting much business and forced herself one night to go around the club and ask everyone there if they wanted a dance. She received forty rejections in a row and had to repeat to herself, "I will not cry, I will not cry." I think about this story as I watch her on a better night give a lap dance to a stone-faced guy who never once cracks a smile or says a word. Is he bored, displeased, critical of her or her performance? Even when they say yes, this profession can be hard on a dancer's self-esteem.

Stripping, I'm coming to see, has fantasy appeal not just for men, but for women as well. When the money is flowing well, part of the attraction of being a stripper is that it allows a woman to indulge in the fantasy of her absolute desirability to men. Heidi Mattson, in her memoir *Ivy League Stripper* about how she put herself through Brown University by working at a local club, writes, "It was a high – being loved en masse (and showered with cash, too). I amazed customers by walking past them, even by merely existing. It was empowering, as only the strongest, highest-paying fantasy can be."[2] Chapter 4 explores this aspect of fantasy as a central facet of striptease culture, but empowerment is clearly not the whole story about stripping, and that rejection, or reality check, can be hard to not take personally. While a good night – depending on dancer, season, and club – can mean earnings anywhere from two hundred and fifty to one thousand dollars or more, a bad night can mean fifty dollars or worse; sometimes after paying out the required house fees and tips to DJs, bouncers, and bartenders, a dancer can find that an evening has cost her money. Such shifts usually bite into one's confidence and self-worth as well.

Mr. Lucky's, Women's Restroom, 10 p.m.

Fantasy and reality thus collide, not only for the leering customer disappointed that the dancer loses interest when his flow of bills dries up, but also for the young woman who finds a downside to stripping that belies the promised magic of its easy cash and imaginative pleasures. The emotional labor of exotic dance is one way to present this downside, but the reality costs of stripping go beyond a mere acknowledgement that it is hard work. Some harsh truths of the industry itself and of the culture within which it operates clash with the fantasy image of the stripper as sexy beauty, whose every hip-thrust beckons and beguiles.

One night at Mr. Lucky's, I hang out in the women's washroom with Marie to learn more about these negative aspects of the profession. Clubs, as public establishments, provide restroom facilities for both male and female patrons, but at most clubs the latter are few indeed. Accordingly, the women's washroom functions as an employee lounge, with dancers streaming in and out all evening to primp between sets or grab a smoke or just take a break from hustling and smiling. The dancers all know that I'm there to research a book, and more than a dozen of them jump in and out of a conversation that I initiate on the downside of their profession, as they mist on body spray, casually rearrange body parts inside costumes, and use the toilet stalls to freshen up. ("Christ," the irrepressible Mia once told me, "we're probably cleaner than most of the people out there because we're wiping, wiping, Baby Wipes, wiping, wiping, all day long.") They want me to know "what it's really like," and weave me a story out of overlapping anecdotes, impressions, arguments, and advice, as I wedge myself between the sink counter and the wall-size full-length mirror.

When I ask about the disadvantages of the job, the women's answers, along with those from my interviews with other dancers, fall into four broad categories. The first two are related: unfair social perceptions and rejection by family. One of the great costs of the profession is the negative stereotype still evoked by the job title "stripper." While the general sexualization of pop culture throughout the 1990s has made it much more socially acceptable, and even chic in some quarters, to be an exotic dancer, women who earn their living on the club floor still do not totally escape the censure of the job. Part of my research involved surveying, in 2002, a representative group of 484 Alabama residents for their opinions on stripping. Although Alabamians often rank as more socially conservative than those from other parts of the country, the attitudes revealed by my survey respondents were not so different from those experienced by dancers I interview in Florida or Atlanta or San Francisco or Toronto.

In response to the question "Do you feel that stripping as an occupation for a woman is acceptable or unacceptable?" 55 percent of the respondents think that exotic dance is unacceptable for a woman. In response to the question asking whether "[s]tripping as an occupation is degrading or demeaning to the women who do it," 45 percent strongly agree that it's degrading or demeaning to the women, and only 17 percent strongly disagree. When asked how they think strippers compare to other women as being more sexually promiscuous or loose, less so, or about the same, 52 percent say that the dancers are more promiscuous. When asked whether women who strip are more intelligent, less so, or about the same as other women, the view of 30 percent is that they are less intelligent. Response of 53 percent to the query about drug use among dancers shows the conviction that the dancers are more likely to be drug users. A high of 73 percent of our respondents see strippers as taken advantage of and exploited. And 33 percent of those surveyed conclude that dancers are more immoral than women in the general population. Even while the industry rakes in billions of dollars a year and while stripping has become undeniably more mainstream, it appears that the public generally still holds the profession in low, if titillated, esteem. The Appendix at the end of the book gives the full range of response to each of ten questions, on which these figures are based.

The dancers in Mr. Lucky's washroom are all very familiar with these social perceptions. Exotic dancers don't get to be Miss America or run for public office (except maybe in Italy) and they worry about job gaps in their resumés when they return to the "regular" work world. They complain about the unfairness of these negative views and name such stereotypes as one of the worst parts of their jobs. Dior, for example, is in the room preparing for her upcoming three-song set on stage. She is a statuesque African-American dancer in her late twenties who has been working in the industry for several years, with long full hair and shiny red lipstick matched by a perfect manicure. Dior is quite indignant about the public perception of strippers: "Yeah, people think you're a whore, they think we're all on drugs. I don't rub dick for a living! I don't touch them there!" And what's more, she says, turning from the mirror and shaking a mascara wand at me, "they can't believe that you're smart or that you have plans outside the club. Like me, I'm a landlady." She tells me about the three area houses that she's bought from her work proceeds and that she rents out. Luckily, her boyfriend understands: "He's a lawyer and he's totally cool with what I do here. He says, 'Let's pool our money and work together.'" They're getting married this summer, she starts to tell me, before suddenly rushing out of the room laughing, "Oh my God!" as we hear DJ Bill announce her name.

Cameo, a strawberry blonde from North Carolina with skin so white that she's rumored to never step out into the sun, looks on, saying little but nodding emphatically. Marie, standing beside me, agrees that strippers are sick of people thinking that they're all stupid or whores or drug-addicts. She says that in her estimation from working a few years in the industry, 90 percent don't fall into these categories, and most women are in fact intelligent and intentional about their work. One of Marie's main motivations in helping me with the research for this book is to counter the derogatory stereotypes about exotic dancers that continue to abound and that fuel instances of discrimination which continue to infuriate her. Within the industry itself, the public record is full of stories of illegal working conditions in the clubs, harassment practiced by management, and inequity in the legal system when dancers seek redress (all issues tackled by exotic-dancers' rights organizations, as discussed in Chapter 6). Outside the industry, dancers suffer slights as well. To cite just one example in the news around the time that I'm in Florida: Christina Silvas, an exotic dancer from Sacramento, California, was "outed" by a parent at her daughter's Christian school, which then expelled the kindergartner for having a mother who stripped for a living. A church pastor associated with the school justified their exclusion of the 5-year-old by saying, "If you choose to do the wrong thing willfully, then God's word instructs me as to what my responsibility is."[3]

Back in the washroom, another dancer picks up Dior's thread. Alexa is a blonde woman from Poland whose name I don't hear at first amidst the lounge chatter when Marie introduces us. When I ask again for her name, she pauses for a second, shrugs and then smiles, "Whatever you want it to be." Her outfit is a white lace stretch minidress with spaghetti straps that she wears under her arms as a tube dress, with a faded jean jacket pulled over top. At Marie's request, she nonchalantly turns around and lifts her skirt to model for me a new G-string, sparkly white with sequins. She is smoking as she talks, flicking ashes into one of the toilets that has a blue shower curtain around it while renovations proceed in the club. Although it's true, she concurs, that strippers are definitely looked down upon in society – "Oh yes, they all think we're whores and coke heads. But I don't even touch my customers!" – the real problem for her isn't the opinion of strangers, but that of family and friends. Her mother and other family members are all still back in Poland. "I send money home. Every month," she tells me, clearly glad that she can help. When I ask if her family knows how she earns her salary, she waves her hands and shakes her head emphatically. "Noooo! My mother would hate it. She'd never understand. There's nothing like this in Poland." She takes another drag on her cigarette and then tells me a story. "I have a Polish friend from New York who was visiting. I told her I was a cocktail waitress. She wanted to come have a drink, and I had to say you can't, it's a private country club, only members can come. I couldn't tell her either." Beware, then, this other major reality cost of the profession, should you decide to enter: your parents will probably hate it.

Alienation from family may, in fact, be the most painful cost of stripping. Family relations are almost inevitably strained around the issue of a daughter's stripping. Examples abound; practically every dancer whom I interview says that her parents don't know and would freak out if they knew, or, at best, that they know but don't want to talk about it. Upon learning of Marie's change of direction from graduate school to exotic dance, her mom said, "Tell me when you quit. But I love you." Her dad quipped, "Well, I won't be telling my friends that!" Beyond expressing their worries over her safety, they don't want to or can't discuss her life as an exotic dancer. While Marie is grateful that she never loses their affection, she does feel shut out, as at Christmas reunions when her brother is asked to update the family on his job life and she is conspicuously not invited to share such news.

Andrea, whose parents live five minutes away and who says of them, "We get along," summarizes her family's reaction: "My mother hates what I do, my father would prefer that I do something else, and if my grandparents found out, they'd probably have a heart attack." Laura admits that her father hasn't spoken to her since the day he found out and "my mother and I have agreed never to discuss it." All are aware that they are being shamed, even if they don't feel ashamed themselves. "I know that when I go to bed at night, I have a clear conscience about what I've done," avows Mia, but she hasn't told her mom either. Dancing can cause problems with one's partner as well, if he or she isn't supportive and is jealous or insecure. Alexa, who is touching up her lipstick after her cigarette, admits that her husband doesn't like it. "He's a round man," she says, turning from the mirror and holding her arms out to indicate a big beer belly. "He's afraid I'm going to find someone more handsome and with more money here at the club. He knows that I like money," she laughs, capping her lipstick.

Sable, of the long dark hair and melting eyes, is one of the few dancers I interview whose family knows what she does and is fairly supportive of her work choice. She comes down from the locker room upstairs into the restroom, having just changed into a long velour dress of midnight blue. (Dancers often switch costumes once or twice midshift.) She is very pretty and girl-next-door sweet and she joins into our conversation that dancers are unfairly perceived as drug addicts: "I never drink or do drugs here." Then she catches herself, widens her eyes, "I never do drugs at all, I mean!" While she dances, Sable is training to get her license as a massage therapist. She's only two courses away from finishing, but she's having problems and has delayed graduation. "I started to hate touching them, especially the guys. Sometimes they'd be really gross, dirty, smelly. I didn't want to touch, like, their gross feet." She mimes a shudder and takes a couple of steps backward. One gets the impression that an occupational hazard of stripping is that one can develop a desire to not touch or be touched. Once she's licensed, she's thinking of advertising for women-only. "Men are just assholes," she laments. "Except for my boyfriend," she quickly qualifies, "but he's been trained." She knows she's lucky that when she informed her mother about her dance job, her mom was sympathetic and even, she marvels, sort of proud: "It takes a lot of courage to do what you do, dear," her mom had said. "I could never do that; it takes a strong woman." Her grandmother, she is grateful, is equally supportive.

Both Andrea and Laura have ways of processing the rejection that they have experienced from their families. Laura tells me that her parents are reacting out of ignorance, based on their negative stereotypes about the industry. "In my mind, that's their problem. They've never been in a club. They don't know anything about it. And in general, people who react badly to stripping as a career are people who really don't understand what it's about. It's all pretty much ignorance." Andrea defends her career choice, although with her parents she says that they can't even talk about it: "I'm not hurting anybody doing what I do. It's not like I'm a horrible person and I'm smoking my money into a crack pipe. I'm an everyday normal person. Just because I take my clothes off for a living I don't think that that should classify me as anything, as a bad person or a good person. I am just who I am; you can't define me by what I do." Both their points, however, probably fail to address their parents' real concern. While it's true that stereotypes and fears about what goes on in a strip club are often worse than the actual working conditions, I suspect that no amount of "Strip Club 101" schooling would reconcile Laura's parents to her current choice of job. And Andrea's parents are probably convinced that her work is in fact hurtful, either to herself or to their vision of ideal male-female gender relations.

Partly, parents react badly because embracing the fact that their daughter is a stripper involves facing and embracing her sexuality. Children are famous themselves for not wanting to deal with the idea of their parents as lively sexual beings. Exotic dance raises repressed Oedipal family dynamics around issues of sexuality and desire. Many of a dancer's customers, for example, are men the age of her father, and her dad may be at least an occasional patron of strip clubs himself. Some element of a father's rejection of his daughter's stripper career may spring from his own discomforting dilemma of finding himself sexually attracted, either in the media sphere or in strip clubs, to young women like his daughter. Sexuality is a notoriously difficult issue for any family to address, and having a stripper in the family brings this issue to light in particularly acute form. I only ever meet one parent who seems truly supportive of her child's occupation in the exotic dance industry. She was a somewhat older woman who came up to me after a conference presentation on my research and who let me know that not only had her daughter worked as a stripper, but her son had as well. She had advised them at the time that they would discover things about themselves through this work that they would never otherwise know and she seemed quite comfortable with this form of self-exploration.

Partly, family members are also opposed to stripping because they worry for their daughter's or sister's safety and physical well-being. There is some truth to the dangers of the job, as in the poor working conditions mentioned above. Ironically, the worries that many concerned parents and friends voice – that she'll get hooked on drugs or lured into prostitution or beat up or raped or implicated with the mob – seem the most exaggerated. These are the dramatic danger scenarios, fed by shows like *The Sopranos* where the strip club is office central for the mafia. I hear two rape stories in my interviews, I hear testimony about a lot of drug use, and I do see the overlap between dancing and hooking. It's not clear to me, however, that prostitution is necessarily or always a problem (as I'll discuss in Part II) or that rape and drug use occur more frequently among dancers in the clubs than they do, for example, among university students, the other context that I know well from my work. One of the rape stories that I hear from a dancer is the exact same scenario that plays itself out all too frequently on college campuses: this young woman had a "date-rape" drug placed in her drink at a club to render her insensible such that she had no memory of the actual attack. Realization of what had occurred came only from a pregnancy discovered some time later. She is now no longer dancing and has a baby daughter whom she loves but struggles to raise as a mom and college student with a full-time outside job.

The situation is the same with drugs and alcohol: they are clearly available through the strip-club scene, but they're easily available through the college club and party scene as well. There's a street near our campus that was nick-named "Crack Alley" until a recent police and redevelopment effort cleaned up the neighborhood. I've had a student tearfully show me the track marks on her arm as she sought help to end her drug use. Statistics about binge drinking on campuses across the nation are truly alarming, and I've heard innumerable stories from students about the pressures to drink and the pleasures of being drunk. In other words, you can go into the world of stripping and be the sort of person who doesn't do drugs and who stays safe. Or you can go to college and become a drug addict or be date-raped – I've seen both situations among students and strippers alike.

I know of no comparative statistical studies as to whether stripping makes these parent's-worst-nightmare scenarios more likely. What is certainly different in the two contexts is that college campuses generally come equipped with alcohol- and drug-abuse counselors, women's crisis centers, and date-rape prevention programs, whereas strippers who slide too deeply into addiction are usually just fired. While clubs do have a system of bouncers and managers to protect the dancers (entailing the monitoring and expulsion of aggressive patrons, escort to a dancer's car, taxi service), there is little structure of support if a dancer does get hurt, other than recourse to a sometimes unsympathetic legal system. The hospital emergency room where my interviewee ended up didn't think to check her for rape, although she was found unconscious with high bloodstream levels of a drug commonly used in date-rape; one suspects that the oversight had something to do with the fact that she was a stripper passed out on a strip-club bathroom floor.

The reality costs of stripping, then, include negative societal stereotypes, alienation from family, and the potentially unhealthy working conditions of the club scene. Laura tells me later, away from the washroom lounge and the other dancers, that she has a different take on my questions about the industry's downside: the negative stereotypes are in her opinion both fair and justified, since she estimates that almost half of all strippers "hook on the side" and a lot do take drugs. They also, she says, regularly mismanage their money. This last issue is what ultimately strikes me as the greatest overall cost of exotic dance: that its short-term lure of easy fistfuls of pink-neon, vanity-stroking, party-palace cash will lead a woman – often truly just a girl, with no experience managing this type of cash flow, and with youth's conviction that there will be plenty of tomorrows to worry about such things – to ignore her goals. It is very easy, in such an atmosphere, to lose sight of one's overall, long-term best interests. Laura has worked with girls, she confides to me, who "buy hundreds of dollars of plastic toys for their kids at the gas station when they stop to get gas. Then the rent's due at the end of that week, and they don't have the money and they're in danger of being evicted, but they just bought three hundred dollars worth of toys or video games for their 4-year-old." There are lots of girls like that, she shakes her head: "You can do really well with dancing if you save your money and you put some back and you go to school or things like that, but there's more dancers who don't, who sniff their money up their nose, or just party all the time."

Each of the dancers in the women's lounge with me that evening has a story of how she plans to use stripping to finance longer-term goals. Some, like Fire, Darcy, and Dior, are saving to buy houses or have already put money into real estate. Others, like Alexa and Jeanette, are investing in retirement accounts. Gina, a sexy little dancer with teeny red shorts, a lip ring, and pink highlights in her blonde hair, is presently in school doing a degree in neonatal nursing. "I'm going to be delivering babies," she says matter-of-factly, swinging her stilettoed feet as she sits on the bathroom counter. She thinks stripping is a good job for a woman in school and that it helps her to get through her program. "Otherwise," she says, "college would be really hard financially." India, 18 years old and just starting out this month, talks about getting into dog breeding.

Brook, a tall dancer with blonde corkscrew curls and dressed in a skin-tight black body suit, announces her goal of opening her own day spa by the age of twenty-five. She is twenty-one now and enrolled to go to school in the fall for cosmetology and massage therapy. She tells me about her daughter, 1 year old, and how she came back to work when the baby was just one month. I'm surprised, as I know the shape my body was in at that point postpartum, and comment that it must have been hard for her, with the strip-club hours and recuperating from the physical strain of birth. Brook just shrugs and explains that "I breast-fed long enough for her to get the colostrum, for the immunities, then I worked out to get my body back in shape." She turns from lowering the neckline of her catsuit – how in the world is she going to strip out of that, I wonder? – and adds, "Now I'm just saving the money I make here for school and for the day spa." Dior, who has tumbled back into the lounge as soon as her set was over, nods approvingly at all these long-term plans. "You can't let the job control you. You have to control the job," she advises them firmly. She's the mother hen lecturing the chicks (so to speak): "When I leave here, I don't take the job home with me. I have an outside life. You have to."

All this is clearly good advice, if you can take it. The problem is that stripping tempts one oh-so-seductively, instead of saving the money, to use it in the pursuit of present-day lifestyle ambitions: in other words, to blow it at the mall. After all, you can always make more tomorrow night. Many of the dancers, like Alexa and Andrea, admit to indulging expensive tastes with their incomes: "Versace, Vuitton, nice cars, traveling. I love to shop. I've got a shopping addiction," confesses Alexa happily. Andrea agrees that "it's definitely hard to save money. It's like I'm never going to run out or have to depend on a paycheck or anything like that. Money comes way too easy. Most strippers don't have an understanding of the meaning of a dollar. I don't. To me, a dollar is nothing. One hundred dollars to me is basically nothing. It's a lot of money to some people, but to us it's not, because we are so used to making so much more."

Of course, it's not only strippers who have trouble saving their money. Economists bemoan the current low savings rate and high debt ratio across all occupations in America. But with stripping, much of the rationale for the job is that it allows a young woman to make more money, with less effort and training, than any other legal occupation. In one reading, if she's not responsibly taking advantage of this fiscal opportunity – if she's merely *enjoying* herself and living the high life – then a whiff of immorality starts to swirl around her pole. A profession that could otherwise be excused were she cleverly using it to save for future respectability becomes suddenly less excusable. And in another scenario, one all too likely, if the dancer is not using her money wisely, then it's quite possible that she's getting into trouble.

Laura's case, sadly, illustrates exactly this danger. When she tells me that a girl can do well with dancing if she goes to school or saves but that most girls don't, she knows of what she speaks. In the end, unfortunately, it doesn't help her. I interview her several times over a three-year period and spend more time with her than with any of the other dancers except for Marie. Before stripping, she had attended one term of college but had also worked sixty hours a week at a restaurant at the same time and, not surprisingly, did badly and dropped out. Instead, she became the restaurant manager. When she started to fall behind with her bills, her boss, a man whom she considered a friend, suggested she make some extra money by stripping. She soon quit the restaurant and was dancing full time. After three years in the clubs, she re-enrolled at college. She wanted to study child development and psychology, with an eye toward an eventual Ph.D. and career as a child psychologist. At first, all went according to plan. She was earning good grades at her local community college and enough money at the club to finance both schooling and a comfortable lifestyle (requiring $40,000–50,000 a year in income, she told me). Her early take on stripping at that time was that more and more women were using it responsibly, as a smart, goal-oriented way to get ahead. But after a year or so at school, she became in our interviews more and more dismissive about how dysfunctional dancers are – "one hundred percent of them are screwed up; everyone has their story," she scoffs – and begins to live out her own evaluation.

The party scene gets to her: she drinks too much, spends money on drugs, and goes to work high. When I had asked her in an earlier interview why it is that dancers are sometimes irresponsible with their money, her words now sound prophetic: "A lot of girls who dance come from a place where they don't feel very good about themselves and they don't feel like they're going anywhere. So if you're a person who has no plan in life and all of a sudden you're making a bunch of money, you have no plan, you don't think much of yourself, what are you going to do with your money? You're just there to have fun." Somehow her own educational goals are not enough to sustain her through her feelings of low self-esteem and the temptations of the strip-club scene. One of the saddest moments of my research is a night at Mr. Lucky's when Laura was drunk and high, chattering away to no one in particular, laughing too loudly, and tottering around on her heels. Dancers don't earn money in such a condition. In her last term at college, she fails all her courses and drops out. The drugs and a chaotic lifestyle lead her to gain weight, which, coupled with her unreliable performance at work, causes management to ask her not to come into the club anymore. Eventually she can't pay the mortgage on the townhome she bought in a gated community of new, look-alike houses. She moves and to the dismay of Marie, who has been Laura's good friend for years, drops out of all contact.

This, in the end, is what strikes me as the greatest danger or reality cost of the profession: that the industry will suck you in and prevent you from going forward with other life plans. It can be very hard to keep sight of long-term ambitions amid the torrent of cash. Managing the money and maintaining focus defeat more than one dancer. Over and over, they repeat to me that if you want to thrive, you have to treat dancing seriously and professionally. Long-term, successful dancers like Dior, Jeanette, and Hallie (the engineer from Atlanta) all emphasize that a wise woman uses stripping as a means toward a clear goal; she does not simply drift into or within the job and let it consume her. But taking good advice, for stripper and layperson alike, is a challenge. I wonder how many of the dancers in the lounge will go forward with the plans that they confide to me. The fantasy that stripping will finance your way through school or set you up as a small-business owner can work out and indeed does for some of the dancers whom I interview. Even when it hasn't yet worked out, this financial success fantasy is a large part of the imaginative pleasure of dance. But the fantasy can also collapse and crash back down to earth. Some women – I don't know what percentage; there are no statistics – get lost in the job. Like quicksand, it pulls them into its neon swirl, and sometimes pulls them down.

Hallie in fact estimates that no more than 20–30 percent of the girls she knows use it well. The lifestyle, she warns, is powerfully addictive; the flow of cash, the workplace freedom, and the flexibility of scheduling all become very hard to give up for nine-to-five and minimum wage or the bottom rung of a corporate ladder. But you mustn't let it completely rule your life, she cautions, or it becomes a downhill slide. Enroll in a local community college – "take PE, take anything!" – because "once it becomes something that you aren't using to get to the next step in your life, then it's an endless cycle." Hallie reflects appreciatively on her family's commitment to education. "I can look at dancing as just an act, whereas some girls were never taught that they could be doctors or anything like that. And now they're making money in a way that their family never made money. You're talking about someone who's 19 or 20 years old who makes $60,000 a year, who with a degree would not make $60,000 a year. They're able to do things they were never before able to do. But then they are 30 or 32 years old, with no marketable job experience and no job skills. They're sitting there and they've got nothing." For a 26-year-old, I marvel at her maturity and wisdom. If Laura is the cautionary tale warning other susceptible young women of the hazards of kidding oneself and losing one's way, Hallie is the poster girl of how to use stripping well to finance life goals of an engineering degree, a condo, and a rainy-day fund.

One final danger, a more subtle one, continues to haunt me. This term, the students in my gender studies class are reading Mary Pipher's 1994 best-seller *Reviving Ophelia: Saving the Selves of Adolescent Girls*. Pipher, a clinical therapist, argues that teenage girls in America are pressured into developing a false self, a notion she draws from Alice Miller and other psychological theorists.[4] The false self is a persona designed to please others and to fulfill a certain set of social expectations. This "Ophelia," in Pipher's provocative metaphor, is thin, groomed, beautiful, compliant, and even passive, but also sexy and conditioned to please men. Is this the stripper, I wonder? Is the stripper a creation and victim of these pressures toward the false self? Or is she thriving despite the pressures? Is she a creative and successful adaptation in response to them?

The peril of this false self is related to the problems Hochschild identified with emotional labor; it is related to the industry's and the culture's unrelenting pressure for girls to look good; it involves an internalization of these pressures and a breaking down of the division between the public stripper persona and her private or everyday self. It involves the issue of gender as a performance. As Marie and I leave the women's washroom and start back into the club, I notice Jeanette working the tip rail and weaving her spell. I watch her throw back her head and laugh, her small hand on the shoulder of a paunchy and balding man easily thirty years her senior. We head out into the steamy West Palm night, and I'm left with this quandary: is this image of Jeanette the false self at work, or is she making the false self work for her? I ask Marie what she thinks, and she smiles, "I know just where to take you next."

—4—

Where Fantasy Becomes Reality

Rachel's

Tonight's club is called Rachel's. Marie and I are here with Anita, our friend from Canada, and Jeff, who is again acting as escort. I don't know who Rachel is. Nothing in the club's advertising explains who she might be, and probably she doesn't even exist. The place does, however, spell out its corporate identity in other ways. This is a gentleman's club, "the finest in adult entertainment on the Florida east coast," according to its promotional materials, and in fact Rachel's turns out to be the most upscale club that I visit in my research. Its interior is large, spacious, and elegantly appointed. It has valet parking and leather upholstery. Two bars line opposite walls of the club, and the bartenders are clean-cut and well-mannered men in white shirts and black bow ties. About forty-five women are working in the club tonight, all dressed in clingy formal gowns, whether long or short. There is a dress code here for dancers; no bikinis or bodysuits or two-piece outfits are allowed, as would be the case in less "classy" clubs. On stage, the dancers do neither pole work nor floor work (no rolling around on the floor, no getting down on hands and knees). Table dances are strictly no-contact; your dancer of choice will strip from clothed to nude while swaying to the music in front of you at your table, but you can't touch. Champagne rooms on the second level offer other possibilities.

As usual in Florida, my first impression on entering was the blast of cold from the air-conditioning. Also as usual, I feel a little off balance. Strip clubs, I've discovered, make me nervous. This whole book is in a sense my attempt to figure out why, but one reason, I've realized, is that they make me feel as if I'm crashing someone else's party. The clubs are made for men. It's as if I'm not quite sure what I'll find at the party or what sort of reception I'll receive. In a way, as Anita points out, this is a very conservative reaction on my part. The clubs are public commercial establishments, open to anyone willing to pay money, and the dancers I meet are unfailingly gracious and receptive to female patronage: a dollar is a dollar and since their desire is a performance anyway, most have no trouble switching from heterosexual to lesbian persona, or simply to playing polite hostess. But still, the feeling persists, and I'm glad that I have my little posse with me for company, guidance, and moral support.

As we had dressed for the evening back at Marie's house, we started to joke that Jeff was our pimp. I had been all set to go out in my standard professor-wear: a calf-length skirt (no slit, no garter), a loose-knit sweater, and flat-heeled shoes. Anita very tactfully suggested – without ever saying it – that I had all the charm and visual appeal of an old married frump, which on many days feels more or less right. She started pulling things out of a massive suitcase she'd lugged down from Canada for exactly such a moment. By the time she, Marie, and I had finished dressing, we were thoroughly tarted up. I found myself in a black stretchy micro-skirt and tight metallic camisole top with spaghetti straps, complete with tinkly costume jewelry. (I did still have on my flats.) I must admit – despite my token protests that a college professor and married woman with children had no business going out in public dressed like a hooker – that I did enjoy it. After having tried on so many of Marie's costumes and having listened to Andrea – "I've always been a prissy little bitch" – and Mia on the joys of buying and dressing up in the stripper outfits, tonight I too let myself be convinced to play dress-up and costume party, to engage in a little fantasy of my own – not necessarily that I'm a stripper but that I'm not yet consigned to the frump-heap of history either.

Once seated in comfy upholstered club chairs at our table in Rachel's, I am struck again by how powerful is this theme of fantasy in the strip clubs. Indeed, Rachel's claims it as central to their experience: another one of their slogans, printed on the matchbook we find in the ashtray at our table, is "Where fantasy becomes reality." Through their grooming, costumes, dance, and conversation, the dancers weave a fantasy image for the customers' consumption: we are sexy, sleek young beauties, here just for you. The picture on the back of Rachel's matchbook is of four women, each looking directly at the camera and toasting the viewer with a raised glass of champagne. They wear identical low-cut tight white gowns embellished with cut-away mesh sides. Their breasts are improbably large, their teeth suspiciously white, their hair monolithically blond, their smiles amazingly wide. We are your fantasy come true, they seem to be saying, except of course that the fantasy won't come true, unless, perhaps, you are a sugar daddy trolling for a new mistress. Here again is that peculiar strip-club twist in which the patrons must buy into – and pay well for – the reality that the club offers only a fantasy of a fantasy comes true.

Sitting there, I feel confused. Is this upscale club somehow "better"? Marie insists not. "Look around," she says, gesturing out at the floor. The competition among girls is intense here, and, as a result, the club lacks camaraderie. Even though Jeff has encouraged her to think about dancing at Rachel's and suggested that it might offer a better clientele than Mr. Lucky's, Marie has never wanted to switch clubs. From my interviews with her colleagues, I have discovered that the Mr. Lucky's girls scorn the Rachel's girls as haughty whores, all looking for sugar daddies, and say that the place has a slimy feel. It sounded at first like a high school complaint between two rival cliques, but now I'm not so sure. I had myself originally assumed that working at an upscale club, with wealthier patrons, would be preferable and entail better working conditions, a safer environment, and less pressure on the dancers.

But following Marie's gaze around the club, I notice that the women seem to have less personality here, less freedom to be themselves or at least to construct their own fantasy vision of who they want to pretend to be for the job. These women are required by management to package themselves into a very narrow persona and, as a result, do all seem rather the same. Their smiles are broad and fixed, their motions slow and controlled, and their attention focused not at all on each other but radar-like on the men. I come to realize that the dancers here are under the strictest emotional management of that in any of the clubs that I visit. Their wardrobe, grooming standards, and client interaction are all closely regulated by the club. As a result, things seem more scripted here, more constrained by the club's sense of itself, and frankly, more bizarre.

This element of the bizarre comes up especially in terms of Rachel's steakhouse, an in-club restaurant where tuxedoed waiters provide "5 Star Dining Until 1:30 a.m." The eating area is set off to one side of the establishment, but still offers views of the main stage and floor action for the patrons enjoying their *filet mignon*. Although many clubs have a kitchen of some sort and offer bar food or advertise a "free businessman's lunch buffet," this option of fine dining is less common. No doubt the business plan intends for the restaurant to attract more and wealthier patrons who might not otherwise frequent a strip club, and thus to contribute to the dancers' take-home earnings as well. The more I think about it, however, the more this juxtaposition of steakhouse and strip club grates on me.

Katherine Frank wrote an intriguing series of short stories that are interspersed with the chapters of her ethnography on exotic dance, *G-Strings and Sympathy*. One of her fictional interludes is a first-person narrative of a dancer entertaining a regular – "the Doctor" – in exactly such a restaurant setting, which goes even further than Rachel's by offering dance on the table top itself. Reading Frank's excellent short story, "The Management of Hunger," I find it hard to maintain a sex-positive interpretation of the strip-club scene: "A brunette dancer … sways high above the breadbasket," "I take off my dress and dance two songs for him to the smell of our dinners cooking in the kitchen," "We dance for him together … placing our feet carefully around the bread plates and wine glasses with each move."[1] The Doctor even orders steak, rare. You can buy a piece of meat; you can buy a female; you can have both served up on the tablecloth in front of you. The equation of woman as raw meat – a consumable commodity, trimmed and packaged – is just too obvious for comfort, the spectacle too truly odd for enjoyment. Don't stilettos ever slide into the herbed butter pats? Hairs land in the Merlot? Women tumble down on top of the silverware? Is this not the most awkward way imaginable to "dance"? The whole thing seems unappetizing, to say the least.

The main stage in the middle of the club is quite high at Rachel's. I later learn that a high stage is a trick used by many upscale establishments to flatter the dancers: it improves the breast line and eliminates any appearance of sagging if the men are always gazing up at the dancers. The stage at Rachel's is more like a long, narrow catwalk that extends through the middle of the central seating area. The tip rail is a narrow counter with a row of bar stools all around the raised stage. The men sit – literally – at the feet of the dancers. They stare up at the women who strut and sway sensuously on stage as they peel off their dresses and G-strings to reveal the perfect, smooth, shaved, tanned flesh beneath. Although many clubs feature a fairly wide range of ethnicities and body types in the women who work there, Rachel's tends to stick to a certain look: their girls are slim, usually big-breasted (often surgically enhanced), predominantly white, many of them blonde, and typically long-haired. The club rotates two or three dancers in different states of undress on the stage at all times. Performing now are a statuesque brunette with an impressive cleavage spilling out of a red velvet halter gown slit up to her thigh and a blonde who is already stripped down to a blue sequined thong.

Our table is behind two men sitting next to each other at the tip rail. They are white, middle-aged, businessmen-types. I can't tell if they're together because they don't speak to each other: they seem almost transfixed, or maybe simply drunk, never taking their eyes off the dancers. The women, for their part, lock gazes with them, knowing that eye contact is their best way to generate income. The blonde dancer undoes the Velcro sides of her thong, slips it off, and then holds on to one of the stage poles as she arches her back and neck to let her long hair fan out behind her. She rocks her pelvis up slowly toward the pole. One of the men smiles and holds up a bill, and the blonde sashays over with a seductive smile of her own. She leans down languorously, bending over on her six-inch heels to accept his offering. Her hair falls forward to sweep the stage and brush against his hand as he tucks the bill into the garter at her thigh. She purses her red lips to blow him a little kiss and then heads back toward the pole, swaying her hips as she goes.

Why She Does It: The Motivational and Fantasy Life of the Stripper

This moment is as good as any to ask the question, "Who holds the power in stripping: the female dancer or the male customer?" Is the man the one in control, because he's the one with the money? Or is it the dancer who wields the power, because she's in charge of spinning the fantasy? Although the question seemed obvious as I sat in Rachel's, I also knew right away that it wasn't a very good question. Clearly both parties hold a certain power, as the dancers will readily admit, and the relationship is a symbiotic one with each providing for, or withholding from, the other. Sable and Fire talk to me about these dynamics one night at Mr. Lucky's. It's more so the dancer who holds power, they claim, or at least it should be if she's doing her job right. "Men have the money, and dancers want the money. They want what men have," Sable explains, "so actually both have power." "Yeah," chimes in Fire, who has worked in places across Florida and southern Ontario, "but if the girl is smart and uses her common sense, then she can control him. She stays in control."

The exchange brings to mind one of my recent gender studies classes, when my student Leila told us about her mom, whom she described as very prudish and conservative. Leila had been explaining to her mother about the class unit we were doing on exotic dance when her mom suddenly exclaimed, "Oh, I get it! You could work at some job and be talented and do a great job, but some man gets the promotion or makes more than you do, just because he's a man. Then you go to a strip club, work there, and some guy – it could be the same guy – is taking off his tie and drooling all over you and handing over the money. Who's got the power now? It totally makes sense! I say more power to them – they should go for it!" Leila was surprised by her mom's reaction, but then agreed, "If I had the guts, I'd do it too."

It's time to dig deeper into this issue of power and its important attendant themes of fantasy and desire. By now, one thing has become quite clear to me from my voyage through the strip clubs. This notion of fantasy is a central and complex key to what is happening in the stripping experience, not just for the men but for the women too. There is the private fantasy life of the dancers as they strip and of the men in the clubs as they watch; there is the shared and performed fantasy of dancer-with-customer, where two very different and essentially conflicting scripts are often going on within the consciousness of each actor; there is the fantasy of the laywomen in the culture as they take stripper aerobics at their neighborhood community center or buy naughty lingerie at Victoria's Secret; there are the fantasy expectations fueled by the stripper icon that are projected by men onto the women around them, whether or not the men participating in these fantasies have ever actually stepped foot within a club; and finally, there is the extent to which the hypersexualized feminine ideal of the stripper functions as a cultural fantasy itself.

One way to begin this exploration of the interrelated dynamics of fantasy and power is by asking, "Given the intense physical and emotional labor of the job, its demands and reality costs, why would a woman choose to strip?" The possibility of making $60,000 or $80,000 a year or more provides a big part of the answer, but money is not the sole motivation nor the sole job benefit, according to the strippers themselves. Much of it also has to do with this question of fantasy and related issues of empowerment and desire. On a later return visit to Mr. Lucky's Lounge, I interview two dancers who help me better to understand these dynamics. I head back to the club with Marie and Jeff on a Tuesday night around 11:30 p.m. I never stay up this late anymore now that I'm a working mom, but Marie has set up an interview for me with Jeanette and Darcy, the dancers who work as a team performing on stage one after the other and doing lesbian play-acting. They paired up a couple of months ago and now routinely go around the club together soliciting dances. They happily play up the lesbian subtext if it strikes a chord with their customer, although both are heterosexual. While a butch lesbian persona does not go over well in the strip club, femme lesbian pairs – glamorously made-up "feminine" women – play very well indeed.

Jeanette seems to be the leader and is the more talkative of the two. She is from the Philippines, 29 years old, and has been dancing for seven years. According to what Marie has told me previously, Jeanette is one of the top-earning dancers at the club. Darcy is from Colombia. Her wide smile is the highlight of her pretty features, unless one counts the impressive breast implants stretching the red-lace, one-shouldered minidress that she wears – briefly – for her last set onstage, before they both come over to our table to collect me for the interview. They lead me to the banquettes at the far side of the club where they normally take customers for lap dances and where a series of small curved alcoves with leather booths lines the wall. The three of us sit down together, both of them bare-breasted, stripped down to their thongs and, of course, their ubiquitous shoes. While dancers often cover back up when they come off stage, depending on the house rules and the proclivities of the individual they don't always bother to do so. It's a little disconcerting to interview naked women, but they seem to think nothing of it and, in truth, I'm the odd woman out in this place, with my trousers, flat shoes, and buttoned-up blouse.

While Jeanette and Darcy have teamed up mainly as a hook to customers, they are clearly friends. Even with me, when they're not performing the "party girl" or "lesbian lover," they sit down close to each other and laugh together often. One pleasure of the job that many of the dancers mention is workplace camaraderie with the other girls. I see a lot of genuine affection at the clubs, although management can disrupt these friendships by fostering competition, either by scheduling too many girls on the floor (since the club doesn't pay them, it has no incentive to restrict the roster) or by not enforcing house rules (thus allowing some dancers to draw customers away from others by undercutting prices or offering prohibited services). Such is not the case at Mr. Lucky's, which Jeanette declares to be a "good club." She and Darcy seem quite willing to fill me in on the details of their work, even though I am conscious that they're losing income by doing so. It occurs to me that maybe they are still performing: everyone in the club can see us, and the two of them talking to someone who looks like me may give them a further hook to use later with the men.

The first thing they want me to know, before I even have a chance to ask a question, is that stripping is all about the pretend. "What we do here is create a fantasy," explains Jeanette, leaning forward. "We let guys have a fantasy that we're here for them, that we want them." Laura had told me much the same thing earlier, that "Fantasy is what we do. This is all *completely* about fantasy. You have to show these men that you think they're sexy, that's part of what they're there for, to feel good about themselves." Darcy jumps in to maintain that their work is not "vulgar." She insists on this point twice during our interview. "It's entertaining.

People think bad things about strippers, but that's not fair. This is dance, it's art." The dancer performs and sells a fantasy; the customer buys it. Marie has often said that the club experience works best when the man recognizes that it's a game and plays along. If he will let her orchestrate their time in a champagne room or the three-song dance set that he's bought, if he'll relax and play along with the fantasy but not delude himself that it's anything but, then it can be fun for both of them, playful and liberatory of tight cultural restrictions around sexuality.

Darcy's point about art figures prominently as well in other dancers' explanations of the meaning and motivation behind their work. The fantasy they conjure up is like that produced by actors in a play or in dance theater; many strippers maintain that they are simply acting out a role in an art performance space where the script is an improvisational one of fantasy and desire. Chrissie, for example, who started out as a theater major, found her background as an actress very useful in stripping: "When I got up there, it was my chance to be on the stage again," Chrissie told me. "It didn't matter what stage it was. All I was doing was playing a role and I was a part in the play." She did exotic dance, she said, "for the theater of it." The benefits of this performance are directed not just at the clients. A big part of the appeal of dancing for Chrissie was its cathartic value. "When I got up there, it was like you can act, you can sing along, you can portray your moods by the songs that you play or the type of dance that you do. You can act out all your emotions." Now that she was back in school, she missed it: "I've always had a vent for frustration and anger and sadness and happiness and all of a sudden I don't have that vent," she explained quite wistfully. "It's wonderful; it keeps you emotionally calm and mentally stable and just happy – if you use it for that."

While this fantasy and play-acting aspect of stripping clearly holds a certain appeal for club patron and dancer alike, I wonder about the complications it poses as well. I ask Jeanette if her husband, who is a police officer, ever minds her work or gets jealous. "No, not at all," she claims. "He knows that I love him and respect him, that I would never cheat. I wouldn't ever be a prostitute. I'm a good girl. This is just for make-believe," she says, repeating her theme. A couple of potential contradictions seem to present themselves here. First of all, Jeanette had told me that she met her husband "through the club, because he was the friend of one of the bartenders." This goes against her earlier statement that the club dynamics are only ever a fantasy of desire. Marie, too, started going out with Jeff when she got to know him through her first club gig back in the Midwest. Mia's current boyfriend was originally a customer as well. These romances happen, not often, but perhaps just often enough to keep the patrons guessing as to whether the fantasy is only ever that, or whether it could actually become real. The possibility of dating a dancer destabilizes Jeanette's claim that everyone knows the dancers' desire is just an illusion for hire for the pleasure of make-believe. This possibility fuels instead another fantasy, that it could all become real. If he's persuasive enough, or charming enough, or generous enough, will she fall in love? Might the passion and interest for which he's paying become real? From this perspective, the man is not entirely to be blamed for paying the dancer to weave a fantasy that she's there for him, and then further indulging in the fantasy that maybe it's not just a fantasy and that she could really be his.

Love, of course, is not the only possibility. Jeanette has raised the issue of prostitution. Thus, the other potential contradiction here is whether the dancers actually are available either for one-time acts of prostitution or as mistress to a sugar-daddy. Can the fantasy become real in this way? The truth is that in some clubs and for some dancers the answer is yes, although for others it is a resounding and offended no. Jeanette has told me she isn't a prostitute, but Marie says that Jeanette will sometimes bring favored regular clients to orgasm through a naked friction dance in a champagne room (that is, she's naked, or wearing only a G-string, and he keeps his pants on as she rubs her bottom against his lap). Is Marie mistaken, or is it Jeanette's claim that such an act doesn't constitute prostitution, or is she just hiding some of the truth from an interviewer she doesn't know and has insufficient reason to trust? This theme of prostitution and the overlap between it and what goes on in a strip club is so complex and significant that I end up devoting space to it in Chapters 6 and 7. For now, I am interested in the story that Jeanette and Darcy tell about themselves, namely that they are hard-working professionals performing a legitimate service. (This is, as well, a story I tell about myself as a university professor, with perhaps the same risks of sounding as if I offer a rationalization for self-aggrandizement.)

Interestingly in this connection, fantasy also functions as the moral justification used by these dancers for their work. In other words, there is nothing wrong with what they do because it takes place strictly within the nonreal world of entertaining fantasy. "The guys know it's a fantasy, an illusion," Jeanette assures me, "so it's okay." As long as the visual display of flesh, the sex talk, and caresses stay safely contained by these bounds of make-believe and illusion, all is permissible. What the dancers do is not "vulgar," as Darcy has said, not immoral or adulterous or promiscuous or sinful or *wrong*, because they don't really mean it, no more than an actor means or is morally accountable for a lustful embrace or a murderous threat performed on stage. When I ask Dior, the senior black dancer who has invested particularly well in real estate, how she feels dancing for married men, she shrugs one muscular shoulder, "I'm not thinking any sexual thoughts about them. I'm not after another woman's man. He wants to play a little, spend some money, needs someone to talk with, that's fine, but then I send him home. I have no trouble with it." Jeanette confides that she likes giving lap dances because afterward, "The men go home to their wives. Girls aren't looking for sugar daddies at this club." What they do is purely a performance and this performance is respectable, they say, because the work remains always – at least for the dancers – in the realm of fantasy. As for the guys, the dancers can't control and aren't responsible for what the men think: "Whatever's going on in their heads is their business," Dior maintains.

Why they do it is for the money. If – from the point of view of the dancer's interaction with her customer – stripping is all about fantasy, from the point of view of the dancer herself stripping is all about the cash. Without fail, every dancer I talk to says that she does it for the money. Financial security and the ability to finance immediate or long-term goals is the number one reason given by all dancers for why they strip. Jeanette and Darcy are both insistent that this is a job and one that they take very seriously. Darcy explains that they don't do drugs, that they never drink alcohol at work (as they wave their water bottles at me), and that they exercise every day at the gym. Jeanette is reluctant to tell me exactly how much she makes, saying her nightly take-home is from around three hundred dollars, four nights a week. She declines to give me a figure for a high night: "The IRS could get suspicious of the low amounts girls report on their income tax if they read how much dancers really earn," she says, laughing. She just repeats that she does well, has a Roth IRA, and saves her money for future goals. Darcy adds that she's saving now to buy a house. Marie, who has been asking Jeanette for advice on how to improve her earnings, later suggests that Jeanette's take-home pay is more often in the range of one thousand a night, and that she makes it a policy to try not to leave the club with less than eight hundred dollars in her purse. Jeanette repeats what she told me earlier, "I'm a good girl. But my thing is that I'm money-hungry." Darcy nods her head. "If it weren't for the money, we wouldn't be here. This job's just a good way of making money." They both strike me as brisk professionals: they've got a job to do and money to make. They'll dance for you, laugh with you, play a game of passion and desire, but they're not there to bond. It's never personal, or to put it another way, never real. "I don't take the job home with me," Jeanette says firmly.

Halfway through my talk with Darcy and Jeanette, a man and dancer fall over at our feet. She was performing a dance on his lap at a table and chair in the row in front of us. I see why the dancers prefer the alcoves with the padded benches – it's a much more stable work site. As they tumble to the ground unhurt, with the dancer on top braced against the man's chest, Jeanette laughs, "She's raping him!" When I tell Marie later, she laughs as well, "No, that would have cost extra." Besides this issue of the money – the dancer's constant refrain – there are other motivations, both practical and fantasy-related, that draw a woman into this profession and that keep her there. Other than those already mentioned – camaraderie, the pleasures of dress-up, a physically active job that keeps you in shape, workplace license for sarcastic banter – there is the flexibility of the scheduling and the party atmosphere of the club. Many of the dancers whom I interview claim they'd never survive in a nine-to-five, Monday through Friday job. They appreciate being able to schedule their own shifts and to call in if they don't feel like going to work one night. Mia's exultant "I'm paid to party!" is a common response from dancers who report that the job is simply a fun one (in contrast to dancers like Jeanette and Darcy, who stress their professional work ethic). "Oh my God!" Mia told me,

"I smoke at work. I drink at work. I act like an idiot at work. I get to be half naked and naked half the time. I've got the perfect job in the world!"

A related emotional pleasure circles back here to the question of fantasy, and especially the dancer's internal fantasy of herself in her role as stripper. Many a dancer whom I interview reports that the work is emotionally empowering: it improves her self-confidence, makes her more comfortable with her body and sexuality, and teaches her to assert herself. From this perspective, an exotic dancer is a strong woman, sexy and the object of much desire, but one who is in charge of these dynamics, who calls the shots in her dealings with men, chooses her own partners, and sets her own boundaries. The fantasy here is Aphrodite, goddess of beauty and love, in whose presence mere mortal men become weak with desire. Mattson, in *Ivy League Stripper,* describes in her memoir the reaction of one of her regular customers to a theatrical dance routine she performs called "the Kinky Cop," complete with handcuffs, black leather, and thigh-high boots. She writes, "'Look at you,' he seemed to be saying. 'You have all the power in the world. Look at you, you are so strong! Jesus!' He swore and dropped to his knees, weakened by emotion. Jealousy. Awe. Wonder." And then she adds, with lovely self-deprecating humor: "*Or was it beer?*"[2]

Laura tells me that she definitely feels more attractive and happier about her body since she started work at the clubs, and even before she got the breast implants. "I feel a lot better about myself now than I did before I was a dancer. Every day that I go to work, men tell me that I'm sexy. It's definitely helped my self-esteem a lot." One can ask questions here about what really has been gained, other than a reinforced notion that a woman's worth resides in her looks. Why is male approval of a female's sexiness quotient a legitimate basis for self-esteem? While I'm irked by this assumption, I recognize too that problems with poor body-image and with eating disorders are endemic among young women (and men) in our looks-obsessed culture, and the feeling that one is physically attractive to others may be at least a starting place for a healthy sense of self-worth. On this point, Mattson goes on to explain about the nature of the power she experiences in the games that she plays with her customers: "The power emanated from the fantasy level but served as a source of motivation. I craved this power elsewhere. I didn't especially want power over men. I wanted power over myself." This element of "power over oneself" or of personal empowerment strikes me as more promising in terms of a deeper sense of self-esteem.

A dancer whom I interview on a research trip to San Francisco helps me to better understand the potential of stripping in terms of these various levels of self-confidence. Brandy works at the Lusty Lady. This club, with a branch in Seattle as well, is a well-known peepshow, nationally famous from several books and from the documentary *Live Nude Girls Unite!* as the first unionized strip club in America and now the first employee-owned locale.[3] The dynamics there are quite different from those in a typical strip club. In a peepshow, there is no physical contact between dancers and patrons. Except for the few women who work in the "private pleasures booth" (still no contact), all that the women do is dance in nude or semi-nude stripper outfits within the enclosed room of the peepshow, with the customers on the other side of glass booths that line the room. These customers pay per minute to have a slide lifted from the window and typically masturbate while watching the women. The dancers are then paid by the club on an hourly wage that increases with seniority up to about twenty dollars an hour at the time when Brandy was working. At the Lusty Lady, dancers don't and can't make as much as at a lap-dance club. Among the women, there is instead more emphasis on the pleasure of dance and on comradeship, as the peepshow is known to attract particularly smart, creative, and feminist-inclined workers, often graduate students from area schools. In one published account of the club that combines text and hundreds of photos by a professional photographer who works at the Seattle Lusty Lady, the author, Erika Langley, confides that her motivations are "exercise, vanity, power, and money. Mostly exercise and vanity, though."[4]

When I talk with Brandy, she explains about this element of "vanity." She is 35 years old and was a lawyer, but after six years in a firm found that she hated it and wanted instead to indulge a long-standing passion for art, namely the creation of large installation pieces incorporating oral histories that she is now exhibiting in San Francisco. She thought dancing at the Lusty Lady would be fun and hasn't been disappointed with an experience that, she says, has been very positive. She echoes Laura's motivation, asserting that "I feel much more confident about my body. I've seen now that there are just so many types of bodies. I don't even worry anymore about tiny imagined rolls of fat." But the impetus runs deeper. "It's definitely empowering. The money is not so great that I would do it for the paycheck alone. I've learned lots of valuable things here."

For one thing, she finds that dancing has been sexually empowering and that she has experienced an "expansion" of her sexuality. She describes her work as enabling her to be both a student and a teacher of human sexuality. "Now," she tells me, "I feel less sexual, less attractive and less in tune with my body when I am *not* dancing." It's also improved her relationship with her boyfriend. She jokes that "I've never felt sexually oppressed or abused, on this job or elsewhere, except with boyfriends who refuse to have sex!" Marie makes a similar point, that dancing has allowed her to play with her sexuality and be more in touch with it: "Being a stripper liberates me sexually. It allows me to let my sexiness out and it encourages me to be more experimental." While exotic dance has improved Brandy's body image and energized her sexuality, it has also given her the time to pursue the change of career that she says she desperately needed. "For me, being a dancer is symbolic of freedom." She makes up stories, raps, and rhymes to use over the intercom with the customers and directs little scenarios with them. "It's a really great creative outlet," she says, and one that feeds her artistic imagination. In fact, her next installation piece is about male-female relationships, drawing on material from the club.

As a final point, Brandy tells me that exotic dance has strengthened her sense of personal boundaries and her entitlement to keep them intact. "I'm much more self-assertive in public. A while ago I pushed this stranger on the street who had asked me if my breasts were real. I know it was a sort of dangerous thing to do, but the guy was just so obnoxious! He looked like he was going to hit me, but then he didn't. He just called me a crazy bitch." She is rather exultant that she survives the encounter so well and concludes with a statement that I hear from many dancers, that she is now much less willing to put up with disrespect from men. Ironically, working in a club teaches a young woman that she's allowed to say no, whereas so much of the training women receive in our culture is about docility and politeness and pleasing others, especially men (lessons perhaps taught with particular finesse in the South). It can be very hard for a young woman to even know what she does and does not want to do with her body sexually and to insist on her right to say no when a guy wants more. I sometimes fear for my young women students getting backed into a sexual corner, so to speak, because they worry it would be rude or hurt his feelings to refuse.

In this connection, there is an important final aspect to the fantasy and motivational life of a dancer. A certain common stereotype has victims of sexual abuse disproportionately entering the stripping industry, in an unhealthy repetition of their abuse. While in San Francisco, I meet also with Johanna Breyer, an ex-dancer and present-day social worker now helping to run the Saint James Infirmary, a free health clinic for sex workers, whose story I recount more fully in Chapter 6. One point relevant here, however, is that Breyer confirms my research that there is a lack of documentation for the popular "traumatic reenactment theory" of why women enter sex work: "Something may have happened to someone in their past and they ended up in the sex industry, but I haven't seen any research projects convincing me that women have more of a history of sexual abuse or sexual violence in the sex industry versus any other sector where women work. I think if you go talk to ten lawyers, they could probably tell you some stories too."

What she has sometimes seen, Breyer continues, are cases where stripping has been healing for survivors of abuse, precisely because it does allow them to repeat sexual scenarios, but this time to remain in control. They can learn to set boundaries and say "no" and be self-assertive. "In some ways, this is where they can feel safe," Breyer tells me. "Maybe because it's sexually charged, and they are able to explore those issues internally or play them out in an environment where sex is 'okay.' And I think that even for people who are doing prostitution and full-service work, that can be a way for them to really find their boundaries and say, 'This is not abusive to me, whereas this was abusive to me,' and you can really have those clear delineations. I was not sexually abused as a child," she concludes, "and I chose to enter the sex industry." The sad truth is, "in America and in the repressive sexualized society that we're in, there are high rates of sexual violence and abuse among women, period."

In this context of rape culture, I start to think differently about the costumes and the diva-esque persona of the stripper. The dress-up and strip-down fantasy seems in some ways aimed at solving exactly this problem of rape. The fantasy of striptease – whether acted out professionally by an exotic dancer or casually by a woman in her stripper aerobics class – is the fantasy of teasing, of tantalizing, of inspiring desire, but – and this point is crucial – always safely and from afar. It is, ultimately, the fantasy of controlling male desire. As I look around the club at the dancers, it occurs to me that, from one perspective, the point of this game is no less than to solve the problem of patriarchy, or at least the problem of the rape culture that is one of patriarchy's most noxious marks. Given that the majority of women live heterosexual lives and are inclined to find romance and partnership with a mate, these women want and need to attract male sexual attention. But women fear such attention as well. Too much, of the wrong sort, at the wrong time, means harassment, stalking, abuse, rape. All women fear male attack. It must be one of the most universally shared female characteristics, acquired early, reinforced by parents, school, the media, shadowy corners, empty parks, and solitary walks home: be careful, you never know who – what *man* – might be lurking in the dark. The fear of rape is an ever-present reality, usually on the back-burner of a woman's consciousness, but there all the same.

From this standpoint, one of the main problems in life for a woman is this problem of male sexual attention. The fantasy pleasure of being a stripper, or even the appeal of dressing up tart-like for a naughty night out, is to have solved this problem. In the fantasy (although by no means necessarily the reality), the stripper has the attention and desire of men, but totally controls how this desire is played out. In the fantasy, she wields the power. She is safe. She gives only what she wants to, and he is prevented by the set-up of the club from taking more. Strippers are not immune to the lure and power of this fantasy. It can fuel their entrance into the profession and keep them working there, despite the gap we all experience in any life endeavor between fantasy and reality. In this sense, playing the role of stripper means that you win the game of patriarchy and solve the problem of rape culture. You still have to play by the rules of patriarchy, meaning that you have to look sexy and pander to male desire. You aren't striking a victory for the feminist side by fundamentally changing these rules of the game, but you do win by the terms of the rules themselves. You get what you want – male sexual attention – and stay safe while doing so. Such, it seems to me, is part of the internal-fantasy pleasure of stripping.

There are, of course, drawbacks or risks to this strategy. The exhibitionist game of tarting it up to win male attention leaves a woman vulnerable, depending on where she plays it and with whom, either within or outside the club. It leaves her half naked, in suggestive costume, balanced on precarious heels. By rousing desire, the game is a version of playing with fire. Furthermore, there's little equality in the game. Looking at the dancers wrapped tight in their spandex, I think about the "vicar and tart" party scene in the 2001 movie *Bridget Jones's*

Diary: the men were to be in long black robes while Bridget is stripped nearly bare in corset and stockings. Why don't men dress up in revealing gigolo outfits for the enjoyment and amusement of women so that the gals can ogle and giggle at them? Why is it only drag queens and men among the gay and leather crowd or the San Francisco-style street fairs who play dress up and put their sexuality on display in ways that are erotic, aesthetic, and humorous all at once? Your average heterosexual guy seems to find it hard to play this game. Is it too threatening to his own sexual identity as a male? This identity is clearly a precarious developmental acquisition in our culture where attention to aesthetics is the province of the female and where there are few rituals and marks of attaining manhood, other than to be *not* female – not a wuss, not prissy in dress, not soft, not a sissy. One mocks a man and his manliness by calling him a girl. Masculinity is a very fragile cultural construct that is actually policed with even stricter boundaries than femininity – women can wear pants, dress in blue, and be doctors, but woe to men wearing skirts, in pink, and with a yen to be a nurse.

The fantasy pleasure of tarting it up to control male sexual desire also makes one a target for the deep ambivalence surrounding women's sexuality in our culture. Women are supposed to be sexual, but not too sexual. Young women in particular are prized for their beauty and allure, but still ideally required at the same time to be, or to act, chaste. Women are supposed to be virgin and whore all at once – a tough act to pull off for anyone other than a prehistoric goddess. Girls of the *nouveau* raunch can more easily nowadays get away with flashing their breasts in a *Girls Gone Wild* video or dancing like a stripper at an office party or practicing *Sex in the City* bedroom mores, but there are nonetheless consequences for such adoption of the stripper persona.

One consequence, and another aspect of this ambivalence, is that stressing one's sexuality still seems to go hand in hand with being assumed to be a bimbo; a woman can't be smart and sexy at the same time. Once when I was in graduate school, my boyfriend at the time informed a male friend of his that I was doing my Ph.D. at Harvard. "In what?" his friend replied. "Cute legs?" The dancers note this phenomenon all the time. Laura, for example, whom I knew to be studying psychology and child development part time at a local community college, told me that a recent customer didn't believe that she was in school. "All dancers say that," he had scoffed, "Do you think I just fell off a turnip truck?" He left their table and sent the driver of his rented limousine over to tell her that it was not a good idea to piss off someone with so much money. Smart dancers seem to intimidate or turn off a lot of men; intelligence doesn't mix well with sexiness in most customers' image of a fantasy girl. The clever dancer thus disguises her brainpower and uses it instead to read her customers' desires and to play dumb whenever necessary, which from their accounts is much of the time.

Jeanette, Darcy, Marie, and these other women help me to see how the internal mental and emotional life of an exotic dancer is a rich one animated by complex fantasy, motivation, and desire. The dancers inspire desire in their customers, but also act out of desire themselves – almost never for the men, and almost always for the financial gains that the job makes possible, but also and perhaps just as importantly want or desire for the job's emotional and imaginative pleasures, for the satisfying internal life that it makes equally possible. Being a stripper allows these women to participate in various fantasies about their identity and to play with different roles. They are motivated by and get to live out the fantasy of the diva, the glamour queen, the temptress illusionist, the artistic performer, the professional business woman. The job allows them to explore, internally, various issues related to their own desirability and to develop confidence and self-assertion in setting and defending personal boundaries, whether as survivors of sexual abuse or simply, like all women, as inhabitants of a culture where women stand on guard against the threat of rape. Work as an exotic dancer can build up a woman's comfort level with her body and can encourage sexual experimentation and liberation from restrictive social mores. It can provide a group membership, in a freewheeling work environment, among a sisterhood of dancers.

In other words, many dancers experience the job as desirable not only because it is financially empowering – although this motivation *is* crucial – but also because the job is or can be empowering sexually, emotionally, and socially as well. The profession can even be spiritually empowering for women who find that it supports a feminist, sex-positive spirituality in a religious world where sex is often the greatest sin. This latter claim so intrigues me, I end up dedicating this book's final chapter to it.

Fantasy, Power, and Performance

Power, empowerment, disempowerment – all are there in these discourses about the strip-club experience, intertwined in and around the fantasy play of both patron and dancer, and in the fantasy imaginings of outsiders about what it's like to be a dancer. But what more can we say to dig deeper into these workings of exotic dance? Here's an idea that feminist theorist Judith Butler helps me with: *gender is a fantasy as well.* Gender may in fact be the ultimate fantasy spinned in the strip club, animating all of its dynamics and fueling its current cultural impact. Butler, in her influential 1990 book *Gender Trouble*, develops the notion of gender as performance, or as what she also calls a style or a strategy.[5] Gender, whether masculine or feminine, does not exist as a fixed essence or natural identity that we then express respectively as a man or woman. It is not something given, a biological condition that determines a person's identity. According to Butler, gender *has* no preexisting, natural, or fixed meaning; there is no primary or interior gendered core to our personhood. This notion of an "abiding gendered self" is, she argues, an illusion, a chimera, *a fantasy*. From this perspective, gender is a fantasy in the "negative" sense that there is no such thing as gender (no abiding gendered self). This is one sense that we've traced in which exotic dance is a fantasy as well, as in that which is not true, as in the stripper's "Not a chance, buddy" to the hopeful customer with a leer in his eye.

But it should also be clear, I hope, that in none of my discussion of fantasy do I simply mean a lie. Along with Butler, I mean something more as well, something deeper. I mean a story or narrative or archetype in which one participates, what Butler calls a "personal/cultural history" that one inhabits. Such fantasy animates and motivates one's internal mental and emotional life, consciously or unconsciously, for better or for worse. From this perspective, gender is also a fantasy in the "positive" sense that it is a performance we create and act out. Butler uses the term a lot: her reading reveals gender as "the disciplinary production of the figures of fantasy," as "the fantasied and fantastic figuration of the body," as "the public regulation of fantasy through the surface politics of the body." This fantasy of gender is ritually enacted by all of us, all of the time, as bodily styles of living that we adopt and perform. Gender, then, is a set of practices that we soak up and imitate and whose meanings we both inherit and collectively construct. Here gender and fantasy are about play, presentation, production, theatricality, roles, lines, make-up, moves, and stock characters. Precisely through the excellence of the performance is created the illusion that there is no performance at all and that there is instead this innate psychological core of gender.

I find Butler's work fascinating as a lens for thought about stripping, for two reasons. First of all, her theory of gender is a way of seeing quite clearly what stripping is all about: the enactment or performance of a certain notion – clearly in consumer demand – of what it is to be a woman. *Stripping is about the provision of a fantasy of female gender*. In this fantasy, womanhood is envisioned as hyperfeminine, hypersexualized, and completely male-focused, even when playing at lesbianism: Jeanette and Darcy are always hot to have a man join in their fun, for example. Drawing on Butler's work, I would go so far as to say that *no one* is more clearly aware than the stripper that femininity is an act, a performance, and a fantasy. If there is anyone who knows that gender is a performance, it is precisely the stripper, especially the lesbian stripper who acts out heterosexual hyperfemininity for her clients.

Gender is literally something that the dancer creates and puts on with every shift. She dons it corporeally with her layers – scanty though they may be – of glitter body lotion, makeup, hair gel, perfume, costume, and shoes. As one does in any playhouse production, she enacts gender with a memorized routine of lines and scripts and with choreographed routines of strutting dance and hip-swaying movement. Hyperfeminine, hypersexualized "Woman" is what she's paid to act out. David A. Scott, in his book *Behind the G-String*, aptly calls such a fantasy "the goddess." This "quintessential male fantasy image" of woman as goddess, he argues, has four aspects. The goddess is the female who is "ever available, infinitely gratifying, monolithically sexual, and physically ideal." In the stripper, this goddess is rendered nude, live, and commercially available for easy public consumption.[6] "The goddess" is a mask that the dancer puts on, a character she performs, a game she plays, a style or strategy she adopts, a fantasy she spins out.

But down to her bones, the dancer knows that this gendered fantasy performance is not *her*. At the very least, it is not *all* of her. In everyday life, she is Jane, with baseball cap and T-shirt; at the club, she is Tigra, with hair extension and false eyelashes. Fire once explained to me, "I tell men this all the time, but they don't believe it: 'You wouldn't even recognize me outside the club!' I come in here in like an old pair of jeans and like my hair is in a fucking messy ponytail, and like my fucking running shoes, and I don't have my eyebrows on." Dior, who was with us, cracked up laughing. Fire is renowned for her dramatic eyebrows, painted on with a heavy pencil in two thick straight brown lines. "Me too," Dior added, "I look totally different!" The fact that dancers are not infrequently bisexual or lesbian only serves to highlight this aspect of performance even more. Dancers perform heterosexual, ever-lusty, hyperfemininity, *as a job*. This is a crystal-clear truth about stripping for the women: it is a fantasy act that they put on for purposes of pleasure and consumption.

Now men, being men (so the strippers would say), sometimes like to forget or choose not to know this truth; instead of crystal-clear, it remains murky for them. Their fantasy is that Tigra is real, that the dancer looks and acts like Tigra all the time, that her performance is not an act but the true or natural essence of who she really is, and that she truly does want him. Laura explains that this dynamic can quickly become problematic if you do end up dating a customer: "He's asking Angel out," she says, using her stage name, "not Laura. That's a fantasy I can't ever live up to." The dancers, of course, to some extent encourage these illusions. For the strip-club experience to really work, all involved must participate in a fantasy and, for the time of that participation, suspend or bracket up-front acknowledgement that it is "only" a fantasy. Part of the fantasy is precisely to pretend and to act as if it were real. So the culture dreams up the fantasy, and the dancers provide it, but the men provide it as well, by supplying the audience and market. In fact, everybody both consumes and feeds this fantasy: the (mostly male) paying customers, the women dancers, and the culture as a whole. Even those who pathologize and condemn stripping consume it, perhaps as a way to maintain a sense of social and moral superiority, or to remain unaware or uncritical about how their own desire is policed, or perhaps to suppress aspects of their own sexuality with which they don't feel comfortable.

It is at this point that Butler's analysis becomes useful for a second time, as she helps us to ask the question, *is stripping subversive of patriarchy?* Is the gender fantasy enacted in stripping in line with feminist and egalitarian goals? Fantasy suggests a realm beyond the everyday, a realm of play where imagination can lead a person to a different kind of knowledge and experience. We probably all benefit from a fantasy life; the richness and flavor it adds to the act of living is hugely appealing. In fact, the escapist satisfaction of fantasy can compensate for much in life that is deadening or dehumanizing. A bumper sticker that I spot one day on campus announces that "Having abandoned my search for truth, I am now looking for a good fantasy." Here I think that the sex-positive defense of stripping can be strong. Fantasy is a powerful yet easily misunderstood category. Much fantasy is not what we would really like to have happen to us. We couldn't handle it. Sexuality, violence, and even gender are often too extreme in their fantasy states to be lived out in reality. But they can be played with. There is a pleasure – as well admittedly as a danger, to quote Carole Vance's seminal book on this subject[7] – to playing with and imaginatively acting out such fantasies. At the strip club both the client and the dancer can experience such pleasures, as they together – more or less safely – get to act out both sexual fantasies and gender fantasies. One of the customers whom I interview tells me that paying for dancers is far preferable to paying for prostitutes, because paying for the fantasy of sex is better than paying for real sex. He doesn't want to have sex with a hooker, he avers, because it's illegal, seedy, risks disease, and breaches his comfort zone in taking a total stranger to bed. Fantasy, in this regard, is far more satisfying than reality.

While fantasy can pleasurably enrich and relieve real life, one can clearly also get lost in it to one's detriment and peril. Butler points out these dangers as well. Her project is to reconceive what constitutes gender identity, but also to critique the hold that fixed notions of gender have on us. Gender is not innate, we have seen that she argues, but learned and performed; furthermore, the problem with this set-up and the reason we should question the pleasure that the fantasy can provide is that this mode of gender identity falsely masquerades as biologically innate, and cruelly punishes those who won't abide within its allotted parameters. In other words, if gender is a game, the trouble is that it's the only game in town. What's more, it keeps insisting that it's not just a game but the real thing and that if you don't play by its rules, then you're in big trouble, buddy. The traditional system of gender identity is "disciplinary," Butler asserts, in that it exists to regulate sexuality; it limits, coerces, and punishes people into living out gender in very narrowly defined and tightly controlled ways. Woe to those who fail to "do" their gender right. Butler wants to "trouble," or to question and disrupt, any and all compulsory norms around gender and sexuality: that reproductive heterosexuality is the ideal, that gays and lesbians are "unnatural," that men can't cry, that women must shave under their arms or else it's "nasty" (as one my students puts it, with a shudder).

To return to my question of whether stripping can be subversive of patriarchy, Butler offers with her notion that gender is a performance, not simply a *redefinition* and a *critique* of the problems of gender identity, but also a *solution*. According to Butler, excess repetition and parody can disrupt or subvert gender norms. She defends drag, for example, as a "subversive bodily act," as a performance that undermines the power of masculinist culture and compulsory heterosexuality by demonstrating, through parody, exactly how "unnatural" gender is and how it is instead an act. Men in drag imitate feminine gender and thereby reveal gender as itself imitative. Here the parody, as she says, is of "the very notion of an original." The message of drag is that there is no feminine "essence," only women and men creating it, in earnest or in parody, for pay or for play. If we could see gender as a performance along the lines suggested by Butler and grant each other, individually and in our collective cultural institutions, more latitude to perform gender in ways other than those traditionally allowed, then the punitive and disciplinary aspect of gender would be lessened, its creative and fantasy aspect heightened. Gender seems best when we get to play with it, when there is choice and freedom: one day Tigra, one day Jane, depending on how you feel when you wake up and what you're up to, or up for, that day.

Here then is my question: if parody helps reveal these dynamics of gender to be at work in the case of drag and thereby challenges the power of narrow and compulsory roles for women and men, does stripping function this way too? Can stripping, like drag, also be a "subversive bodily act"? Does stripping resist and undermine patriarchy? This is admittedly a high bar for exotic dance to achieve. Such a definition of subversion, or requirement for it, poses difficulties for the stripper since her purpose at the club is to make a living, and not to subvert patriarchy. Customers are paying her to create a fantasy, not to poke holes in it for them. Her financial success seems to depend, in fact, on men *not* realizing or being made to think too deeply about how she is very deliberately creating and enacting femininity. In most ways, the stripper simply repeats gender norms, she doesn't set them up for questioning.

From Butler's perspective this lack of questioning is a problem, since subversion requires that one disrupt or "trouble" gender categories by creating ambiguity and acting unexpectedly; otherwise, even parodies simply become "domesticated and recirculated as instruments of cultural hegemony." Highlighted here is perhaps the most trenchant feminist critique against exotic dance: while it may benefit some individual dancers who are clever enough to make it work for them, it harms women overall by perpetuating sexist notions of what women are or should be. According to this critique, stripping does nothing to change the status quo, in which it's still a man's world, and it fails to advance goals of social justice and gender equity. While the stripper may profit from a flawed system, she still simply perpetuates it.

There is some justice to this critique. To the extent that the stripping industry fuels male fantasy – and female fantasy as well – about how a perfect woman should look and act, the "average" woman can never measure up. To the extent that these fantasy images of female beauty and sexuality – the busty, lusty goddess – dominate the strip club, then men's sexuality may well get honed on such images in a way that becomes problematic for all women. DJ Bill's words one night at Mr. Lucky's reinforce this suspicion. I've met him a couple of times now, and it turns out that he is the husband of the dancer Andrea. He is a beefy guy, renowned for his crass commentary, with tattoos emerging from his tank top. He looks like the bouncer he used to be before he was promoted to DJ and announcer at the club. One night, as the feature mimes oral sex in the crotch of a guy who has paid five dollars to lie onstage for the privilege, Bill's voice booms: "That fucking bitch at home won't do it unless you promise to buy her a Porsche!"

In such ways, the stripper image shapes sexual desire and expectation, and probably not just for heterosexual men. Gay or straight, male or female, and everything else in between: our sexuality is formed and influenced by this fantasy ideal. There are definite dangers here for the dancer: to the extent that she buys into this ideal herself, she can become trapped within the false self (to use Mary Pipher's phrase) or burn out on the emotional labor of maintaining her customer façade (as Hochschild warns) or lost within the performance and fail to see it as just that (in Butler's terms). Just as strippers know they can't be "the goddess" all the time with their partners, laywomen may believe they can never compete or match up to this epitome of feminine hypersexuality, and men may feel perpetually unsatisfied by their partners and their own male performance. All involved may sense that they haven't actualized some ideal that the culture tells them they are supposed to achieve. In other words, when fantasy becomes a norm that we try to live out in reality, we're all in trouble.

There is, of course, a stripper rebuttal to all of this. Don't blame me for this goddess ideal, she says; I certainly haven't created it and the exotic dance industry is by no means its sole or even main sponsor. As Hallie points out, stripping is no more to blame here than advertising or fashion or movies or any other form of entertainment and media in our society. In fact, she argues, "in a lot of ways we can be more like the women that you normally see rather than the models and rock stars who have personal trainers and chefs." And don't take it so seriously; as Jeanette and the others insist, it's just a fantasy, just make-believe, just a game that we can all play along with but that no mature adult should ever believe is real. Finally, strippers freely admit that they're not undoing patriarchy. Much of stripping and striptease culture simply comes down not to trying to change the world, but trying to make it work for you, to get the most out of it as it exists. In truth, how many of us have the right to claim more about our own workplace endeavors? Dancers are often cynical about how much change is realistic to expect in male-female gender relations. Men are always going to want to ogle, they maintain, so instead of just suffering it on the streets, why not turn it to your advantage?

Despite all these acknowledgements of the extent to which stripping is not a "subversive bodily act," there are nevertheless some important ways in which the work of the dancer does indeed qualify. Primarily, stripping is subversive in just the same way as is drag, by showing how gender is an act. On the one hand, it is certainly true that a dancer doesn't disturb her male clients' gender expectations; in fact, she works very hard to fulfill them. But on the other hand, it is also true that the dancer does disrupt norms of femininity by parodying them in her excess. Strippers deliver these parodies in over-the-top performances that – for those with eyes to see – show off "femininity" as a cultural creation and a fantasy and that thereby expose the idea of naturalized or essentialist gender identity as a sham. Tigra or "Sexy Girl" is not the essence of who she is, the soul and sum total of her being, but a paid performance. The dancer doesn't just play into patriarchy, but does resist it by commodifying this patriarchal norm of femininity; she points out through her performance and profession that the norm is not natural but is a market creation. This is what is most subversive about the profession, but also most easy to overlook. Her parody is a subtle one, often too subtle for most customers to "get," and one that she herself habitually presents not as performance but as real.

If you ask the dancers themselves how stripping most rocks the gender boat, their answer is the cash. Strippers measure their success by financial gain. Here is a profession that refuses second-class economic status to young women. To the extent that dancers can capitalize on the options available in the club for fiscal security and freedom, exotic dance is financially subversive of a patriarchal economy and – at least theoretically – allows dancers to escape the gender norms that consign women to a lower-earning status than that of men. If it is true that men will always ogle, making them pay for it in a controlled and safe environment does in some ways seem to shift the power balance. Stripping does so, however, only by agreeing that women's looks and intimacy have cash worth and that what is valuable about women is their sex appeal to men. Dancers don't mind making such admissions because they believe that these valuations will continue as inevitable aspects of the culture regardless of their assent or protest; thus, again, you might as well make it work for you. From this perspective, if you can focus on earning and saving money, the job of stripping can be radically subversive, although perhaps not in the way that Butler meant.

Exotic dance also partly subverts the compulsory heterosexuality that Butler seeks to undermine, even if not as thoroughly as she'd like. Many dancers self-identify as lesbian or bisexual (including Mia's wisecrack, "I'm very bisexual – you buy me something, I become sexual!"). The lesbian narrative is extraordinarily common in the strip club, acted out all the time, but always for the paying pleasure and titillation of the heterosexual male audience or, more rarely, of the heterosexual couple or lesbian/bisexual female customer. Another one of DJ Bill's oh-so-enlightened lines one night is, "It's cool to be bisexual, if you're a chick. But no cock-fights, gentlemen!" The subversion clearly only goes so far. It is largely motivated by capitalism – men will pay for lesbian femme play – not gay rights, and remains homophobic.

The industry subverts as well the cultural text that women should be sexually passive and submissive or that they are naturally less sexually desirous beings than men. As I've discussed, many dancers report that their profession leads them to feel more comfortable with their bodies and their sexuality. The stripper can function as a very sex-positive example of a woman confidently in charge of her sexuality, deriving pleasure from it and from her body. Cultural narratives about women's sexuality are complex, however, and by no means deliver a monolithic message. While the stripper does disrupt the text of woman as asexual submissive (the "lady wife"), she really only does so by playing out the opposite time-worn cultural narrative of the sexual insatiable (the "whore" and "slut"). As long as the stripper is viewed as deviant and "bad," traditional gender norms for how "good girls" should behave remain intact. Stripping only becomes really subversive in terms of these messages when it goes mainstream. Then the question becomes whether it is changing these standards and rules that govern laywomen's sexuality. If the stripper's performance of gender and sexuality as uninhibited, flaunt-it, hypersex glamour-puss becomes a more or less respectable option for everyday gals, one that they can pull off without suffering undue social censure, then that's when striptease culture starts to become truly subversive. If it means you can still be a good girl while also being a bad girl, then that does start to "trouble," to disrupt and subvert and melt down, the rigidity of the old Madonna/whore split.

Is all of this subversive enough to qualify under Butler's definition? Perhaps not, but I think it suggests a way to expand her definition. I don't think that the gender performance necessarily has to be disruptive and troubling to its immediate audience in order for it to be subversive. Sex-positivity is making its way through the culture, and some would say that it has already won the day. It allows for a public stripper persona to be adopted and enacted as a gender performance by any woman, by Everywoman, from the 13-year-old shopping for a thong to the Sweet Potato Queen in her golden years. In these enactments, there is a very fine line and one often hard to judge as to what is gender-subversive in a way that is positive for the individual woman and for the culture as a whole. These are very important questions, and the work of Part II will shortly take them up.

At times during the repeat visits that I make to the clubs, the spectacle at places like Mr. Lucky's and Pearls strikes me as seedy and tawdry. The physical set-up is rather low-end to middling in terms of the quality of the tables, chairs, and décor. The commentary of the DJs often strikes me as annoying and puerile: "fucking awesome," as a dancer arches her back with a leg wrapped around the pole; "We've all jerked off to her," as he calls the next dancer up on stage; or – my personal favorite one evening – his excited, "She's going to floss for us, boys!" as a dancer rocks her G-string back and forth between her legs. Are there really men who think like this? Do they find such commentary erotic? Is it just that I am too old, too sober, or too much of a female heterosexual to find this spectacle erotic? Am I too female-identified to enter into the spirit of male lust that drives these places? Is it only drunk and straight men who find this scene a turn-on? But are most of the men even finding this sexy? I look around and see a lot of deadpan-faced guys having breasts and buttocks waved at them. While some certainly seem to find it fun and look relaxed and entertained (like the guy with the dancer draped over him in the semi-private room at Pearls), a surprising number aren't smiling at all and instead seem tense and expressionless. Are they bored? Scared? Shy? Embarrassed? Intimidated? Wildly excited but just not letting it show because of some macho tough-guy display-no-emotion requirement?

While I have no bisexual experience, I appreciate feminine beauty and have always looked upon women as my natural allies. But gazing around at the sea of naked and semi-naked female flesh around me, I realize that not only do I not feel desire, but I don't even feel aesthetic appreciation. The whole spectacle strikes me as surprisingly unsexy in its blatant sexuality. As one dancer after another takes the stage and rips off her top in seconds flat, my impression is confirmed that there is no art of the striptease here, no slow unveiling, no peeling of the glove, no narrative or character creation in the dance. It's just a mass of naked boobs and cheap spandex. I rather quickly become inured to the nudity. DJ Bill, in one of his softer moments, woefully confides to me that the saddest part of his job is his lack of reaction to undressed women: it's no longer special or even very interesting to him. The unrelenting, in-your-face nakedness of it all has the effect of a European bathing spot where everyone takes their clothes off as a matter of routine. It's hard to get excited about a breast, buttock, or vulva when everything's displayed for public view and where there's more of the same everywhere you look. Then again, maybe you've just got to be an inebriated 22-year-old heterosexual guy to really appreciate this place. It's made for him, after all, not for me, and there are clearly buckets of money to be made off such men with these offerings.

Sometimes, by the end of my Palm Beach visits, I do get it. The spirit of the place captures me, and I start to relax and enjoy myself. At times, the spectacle seems playful, celebratory of sexuality and the body – the laughingly done titty rubs at the tip rail, the five-dollar mock cunnilingus sessions offered by the evening's feature dancer. It seems almost fun, like a naughty game, like a liberation of sexuality from repressive or hypocritical restrictions. At such moments, the strip club seems like an adult and comedic version of a sex ed classroom, proclaiming the message that sexuality is a positive good and a healthy part of being human. America remains in many ways very puritanical about the naked body; sex is simultaneously both everywhere and taboo. Where else in the public sphere do you get to be playful about sexuality other than in strip clubs and their *nouveau*-raunch culture spin-offs in the wider pop culture? This sex-positive message is probably what I come to like most about the clubs (aside, of course, from the pole tricks). Yet from another perspective, I remain ever aware that the message is compromised in all sorts of ways by other aspects of the club experience: the relatively narrow ideal of female form and beauty presented at the clubs, the implied claim that women enjoy nothing more than sexually pleasing men, the misogynist commentary of the DJ. I think yet again of Jeanette, laughing on the job as if she loves it, holding a man's head between her breasts, and then in our private interview shaking her head angrily, declaring how she'd happily take the men's last dollar because they are all rapists at heart.

My last night at Mr. Lucky's, I sit at a table with Jeff and Marie. We watch the stage show for a while until, feeling rather bold, I go up to the rail to tip a dancer who has just completed some particularly impressive upside-down pole spins. She is a young, perky blonde in a ponytail, with a natural and muscular look. She seems surprised when I come up to the rail. "Oh, hi!" she chirps. Then she smiles and thrusts her cupped breasts forward at me to take the tip that I'm holding out. I had planned to just hand it to her, but it seems rude to decline the offer of her breasts, like refusing to shake someone's outstretched hand. So I place the dollar bill in her cleavage, and she closes her breasts around it. It's the first time I tip anyone other than Marie, and I'm surprised at how normal it feels for a near-naked women to push her breasts around the money I extend. It even feels sort of fun, like some sort of moment of sisterly bonding.

Is this strip club thing starting to grow on me?

Part II

Stripping and Popular Culture

–5–

Striptease Culture: Thongs For Everywoman

Playgroup Moms Gone Wild

A man is rubbing his naked buttocks across my chest. No, I take that back – the buttocks are not entirely naked. A black thong is nestled between them. (It turns out that there are male thongs as well – who knew?) My one coherent thought is that the friction is about to trigger a breastfeeding let-down and that milk will stain the front of my white T-shirt. It will glow neon-bright under the black lights of the club for all to see. My next thought is that he smells nice. I imagine the dancers in a back room, debating the merits of various colognes and warning new guys that you have to smell good or the women will never buy dances from you. My stripper is also wearing glasses as he performs his lap dance. It's all somehow quite endearing.

For comparative purposes, I have decided that I need to visit a club where male exotic dancers strip for women. There are not really that many of them. In some places with male dancers, the clientele is primarily gay men, and in other clubs one night of the week or a certain section of the floor space is set aside for women customers to enjoy the gyrations of male strippers. But tonight's club is meant just for the ladies. "Canada's Hot Shots" is located in a nondescript commercial neighborhood of Gatineau, the French-speaking Quebec city directly across the river from Ottawa in the national capital area of Canada. (My family and I are back up North again for the summer.) The club is located in the basement of a building where upstairs, in a sister club, women disrobe for a largely male audience. The stairs down to Hot Shots and the lobby where you pay your cover charge open up into a large rectangular room, rimmed all along the ceiling with neon tube lights in fuchsia and blue. Banquette seating and tables line the walls, as well as a long bar. A large semi-circular stage, mirrored at the back and lined with seats for patrons (if not Gyno Row, then Procto Parade? The Cockpit? The Penis Gallery? The Cocktail Club?) takes up much of the space.

For tonight's venture, my enterprising sister-in-law Danielle has rounded up a posse of women from her mommy-and-me play group and from her family. We've actually been here once before, about eight years ago, on the eve of Danielle's wedding to my brother. Memories of the event are somewhat hazy, but I do remember being fascinated even then by the dynamics of the club, and I look forward now to a more focused study. Danielle is renowned within our circle as the organizer, a woman of high energy, humor, and efficiency who holds down a successful career as a social worker, folds laundry with Origami-like precision, and is raising two young children with my somewhat slower-moving brother. Both of Danielle's older sisters are here with us tonight, as well as her friends Sofia and Phaedra (currently nine months pregnant) from the mom's group, and Anita and myself.

The women of my focus group have engaged in various negotiations to join us this evening at the club. France, Danielle's oldest sister, is a 47-year-old single mom with two sons aged 21 and 17. She laughs that her younger boy was not too happy about her destination for the evening. He had admonished her, "Mom, that's not a place for you!" But she countered that this outing was her first girls' night in years and – wink, wink – that "the only reason I came is all my sisters were here." Sofia waves in the air the consent form that I request all my interviewees to sign: "I'm going to show this to my husband, to prove this is a research project. I told him and he was like rolling his eyes, 'Oh, yeah, right!'" Danielle is financing drinks all around with a roll of bills that turns out to have its provenance from my brother, who had slipped them to her before she left the house this evening. Michael (he briefly toyed with the pseudonym "Thor" for this project) is a lawyer for the Department of Justice and has for years fondly accused me of inhabiting a super-elitist academic ivory tower. Now he pats me on the back approvingly when the topic of my book comes up: "You're finally writing something I'd actually want to read!"

It's fairly early when we arrive, with the crowd still thin, so we're able to snag a row of chairs, center stage. I go exploring and find a short hallway at one end of the club that leads to ten empty champagne rooms that are little more than booths. In the women's washroom, there is graffiti in the stalls: *Dean is the man – thank goodness you are back! Derek is so cute when hard. I love Flex.* There's also a dance floor. This is something new for me. The women patrons here can either dance with one another or pay one of the men to dance with them. Why, I ask myself, have I never seen this set-up at any of the other clubs I've visited? Why would women be more interested than men in buying a service where they actually get to dance *with* the stripper? It's an interesting question that begins to reveal some of the differences in dynamics between the two sorts of strip clubs.

As the dancers start to come out one by one for their stage shows, other differences become apparent. The men – or should I call them boys? – are dressed mostly in jeans or khakis and a T-shirt and shod in running shoes or work boots. I wonder about this, since the women dancers invest such time and money into their costumes. Are their male counterparts not willing or able to pay for such expenditures, or have they actually discovered – market research, survey says? – that women find jeans and work boots to constitute the sexiest outfits? Or does the fashion industry simply lack outré choices in garb for men? The dancers also sport chain necklaces or stud earrings and tattoos or body piercings (with nipples seeming a popular choice). They are muscled, some more so than others, but all are in good shape and generally look to be in their twenties. Like the women dancers, they've put considerable effort into depilation: smooth, hairless chests are the rule, as well as a close facial shave.

Unlike the women, however, there is a lot of tease here. The men take the stage and dance to either slow or fast songs, as they also pose and stroke their bodies. The good ones grin and flirt as they make eye contact with the women in the audience. One guy introduced as Chico with tattoos all over his back fails to look at us at all: "Cute butt, nice tattoos, horrible attitude," dismisses Anita. The dancers slowly pull down the waistband of their jeans or underwear to partly or totally reveal their bum or groin and then quickly pull the waistband up again. They flash a glimpse of their penis, flaccid or erect, and then turn away. Dean, for example, pauses in his dancing at the side of the stage and smiles at a woman sitting there with some friends. He gestures at his belt and arches an eyebrow. It cracks her up, as she leans over laughing with her face in her hands. It's a move the men repeat often, and the women laugh in self-conscious delight every time. As Danielle admits, "It's embarrassing, but it's fun. When they show their penis, I can't look," she cringes, holding her hand up in front of her eyes. "You don't look?" I raise my own eyebrows. "Well, I *look*," she admits, laughing again. Sofia leans over to chime in, "I couldn't look them in the eye at first either, but it's getting better!"

There is, in fact, far more mirth in this club than in any male-audience establishment that I ever visit. The women respond to the dancers onstage with whoops of thrilled and embarrassed laughter. By eleven p.m. the place is packed, there's a conga line out on the dance floor, and the swarm of female customers is screaming full-throttle. This is, in fact, the loudest crowd that I've ever heard in my life. Strip clubs with male patrons are much quieter than this. Unless there's a bachelor party going on, the guys are usually fairly subdued. Here, the gals are constantly hooting, hollering, yelling, laughing, and clapping. They howl "Take it off!" at the dancers, which despite the iconic status of the phrase, I actually never hear in any other club. They – we, I – are clearly reveling in it.

We women are in fact *required* to create such a noise level by the MC. This man, whose name I never catch, plays a different role than that of the DJs in the male-patron clubs. The MC at Hot Shots doesn't spin the music but is often out on the stage introducing the dancers and revving up the crowd. His job seems to consist primarily in getting us to scream as loudly and as often as possible. "How many of you ladies want to see Dan naked?" he shouts into his mike. "We have to work for it?" Sofia asks me. "Didn't I pay at the door?" The MC is constantly inviting us to show our enthusiasm, and we generally oblige, despite our sense that we're being cajoled into a type of performance ourselves. Anita, in particular, reacts in mock outrage, banging her fist on the bar: "Men are so spoiled, this is ridiculous! It's like they need active encouragement. Women strippers wouldn't get away with that!"

But perhaps the crowd needs the MC's persuasion as a form of permission to shun time-honored feminine modesty and decorum and to perform instead the usual male gender role of raucous, raunchy oglers and consumers of naked flesh. Phaedra, for one, is having a hard time making this switch. As a cocktail waiter weaves by selling shots from a holster and row of plastic glasses dangling down in front of his legs like a giant penis, she confesses that she'd be having more fun if she could drink. "Part of why it's hard for me to relax and enjoy it here is because I'm so pregnant. I think because I'm pregnant, I feel like I'm not supposed to be sexual – I'm just all maternal now," she says, rubbing her belly and raising yet another cultural script about femininity, namely that maternity desexualizes us.

Niko comes out next for a slow dance, oiled up and already naked. "C'mon, ladies, scream!" urges the MC. Niko leans back against the mirrored wall lining the rear of the stage and arches his back as he strokes his chest. When he steps away to grab one of the ceiling rails affixed above the stage, he leaves a bum print on the mirror that stays there for the rest of the night. He then swings butt naked over France's head while hanging onto the rail, as she turns to me and grins, "C'est bon, ça!" Two feature dancers also perform for us tonight. One is a slim man from Toronto – "C'mon, give it up, ladies!" – who comes out in a Mexican outfit. Unlike most of the other dancers who are simply flirtatious and suggestive, his act is blatantly sexual although oddly cold. He makes little eye contact and is judged down by my group as insincere. Dressed in his pouch thong and sombrero, he seems to turn off the crowd, and when he offers simulated cunnilingus and fellatio for toonies, there are few takers.

"Oh God," Danielle fans herself afterward, "I'm scandalized – that was too much!" When I inquire as to which part of his act was too much, she screams back, "The asshole!" Phaedra, however, who is starting to get into the spirit of it, asks, "Hey, if I become a stripper, can I be 'Connie Lingus?'" The other feature goes by the appellation C-12, named apparently for the length of his male member. Much of his act consists of fiddling with it like it's a toy, waggling his willie at the ladies and twirling it around. The crowd reacts more favorably to his goofy play than to the other dancer's brazenness. Over another round of drinks, we agree that we prefer dancers who aren't too overtly sexual – too crude or in-your-face – but who flirt a little, look you in the eye, show personality and some humor by poking a bit of fun at themselves and at the whole strip-club scene.

For what I swear to God is the twentieth time tonight, the MC asks us, "How do you like it so far, ladies?" This is our invitation/command to scream and clap our delight, and we unfailingly comply, as the place erupts yet again in ear-splitting decibels. I start to realize that being here feels oddly mainstream and socially acceptable. As we were rounding up the posse, a widowed friend of my mother's who is in her late sixties agreed about the appeal of a night out at such a club – "It's a hoot!" – and told me to have a good time, dear. There are at least six young brides in this Friday evening crowd (identifiable by the short white veils they wear on their heads, supplied, I assume, by the cashier when the bachelorette party comes in), most of them probably getting married tomorrow and each accompanied by a tableful of bridesmaids, all screaming away.

The place strikes me as poles apart from the male-patron female-stripper clubs. It engages in no pretense at upscale, high-class "companionship," nor does it feel seriously sexual or slimy. For a woman to visit a club like this entails an entirely different dynamic than for a man patronizing a female stripper club: more playful than sexual, more amusing than arousing, more entertaining than erotic. At one point near the end of the night, the dancers all come out on stage to do a choreographed "Greased Lightning" medley dance number, tumbling over each other and joking together as they dance, clearly not taking themselves or the steps too seriously. I never see anything like that in a male-oriented strip club.

The bridal parties reveal another difference in the audience dynamics. Women, more so than men, come to clubs in groups of friends and when they buy private dances, they tend to do so for each other. The women ambush someone in their party with a dance paid for on the sly and then look on gleefully from the sidelines as their companion gets her dance. The pleasure of the lap dance isn't merely for the woman who receives it, but is a group pleasure equally shared by her squealing and finger-pointing comrades. Men may on occasion spy surreptitiously on another guy's private dance and buddies may well arrange a dance for a shy bridegroom, but they don't generally take turns buying each other lap dances and then watching and laughing uproariously as they get them. They just don't. Here, however, such behavior is standard, and the male model is held in some suspicion. Danielle asks me what goes on in the champagne rooms: "You're in there all by yourself. Isn't that sort of perverted? You're not there with your friends!"

We have two ambush dances in our group, both orchestrated and paid for by the highly efficient Danielle. She first arranges a dance for her sister Julie, who is on the eve of both a divorce and her forty-fifth birthday. Paul shows up at her chair, turns her around to face him on the floor, and begins to sway to the music as Julie blows Danielle a kiss. Paul strokes and brushes up against her with his hands, face, and bottom. France is screaming "Oh my God!" and falling off her seat laughing. Danielle is yelling "Go, Julie! Go Julie!" We're all watching and wildly cheering. Afterward, we huddle for a debriefing: "I can't believe I just did that!" Julie collapses backward in her chair. "It wasn't embarrassing, although I wouldn't have done this twenty years ago; I was too shy." She is still blushing now, but with a huge smile on her face. "It was fun, though. He had a nice personality, which was good. I just decided to enjoy it," she says, giving her sister a hug.

And then, of course, it's my turn. Danielle uses the money that my brother gave her to buy me a dance with Niko (at twenty dollars a song, the same price that the women dancers usually get). Her purchase is without my knowledge and despite the fact that I had earlier tried to head her off, sensing her intentions, by insisting that I didn't need such an experience for the purposes of my research. She correctly intuited that my protests could be ignored. She further figured out – I don't know how, Danielle is truly legendary – that Niko was my favorite of the dancers. Perhaps it was because of a routine he had done earlier in the evening when he managed to seem both sensitive and silly by spoofing the words and gestures to some sappy love song about a broken-hearted boy pining for his girl. There was also that bum print still up on the mirror that somehow seemed charming. Or maybe it was the fact that he wore glasses, as do I.

At first, he stands in front of me straddling my legs and, not exactly knowing what else to do with my hands, I lay one on his hip. He gently removes it by the wrist as he explains, "Le contact n'est pas permis ici. En arrière du club, oui, mais pas ici." Only in the champagne rooms in the back is contact permitted; I should have known, of course, that one pays more for the privilege of touch. He turns his back to me and pushes his bum up against my breasts and then bends around to brush my chest with the side of his face. I worry again that he'll start my milk and what then, but it doesn't happen. The whole thing is just pleasantly silly and naughty and fun. I'm aware that I too have a big goofy smile on my face the whole time. It's partly embarrassment, partly the novelty of the experience, partly the knowledge that Anita, Danielle and her sisters, and everyone else in the mom's group are all staring at us and cackling away. As my mother's friend surmised, it is a hoot. To some extent, the gratification is the same that I get from a visit to a masseuse or hair stylist: a professional's attention focused entirely on me and my pleasure, allowing me to connect with and enjoy my body.

At one point in the song – and I have to confess that I can't remember what song it was; I'm not even sure I was aware of it at the time – Niko dances slowly in front of me and pulls open the waistband of his tight black thong. I follow his gaze down to his flaccid penis as he fondles it. It seems that I'm supposed to watch, that it would be churlish or rude not to look, but it doesn't even feel all that remarkable to be getting this private glimpse down at his groin. Nor does it strike me as erotic – with all due appreciation for the not inconsiderable talents and endowments of Niko. We've been sitting front and center all night long and I've already seen more penises than in my entire life. Oh my God, I suddenly realize – I'm jaded! Is this what it's like for a regular male client at a club? Ho-hum: another breast, another vulva?

Maybe I'm naive, but the whole point of these clubs doesn't seem to be sexual titillation. Here's another of the MC's comments: "Oh, you ladies must be loving this! I bet you're getting wet now!" On the way home, Danielle, Sofia, and Phaedra talked about how they found his suggestion crass and off-target, a clueless male fantasy that assumes women's sexuality to be visually stimulated, like men's. But no one here seems aroused. The men are faking it with their rubber bands. (I learn about the backstage "tying off" technique from a male stripper I later interview: "Get a magazine or if you're lucky enough get a girl from the crowd to come up – they're called fluffers – then you get a hard-on, take the elastic, tie it at the very base of your penis, tie it tight and push it even further, almost inside your stomach, wrap it around your balls to hold your penis up and do your show. You've got twelve minutes maximum.") Nor do the audience members seem aroused, the way some male patrons undeniably are in their clubs; the women here are laughing and talking with each other too much for that.

Instead, the point of this spectacle seems to be the all-out mega-thrill of upending patriarchy for the night. It's about making a joke out of the norms for feminine demureness and masculine dominance laid down by the culture, and to judge by the level of laughter in the place, the joke is hugely funny indeed. We catch on quickly to the game. As Anita soon discovers, "I like seeing them as sex objects! It's a good turning of the tables." Danielle had prodded me earlier in the evening, when she was plotting my lap dance, "Is there one that you like – black or white? tall or short? It's like being at the shopping mall!" Afterward, she confessed that when "I ordered Niko for you and he didn't come right away, I got mad at him … I felt like a pimp," she chortled, marveling at this strange and newfound sense of self.

We're aware that we're in the middle of a situation that completely turns around the gender scripts of patriarchy: here we're encouraged to objectify these men, to unabashedly view their value as residing in their looks and charm, to treat the dancers as if they exist to provide for our pleasure and cater to our whims. We scrutinize their physiques; Phaedra notes, "I keep looking at their flaws, checking for pimples and flab." We revel in the quite extraordinary knowledge that these men devote themselves to tending their bodies for our enjoyment: they groom, shave, shower, choose clothing, put on cologne, develop dance routines, all for us.

There is, one must admit, just a tad of the sweetness of revenge at work here: of letting men know how it feels to be caught in the double bind of a masculinist and lookist culture wherein a woman has to look good or be ignored, but wherein looking good can get her unpleasantly ogled. Here, now, we get to ogle the men all we want, as we have all felt watched by men ourselves. There is undeniably a pleasure in ogling and, in the case of this reversal, a transgressive and liberatory thrill of us women getting to do it ourselves. The satisfaction of the ogle exists even if, perhaps *because*, this sustained and assessing gaze can make the person so regarded feel self-conscious and vulnerable. This act of looking stresses the power of the viewer. Depending on the context, it can either grant and share this power with the object of the gaze, or demean and humiliate them. This is one dynamic that functions no differently in either a male or a female strip club.

When we finally get up to leave, our ears are ringing and deadened by the night-long blast of unleashed feminine ribaldry. I think about how men go to opposite-sex strip clubs for a variety of reasons, one not inconsequential motivation being that they thereby prove their masculinity. Women, on the other hand, go to places like Hot Shots to shed their femininity, at least in the form of some of its traditional trappings. They go to try on instead a new and very different form of femininity, one being crafted right now in the crucible of striptease culture. Women go to places like Hot Shots because, in striptease culture, now as never before, *they get to*.

All the World's a Strip Club

From the perspective of contemporary popular culture, sex-positivity has won the day. The mainstream aura of male stripper clubs like Hot Shots is just one proof of that. On the face of it, these developments are all rather strange. Being a liberated woman now means letting an unknown man rub his buttocks across your breasts, and even paying him for the privilege. "This is liberation?!" a first-wave suffragette feminist may well screech, rolling in her grave. "It is for such gains that I marched?" demands the 1960s-era, second-wave women's activist. But third-wave feminists today of the sex-positive stripe would call such foresisters' questions sex-negative and reply, with a grin, something along the lines of "Hey, honey, don't knock it 'til you've tried it."

We live in an increasingly sexualized society, one in which the stripper and the stripper-look have gone mainstream and indeed become ubiquitous in pop and youth culture, music, fashion, publishing, movies, and television. Women who look, dress, and act like strippers are all over the media and the entertainment industry. Britney Spears, for example, whom one of my students dubs "the sex icon of my generation," lolled across the cover of *Rolling Stone* offering cleavage to the viewer like a stripper in the middle of a floor-work routine.[1] Janet Jackson infamously bared her breast – or had it bared for her – at the 2004 Super Bowl half-time show. Stripper-themed songs such as Sisqo's 1999 debut single "The Thong Song" ("Baby, I know you wanna show that thong") and T-Pain's 2005 "I'm 'N Luv Wit a Stripper" are so routinely played that the roommate of one of my students had the latter as her ring tone. Witness as well SpikeTV and Stan Lee's recent superhero cartoon series *Stripperella* in which Pamela Anderson provided voice and image to the stripper Erotica Jones (tag line: "Stripper by night, superhero by later night").

Erotic dance has made major incursions outside its own industry not only in the entertainment world of popular culture, but also into very mainstream and even high culture. As a result, stripping is having an important impact all across the wider cultural landscape. Pole dancing, for example, is starting to show up in the rarified world of the high performing arts. A San Francisco ballet company recently unveiled the well-reviewed *Bluegrass/Slyde*, a newly choreographed work set to bluegrass music. The piece featured dancers spinning on three metal poles set up on stage. While the choreography was not overtly erotic nor were the dancers costumed as strippers, the moment was still a telling one in the spread and acceptance of strip club accoutrements and stylings outside of the club and into the arts and culture of our day.[2]

Even everyday girls and women who are neither singers nor professional dancers now routinely take on stripping personae and styles. They can even take on a stripper name at a site such as Blogthings.com, where an "Exotic Dancer Name Generator" spits out stage monikers.[3] (It dubbed me "Foxxxy." When I entered a slightly different version of my name, it suggested "Thumper." Hmmm.) For them, being a stripper is almost chic, and stripper-style definitely so, except that it's all already so very ordinary. We inhabit a culture of strippers, wherein "porno-chic" fashion is all the rage. Skin is in, and trendy women's garb is tight and small. "Porn Star" T-shirts and Playboy bunny head decal clothing seem just about as commonplace as skipping ropes and school backpacks. Stylishly edgy young belles now routinely offer up posterior cleavage framed by visible thong straps and low-cut jeans. Indeed, such thongs have become quite conventional in the malls and hallways of America. Sales of this original stripper underwear have skyrocketed, up to $610 million U.S. sales in 2003. An estimated nineteen million North American women now own at least one pair, with about a quarter of the purchases going to teenage girls.[4] I have to admit, I've started wearing them occasionally myself; as a good friend said, "At first, I didn't like them because they tickled, but now I like them because they tickle."

The Bad Ass Café near our campus – my 7-year-old and his friends, in on the joke, cackle in a mock-parental voice that we should call it the "Inappropriate Donkey Café" – offers thongs with its lattes. For $7.95 you get a black cotton thong with – you guessed it – "Bad Ass" stamped across the back. My neighborhood drug store stocks thong panty liners. All the different brands seem to offer them, as if this product has suddenly become absolutely necessary. I own up to being stumped by this one. It's hard for me to imagine a menstruating woman feeling that she needs to wear a thong. Presumably, however, companies wouldn't make and market these things unless someone was buying them. I'm apparently even less hip than I realized.

The sum total of all these developments is what I have been calling "striptease culture." Its dominance of the social scene was not the case even back in the early 1990s, when Heidi Mattson first started dancing at the Foxy Lady and then published *Ivy League Stripper* in 1995. Her decision to strip her way through Brown University was a very controversial one at the time. She found few supportive allies among her fellow students who were tolerant, as she put it "of only the cool abnormalities such as homosexuality, homelessness, and ultra-radical feminism."[5] A part-time job in sex work backed up by the philosophy of sex-positive feminism simply didn't make the list. At that point, the cultural climate hadn't changed much since Vanessa Williams lost her 1983 Miss America crown for having earlier posed nude in girlie photos.

But times have certainly changed. In just the past decade, stripping has gone from fallen to fashionable. As Lily Burana, ex-dancer and now successful author, notes, "About ten years ago, feminism took a switch. It was no longer women saying, 'To be taken seriously, I need to be asexual.' Sexuality became more egalitarian."[6] Which is another way of saying that women can now successfully pull off, with far less social censure than before, the sort of sexual exhibitionism and promiscuity – or play-acting at promiscuity – traditionally regarded as the province of males. Yet, from another perspective less impressed about supposed gains here on the front of women's rights, the prevalence and intensity of this material might suggest not only that an everyday woman *can* now act and look like a stripper, without censure and just for fun, but that she *should*, or else risk being left behind as a prudish frump by pop culture's sashay ever forward into these new sexual borderlands.

Marie told me a story about a cruise she went on last year with Laura and how they had ended up seated together for the week at a dinner table with four older women. "Maybe by stereotype you would think, 'Oh no, we don't want to say anything because they're going to be offended and upset that they're sitting with strippers.'" But then, Marie recounted with delight, "It ended up being the opposite! It ended up taking over as the topic at dinner two or three nights of the five because they were fascinated and had all of these questions about it. … I've actually been amazed at how many connections people have to strippers. Not first-hand usually, but second- or third-hand, because a lot of women do it at some point in their life." Marie is right; most of the people whom I talk with about my book have a stripper story to tell. I hear about a friend in college who worked at a club, or an ex-student who's currently making costumes for dancers down in Florida, or a client now retired who tells stories from back in her day.

Examples of striptease culture are in fact almost endless, with new ones cropping up almost every time I open the newspaper or scan the Internet. Here is a smattering of recent cases in point:

- Mattel recently released a new line of Barbies dubbed "Lingerie Barbie" in which the iconic American doll is decked out strip-club ready in various risqué outfits featuring thigh-high stockings, short stain slips, Merry Widow bustiers, lacy garters, and spike heels.
- Popular clothing retailer Abercrombie and Fitch markets thongs to girls as young as 10 years old that have emblazoned on the crotch the words "eye candy" or "wink wink." Other chain stores offer Muppet thongs, Cat in the Hat thongs, and Hello Kitty thongs. Such simple cotton thongs have in fact become quite common in teen stores, bearing designs such as cherries, a teddy bear, a padlock, or – striking a different mood – "Feeling Lucky?" with a four-leaf clover, or even a dollar sign with the slogan "Pay up, sucker!"[7]
- Stripper aerobics classes are now familiar offerings at the local gym. While actress Sheila Kelley seems to have started this trend after learning pole dancing for her role in *Midnight at the Blue Iguana* and then penning *The S Factor: Strip Workouts for Every Woman*, cardio strip classes have now

exploded in popularity. The trend makes for great media coverage, with bemused and titillated stories on the front page of business sections about pole-dancing start-ups with names like "Polates" (Pilates with a pole) and "Sensual Fitness Studio." Some even hand out color-coded G-strings for advancing a level. The craze seems to attract everyone from grandmas to sweet-sixteen birthday parties, and classes are bursting at the seams. My local community centers presently offer "Strippersize Me" ("gently condition the entire body and release the feminine spirit"), "Yoga-Licious" ("a sensually inspired yoga workout" that combines "exotic dance postures and meditation designed to enhance libido, self-confidence, balance, flexibility, and strength"), and even "Dirty Dancing for Seniors." If you'd rather not try out your moves in public, you can also get a home workout with DVDs such as *Carmen Electra's Aerobic Striptease* (Paramount, 2003) or the *Urban Striptease Aerobics* series, with their most recent installment "Booty Call" (Sparkworks Media, 2006).[8]

- Add to this material the recent spate of "how-to" stripper books and videos for the non-professional woman seeking not just fitness, but fizzle: for example, Rebecca Drury's *The Little Bit Naughty Book of Lap Dancing for Your Lover* (Amorata Press, 2006); Jennifer Axen and Leigh Phillips's *The Stripper's Guide to Looking Great Naked* (Chronicle Books, 2005); and DVDs with titles like *The Art of Exotic Dancing for Everyday Women* (Philadelphia Films, 2000); Susan Bremer's *Striptease for Real Women* (Bayview Films, 2005); and *Introduction to Lapdancing and Entertaining Your Man* (Bayview Films, 2006).
- In a contemporary spin on the use of nudity in political protest – with ancestors stretching back to Lady Godiva and the Doukhobors – nude biking rallies now take place annually in cities like Vancouver and London as part of "World Naked Bike Ride." In 2005, other participating countries included Australia, the United States, Italy, Latvia, Israel, and Ireland. Enthusiasts gather to bicycle together – nude – across the cities in a rally to support bike-friendly policies and to protest dependence on fossil-fuel transportation. While the political edge is real, at another level, the nudity is happily gratuitous, a publicity stunt done to get press attention and, perhaps, just for the hell of it.
- The *Girls Gone Wild* multimillion-dollar franchise has now expanded from soft porn videos to a clothing line and its own restaurant chain. In the videos, young women flash their breasts and sometimes bottoms to the camera while on spring break, at Mardi Gras events, on college campuses, and in sports bars. The appeal is largely predicated on the idea, brainchild of founder Joe Francis, that these are "real girls" in unscripted encounters, induced to unleash their inner wildness by no more than the GGW camera crew's invitation, "Ladies, show me your thongs!" and the promise of a hat or T-shirt.[9]

- Best-selling humor author Jill Conner Browne has built an empire around the concept of Sweet Potato Queens, which translates into something like graciously-aging Southern belles gone bad. While none of them is taking it off, they do put it on – green sequined mini-dresses, pink majorette boots, tiaras, and poufy red wigs are their standard aesthetic, as well as a glamour-puss, stripper-strut, "Look at me; I'm fabulous!" persona. Tending toward a demographic of fifty-something white women, they embrace slogans like "Never wear panties to a party" and "Say it loud: we're fat and proud!" The movement started when Browne, in the grand Southern tradition of beauty pageants and local festival queens, declared herself "Sweet Potato Queen" for the newly inaugurated Saint Patrick's Day Parade in Jackson, Mississippi in 1982. A series of best-selling fallen guides to life and love eventually followed, with titles like *The Sweet Potato Queens' Book of Love* (1999) and *The Sweet Potato Queens' Wedding Planner/Divorce Guide* (a one-stop-shopping how-to book). Now with a reputed five thousand chapters in thirty countries around the world, SPQs embody kick-ass, flaunt-it charm and "I'm worth it, I deserve it" high humor, along with a love of trashy lingerie, all worthy of a retired strippers' convention.[10]
- CAKE is a new women-led organization designed "to make female sexuality a public, political movement." Aggressively sex-positive, it espouses the philosophy that "the new sexual revolution is where sexual equality and feminism finally meet." CAKE is most renowned for no-holds-barred night-club parties in New York City and London featuring amateur stripping, sex ed demonstrations, and live porn. At one, stickers are issued at the door "Ask me: If I know where my G-spot is" or "Ask me: Have I ever had a threesome."[11]
- A full-page advertisement for "medical weight loss treatments" in a mainstream news magazine features a side shot of a woman's curved buttock in black lace garter, bikini brief, and stockings. Accompanying it is the caption, "I am Julie. Last night, I did a striptease for my husband. What would you do with a few pounds less?"[12]
- The original "Calendar Girls" – a group of older women in England who posed nude for leukemia research in their 1999 Women's Institute charity calendar – spur a whole rash of copycat fundraiser calendars, as well as a hit movie. Nude and semi-nude calendars, usually featuring volunteers coyly posed and half-hidden behind concealing objects, have raised money for women and men's sports teams (French men's rugby, women's international curling), firefighters, bowling leagues, and church choirs. The town of Well, British Columbia (pop. 200) released a 2004 "Nude Cariboo History Calendar" as a fund-raiser for the local non-profit arts organization. The mayor – an older, balding man – and other municipal leaders pose naked in various tongue-in-cheek tableaux: scrubbing laundry behind a pioneer washboard or holding a well-placed fishing rod. The arts group reports no trouble finding volunteer models, and the calendars sold "like hot cakes."[13]

- "Human billboard" advertising now uses naked people as a medium for pushing products. The Internet casino Golden Palace recently paid for human "ads": a topless female porn star at the U.S. Open golf tournament and a nude professional male streaker at the French Open tennis tournament, with the casino's web address inscribed respectively across her chest and his back. This new trend in body-art advertising is seen as a form of guerrilla marketing and raises eyebrows in the world of product promotion but, the business professors sigh, is probably the inevitable next step in efforts to cut through the clutter of contemporary mass marketing.[14]

The Sex-Positive Defense of Striptease Culture, or Why It's Okay To "Take It Off!"

If everyone and her grandpa are now taking it off all the time in the name of personal fitness, political protest, fund-raising, or a search for the inner sex goddess, how do we explain this dynamic and what do we make of it? It was in talking with the dancer Jeanette that I first came to appreciate the nuances of the sex-positive defense of stripping, sex work, and striptease culture. I started to realize that this sex-positive apologia takes on more than one form and that there are actually three different intertwined strands of argumentation going on in the justification for sex-positivity. The defense offered by the long-term, professionalized strippers such as Jeanette, Darcy, and Dior in support of how they earn their living is what I came to identify as (1) "sex-positive capitalism." The other two lines of reasoning are (2) "sex-positive feminism" or "woman-centered sex-positivity" and (3) "sex-positive spirituality" (a fascinating movement whose discussion I will leave to Chapter 7). Striptease culture weaves together all three of these justifications to validate its shimmy and shake, despite some real tensions and even contradictions among the strands.

Of these three, the sex-positive capitalist argument is actually the most conservative and the least disruptive of the current cultural status quo. It's one of the main arguments used by those who make their money off the spread of striptease culture (such as the *Girls Gone Wild* empire) in order to justify this form of income or sales. In particular, this line of reasoning is often the first and foremost line of defense for sex work. Drawing on it, strippers and other sex workers claim that what they do is a job like any other job. The assertion is a common one among the women I interview. A compilation of their responses runs as follows: "I offer a service and I get paid in return, like all workers. If I want to exchange nude erotic dance or titillating company" – or sex, the prostitutes add – "for money, that's my business. It's my body and I should be allowed to decide what to do with it." Evoked here is the language of anti-censorship, freedom of expression, and freedom of choice, including links to the pro-choice abortion-rights rhetoric.

Part of the contention of sex-positive capitalism is that we're pretty much all selling something most of the time. (I'm selling this book, and my services as a professor.) Once the lobby against striptease culture admits to that fact, the argument goes, it just needs to get off its moral high-horse in claiming that the escapist entertainment and sexual fantasy offered by the stripping industry is any worse or fundamentally much different from that offered by other segments of the sales, service, and entertainment industries. Sure, the clubs are taking it a little further, but if the girls participate in spinning the fantasy based on their informed consent to the industry, where are the grounds for protest? As one dominatrix and sex-work theorist writes, "It's worth noting that many service-industry jobs require more or less continuous servility toward bosses and customers; a typical waitress or secretary must play a submissive role for an entire full-time week to earn what a professional submissive can make in a few hours."[15]

The strippers make the further argument, as we saw in Part I, that their work is morally justifiable because it is just a performance, only make-believe, and most definitely not for real. "The guys know it's a fantasy, an illusion," Jeanette had assured me, "so it's okay." Her dance partner Darcy had added, "If it weren't for the money, we wouldn't be here. This job's just a good way of making money." Because all is pretend and there is no actual sex taking place – no exchange of bodily fluids, is how Andrea put it – no one is cheating on a partner or breaking any laws or doing anything "wrong." The dancers are simply there to make a living, like any other capitalist worker in the marketplace who is offering a service that is obviously in high demand.

I find that I am somewhat sympathetic to this capitalist sex-positive argument, although also still aware of the costs that this path entails and of the frequency with which it can fail as a life strategy for a dancer, or at least fall short of her original plan. As noted in Part I, many of the dancers are indeed serious about intending their work as a way to finance longer-term educational and career objectives. Like Heidi Mattson before them, they maintain that they couldn't afford to put themselves through school on their earnings from "regular" jobs. They are certainly right that it's hard financially. I have taught college students who graduate with crippling debt loads of $50,000, or who drop out for lack of money, or who work fifty hours a week while sleep-walking through class schedules with no time to study. Most of my students seem to have financial difficulties, unless they have well-off parents supporting them. I even know colleagues with full-time jobs in academia who have to declare bankruptcy because of loan debt accumulated during their graduate-student years, debt that can reach to $100,000 and more.

From the perspective of sex-positive capitalism, exotic dance is one answer to such problems, and some women do successfully finance their schooling by stripping. Among my interviewees are a lawyer, a social worker, an engineer, and a humanities graduate student, all of whom completed degrees while dancing and who chose to strip largely because it paid more and left more time free for school than any other way to finance their education. I have also spoken with dancers, most notably Laura, whose plans for university never came to fruition. While Laura's decline might have happened even had she simply been a full-time student (and I have seen students lost to drugs, alcohol, partner abuse, homelessness, mental illness, or a simple lack of commitment), in her case the temptations of the strip-club scene seemed clearly not to help.

As stripping struts its way into the mainstream, recruitment campaigns and the ease and conventionality of taking on a job as a dancer become further evidence of striptease culture. An owner of three strip clubs in Windsor, Canada, made headlines in 2003 by advertising for dancers in the student newspaper of the University of Windsor. The clubs promised to pay tuition for dancers who worked at least three shifts a week and maintained a B average or better in school. Partly, it was an effective way for the clubs to get free publicity, as the story was soon picked up by newspapers across Canada, but it also highlights this stereotypical link between stripper and student. Clubs find that undergrads appeal to their clientele, many of whom are college-educated and middle-class professionals themselves. (They generally have to be in order to afford the hundreds of dollars in charges that can routinely result from a night at a club.) The university student easily fits the image of the hard-working good girl or the girl next door and, to top off her appeal, as explained by the clubs' marketing director, "a serious student usually makes a serious employee."[16]

Not all dancers, of course, are students; some are just hoping to make money and have a little fun, but many do have something else – or at least the plans for something else – going on the side. Julia Query, for example, is stripper, comedian, and co-director of the documentary *Live Nude Girls Unite!* about the unionization campaign that took place at the San Francisco Lusty Lady. In her film, she makes the claim only half-jokingly that strippers are simply smart feminist women who have finally figured out what to do about the problem of patriarchy: *take their money*. As I said before, for a woman without higher education, exotic dancing is the single most lucrative legal profession open to her in a labor market that still pays women only cents on the dollar compared to incomes for men. If the world we live in overvalues women's youth and looks and devalues her economic contributions, from a capitalist sex-positive perspective, working for a while as a stripper makes perfect sense.

But it's also not hard to poke holes in this sex-positive capitalism. We can wonder, on the one hand, whether it goes too far. Does the free-market economy mean that everything can and should be commodified for sale, including the charms of a woman's sexual intimacy? As the title of one woman's magazine article wonders, does such "do-me feminism" mean that we've become "stripped of our senses"? Are women's newfound freedoms to take it off just the latest set of pressures to conform to the raunch femininity that now reigns as the pop-cultural script *du jour* for today's liberated woman? There is a lobby against striptease culture, as advanced, for example, by journalist Ariel Levy's recent and much-quoted *Female Chauvinist Pigs* (2005). Levy sees little liberation and only the palest empowerment in the equation of consumerism and women's sexuality presented by sex-positive capitalism. What looks like "liberating rebellion" is really, she argues, just "limiting conformity." "The truth is that the new conception of raunch culture as a path to liberation rather than oppression is a convenient (and lucrative) fantasy with nothing to back it up."[17]

While dancers, ex-dancers, and theorists disagree on this question, sex-positive capitalists say that the debate looks naive. Women's looks and sexuality are already commodified; that's just a given. Pretty, sexy girls are used ad infinitum in advertising to sell everything from tampons to cars to banking services to real estate, and women's sexuality has been the object of male consumption for what feels like an eternity. Social critics like Levy ask the important question of why women should give their stamp of approval to this dynamic and become complicit in their own objectification. Sex-positive capitalists for their part don't try to change this dynamic, but simply suggest that the smart entrepreneur – not just men, but now women too – might as well make money off its inevitability and current mainstream conventionality.

While we can ask whether sex-positive capitalism goes too far, the more interesting question for me is whether it actually doesn't go far enough. If sex-positivity is supposed to challenge and improve the current status quo – to maximize possibilities of responsible sexual pleasure and gender liberation for all – then this particular form of it doesn't seem radical enough to accomplish much toward this goal. When the dancers use this justification, they say that their work is defensible because it is merely make-believe and fantasy. Their implication is that there *would* be something wrong with what they do if it weren't just a performance that they didn't really mean and weren't just a job that was motivated solely by financial need. Because capitalism is motivating them and not lust, what they do should be considered morally and socially acceptable. Because they only pretend to be aroused and only mime sex but never really mean it, they are still, as Jeanette said about herself, "good girls."

If, on the other hand, they *did* really mean it, if they *were* motivated by lust and lasciviousness, if they *did* actually want the sex they pantomimed and then went out and had it, then by their own argument what they do would be wrong. They would become the "bad girls." The dancers with whom I spoke were almost universally against prostitution and "promiscuity," at least in their comments to me. They just about all agreed that if you regularly bed down with the customers for either profit or pleasure, then you're a "whore" or a "slut": derogatory terms they use to indicate you've crossed a line in the sand. Here is what I mean by this version of the sex-positive defense being oddly conservative and status quo. It's okay to be a good girl sleeping with your boyfriend and faking arousal with others, but not a bad girl actually doing it with a range of partners for a variety of reasons.

It's okay to be sex-positive as long as you're a capitalist working for the money and you're not actually having sex. It's okay to be motivated by greed or financial desire, but not by lust or sexual desire. This all seems rather strange and, in the end, not even very sex-positive.

As the dancer and theorist Tawnya Dudash notes in her workplace study of the Lusty Lady, "Patriarchy and capitalism … play a large part in the conceptions of female sexuality."[18] Sex-positive capitalism, it seems to me, just doesn't shake that up all on its own. It's still about women looking traditionally sexy – the young, hot babe – in order to appeal to men and make money. There needs to be more going on, deeper values engaged, more of a critical edge in examining who really benefits from the male gaze. I'm looking for a wider vision of women's sexual agency and women's beauty, for more interest in social justice and a political edge. All of these changes start to happen in another form of sex-positivity that is sometimes seen in the strip club, but that more often thrives outside of it. This form does try to take capitalism and economics out of the equation, and its come-hither stare ends up looking quite different as a result. I call it "woman-centered sex-positivity," or to use its more common name, "sex-positive feminism." And it was at Tease-O-Rama, a neo-burlesque festival, that I was enveloped in its bosomy embrace.

Tease-O-Rama

I am in San Francisco in late September for Tease-O-Rama 2005, the premiere annual convention of the neo-burlesque. This growing movement seeks to revive and celebrate the old-style, Gypsy Rose Lee form of slow burn, glove-peeling striptease. Onstage at a red velour vintage theater and speakeasy, performers set carefully choreographed dance routines to music that ranges from classic bump-and-grind to early Frank Sinatra, French and German lounge songs, techno pop, and more. In between acts of beautiful slim women in gorgeous costumes with elaborate skirts and coordinating corsets, brassieres, headdresses, and gloves who strip down to G-strings and nipple-covering pasties (sometimes adorned with tassels for twirling action), more unusual acts also take the stage. Here is some of what I see:

- Eva von Slut strips down to a tight black corset. She is heavily tattooed and proudly fat, with a soigné blonde-bombshell dominatrix look highlighted by a bat motif.
- Satan's Angel, the Devil's Own Mistress, tells tales during daytime workshops from her glory days as a headliner. Now in her sixties, on the last night of performances she makes her comeback, going from peignoir to her trademark tassels (she used to twirl five at a time), as she bumps, grinds, shakes, and twirls to Santana and an adoring crowd.

- Roky Roulette, the only man doing a strip routine at the event, exuberantly tears off a spaceman costume and then three G-strings one after the other, each stuffed with sparkly glitter that floats about the stage, while he bounces nonstop and sky high on a pogo stick.
- Pussy Flambé of the Fat Bottom Revue, a large woman stylishly dressed in drag in a man's dark suit, takes it all off with a sly grin to "I'm a Woman."
- The tassel-twirling workshop. Ninety naked breasts – big, small, young, older, pendulous, artificially plumped, pierced, and tattooed – are decked out in a kaleidoscope of glued-on decorations. Our teacher, Miss Indigo Blue, informs us, "So, darlings, the tassels want to twirl. We're going to help them." Ouch.
- A big butch rapper in a corset who never even disrobes makes the crowd beg for more: "I'm an Amazon Queen with more bounce in the chassis; hear me mother-fucking ROAR!"
- Simone de la Getto and Alotta Boutté (get it?) of Harlem Shake Burlesque, two women of Rubenesque voluptuousness who team up as one of the few black neo-burlesque troupes, do a parody of church ladies in a paroxysm of song and dance that just happens to leave them stripped down to pasties and panties.
- The Wau Wau Sisters, wearing peace-symbol pasties, sit side by side on the piano bench and play Lennon's "Imagine" with one hand each, as the audience waves candles and lighters in the air.
- The gorgeous Summer Peaches comes out in a banana costume and peels herself down to tassels for a fast shimmy dance of gyrating hips (what's known in the trade as a "hootchie kootchie" dance).
- Catherine D'Lish, the grand finale and weekend headliner, an elegant beauty in long gown and gloves with a waist cinched impossibly Scarlett O'Hara tight, wows the crowd with a graceful striptease of look-at-me, drop-dead, high-end glamour.
- Miss Satanica, "the world's only one-woman, three-ring circus," sports a messy, dressy, goth look in a trashed ball gown. She does a little show with a puppet sewn into her voluminous black netting skirts. "Haven't you seen enough tits?" she snarls. "Want something else?" She then proceeds to eat a light bulb in its entirety.

The crowd could not be happier. They are a fairly equal mix of men and women, mainly young and hip and often glamorous themselves in long gowns and skinny ties, retro fashions and urban chic. The two main performance nights of the convention are sold out far in advance. Neo-burlesque has been gaining popularity across the U.S. as another aspect of striptease culture, with mainstream events in cities like New York, New Orleans, Los Angeles, and San Francisco. The acts at Tease-O-Rama come from as far afield as Australia, the UK, Japan, Denver, Seattle, Nashville, Atlanta, and Madison, Wisconsin.

The genre, I soon realize, is entirely different from exotic dance. The women here are "performers," not "strippers." They have choreography and wear dance shoes, as opposed to unscripted routines carried out in stilettoed platform heels. There's lots of flesh at Tease-O-Rama, but it is unveiled slowly (in contrast to performance in the strip clubs), with all the promised tease, and full nudity is always withheld. There is also no tipping, and there are no private dances. Except for a small handful of women who perform professionally, these gals don't make much money at all. In fact, the costumes and travel to such events can cost them a lot. The vast majority are amateurs with regular day jobs, doing these gigs for fun, as a hobby, for the fantasy kick. As I've described, their look varies widely, from stunning to butch to art house to clown; from slim to fat; from pin-up polished to deliberately anti-glam. In comparison, the strip club insists on a much more monolithic and conventional vision of female form (slim, big-breasted, pretty, available). These differences illustrate that the definition of beauty and femininity in strip-club exotic dance is a comparatively narrow one driven by men's pleasure and pocketbook. Women, left to their own devices – that is, not motivated by finances to act, dress, and self-present so that men will pay for their time and services – strip very differently from the way they do in the exotic dance clubs. As burlesque performer and Ph.D. candidate Lola the Vamp explains, "Stripping is about a financial transaction between a stripper and client. Burlesque is more a theatrical show that takes the icon of the stripper and makes her a goddess."[19]

Herein lies the gap between sex-positive capitalism and sex-positive feminism. The latter is not ultimately about winning the game of capitalist patriarchy or being content to simply make money off the world as it is, as I have suggested is the case with sex-positive capitalism. When you take capitalism and economics out of the equation – when the motivation is no longer trying to earn money – sex-positivity starts to become more radical and more interesting. Indeed, sex-positive feminism does set out to actually change the game. In the standard script, the rules of the game say that women should look a certain way and express their sexuality according to prescribed norms – oriented toward men, compliant or subservient to male desire, and monogamous in at least a serial fashion – in order to be validated as "good girls" (as Jeanette said about herself) who are doing their gender and sexuality right. Sex-positive feminism, in contrast, says *ha!* to all that.

Instead, it's about women and men celebrating sexuality in an open and affirming way as a means to oppose restrictive gender roles, to empower women as the agents of their own sexuality, and to support gay, lesbian, and other alternative lifestyles. Sex-positive feminism, much more so than sex-positive capitalism, defends all forms of consensual, responsible sex. Its message crops up in such varied places as the writings of central theorists in the field (Carol Queen, Pat Califia, Carole Vance, Gayle Rubin), practitioners' performance art (Annie Sprinkle), sex toy and sex ed shops like San Francisco's Good Vibrations, the marketing rhetoric of the stripper aerobics classes about the strong and sexy woman, the mission statement of CAKE, and the *woo-wee!* take-it-off empowerment glee of the *Calendar Girls* copycat phenomenon.

The central claim of sex-positive feminism is that we live in a world still burdened by limiting and oppressive gender expectations and restrictions, for both men and women, and that this burden is inextricably linked to limiting and oppressive norms for sexual identity and sexual expression. What Queen calls our "erotically benighted culture" prohibits many forms of sexual identity and expression it deems "perverted" and "abnormal": gayness, lesbianism, bisexuality, transgender, swinger lifestyles, sexual performance art, paid sex work, and forms of role-playing and erotic power exchange known as B&D (bondage and discipline), SM (sadomasochism), D&S (dominance and submission), or just BDSM (a collection of initials that seems to cover it all).[20] Sex-positive feminism argues that women in particular have been sexually constrained and punished for far too long and that they are sexually adventurous beings, with an equal right to explore their sexuality and pursue their desire. On some of these fronts, attitudes are changing – for example, in terms of support for same-sex partner rights, particularly if the couple is family-oriented and monogamous, and, through striptease culture, in terms of the sexual latitude increasingly allowed to women. But change is slow.

Two points are central to this movement of sex-positive feminism. First, it is woman-centered. Not all the women performers I meet at Tease-O-Rama are comfortable with the label feminist, but all do agree that this form of striptease culture is about women's fantasy and pleasure. At a press party to kick off Tease-O-Rama, I speak with the burlesque performer Olive Oil, who tells me, "This is my superhero persona." Another, who is a member of the Devil-Ettes, fondly describes her go-go troupe as "a rock and roll sorority." A third says to me, "I can't be an insurance adjuster all the time." Neo-burlesque is about the performing women's fantasy, not about the male strip-club patrons' desire. The audience is as much women as men, and many performers self-present as lesbian. The genre is convincingly closer to a non-patriarchal expression of women's sexuality and fantasy of sexual play. It's about beauty, not money; performance, not customer satisfaction; glamour, not sex; look, not touch. As suggested by the presence of Roky Roulette, neo-burlesque can also be about men's sexual fantasy and play, although this aspect awaits development until more male performers sign up.

Secondly, woman-centered or feminist sex-positivity is about expanding definitions of beauty and sexiness. Tease-O-Rama, like Hot Shots, is a type of joke on patriarchy. Sex-positive feminism, as exemplified in the neo-burlesque movement, is a parody of patriarchal norms for women's beauty and sexuality. Parody is a tricky genre and, as Lola the Vamp said in a morning lecture about her own burlesque performances, it can be very subtle and can make people uncomfortable by recreating too closely that which it is supposed to parody. (Think Spike Lee's 2000 film *Bamboozled*, which plays with this dynamic.) If it is too very subtle, it can even fail and bamboozle its own practitioners, while merely strengthening the norms it intended to parody. But it can also succeed brilliantly and offer a more piercing critique than any straight expository argument. The fat and the lesbian burlesque dancers, the ones in drag, in dominatrix or goth stylings, inside a gorilla costume, or dressed as a Frankenstein monster or a baby (squirting milk out of the nipple of a baby's-bottle pastie), are all making this point, as are even the ones in Himalayan-over-the-top, ultrafemme frills. They are all mocking and thereby deconstructing traditional norms for what counts as standard female beauty, sexiness, and compliance.

Olive Oil tells me that for her, the "emphasis is on exaggerating and thus mocking and interrogating these stereotypes about women and beauty. I don't strip so much as make people uncomfortable with their desires for me to strip, to make them ask why and think about it." In neo-burlesque, performers revive but also parody the genre of American burlesque that took off post-Civil War and that thrived into the first half of the twentieth century. *Burlesque* literally refers to a parody that mocks and ridicules through exaggerated imitation, especially a parody of high or pretentious art. The Tease-O-Rama performers are burlesquing the art of gender, the script of femininity. To use the parlance of contemporary theory, they are "queering" standards of beauty, by which is meant critiquing the status quo or conventional norm and embracing the non-normative. A queer notion of beauty or expression of sexuality is one that lies outside traditional standards and mores. The resultant message is that any woman can do burlesque: on stage are vibrant senior citizens with sagging breasts, dazzling fat women galore, and alluring women of plain face. The slogan here is "Flaunt it!" At its best, when taking capitalism out of the equation, woman-centered or feminist sex-positivity proves that all women, of all body types, are beautiful and sexy.

At a session entitled "Revolution through Joy (Sometimes): Burlesque and Women's Liberation," a panel of performers discuss the degree to which burlesque achieves feminist goals and resists patriarchal conditioning, despite the paradox of glorifying the corseted woman with the 18-inch waist. Indigo Blue, for example, talks about burlesque as a means of personal transformation that helps women to access their own power and to feel good about taking up space. As a founder of BurlyQ, a queer cabaret group, she also evokes the concept of the "cross-over gaze" and says that "our sexual power and eroticism can be for women too." Michelle Baldwin, author of *Burlesque As It Was*, argues that "enough time has passed that we have choices now." Curling your hair and shaving your legs means one thing when you're 15 (or 55) and have been led to believe that such a display of femininity is the only natural and normal way to be a woman. To adapt an oft-cited concept from the French philosopher Paul Ricoeur,[21] this state of "first naïveté" calls out for feminist consciousness-raising. Once one has been enlightened, however, one could then choose to return to these rituals of femininity in a playful, self-aware, ironic state of "second naïveté."

The neo-burlesque performer is high mistress of such second naïveté. Her curling and shaving and more are not because she thinks she has to, but because she now chooses to come back to these norms and to play with them in full consciousness of what she's doing. Through her act, the point she makes for audiences is that beauty and femininity are a construction that changes over time and place and that these are styles of femininity that we can create, for the fun and for the artistic and political parody of it all. Alotta Boutté adds that "the most powerful moment for me was when another big woman like myself came up to me and said 'Seeing you onstage was so healing.'" Listening to these panelists, I think of a critique that Ariel Levy offers in her *Female Chauvinist Pigs* of the two women founders of CAKE. Levy asks, "How do you publicly express the concept 'sexy' without falling back on the old hot-chicks-in-panties formula? It's a challenge that requires imagination and creativity that they [the two founders] do not possess. They haven't yet found a way to enact the redefinition they are advocating, so they are wishing for feminist justification where none exists."[22] Neo-burlesque, I believe, much more successfully enacts this redefinition and earns such justification.

I do still have one concern. If sex-positive feminism works within striptease culture with more revolutionary verve and a more effective bump-and-grind than sex-positive capitalism to actually open up possibilities for women to live out their gender and sexuality, if it removes some of the constraints of "pleasing the customer" entailed by capitalism and of catering to male fantasy entailed by patriarchy, I worry that it may still be what we could call "lookist." It loosens the straitjacket of the patriarchal capitalist economy, but it doesn't seek to shed the corset of the visual economy. When *Playboy* celebrates the beauty of women Olympic athletes in spreads that still have them looking essentially like centerfold models, when Sheila Kelley designs workouts based on the affirmation that all women are beautiful but still adjures them to shave their pubic hair every day, I worry about such lookism. Society accords an unearned and unfair privilege to those who look "good" or better than others, judged on conventional criteria of symmetry, weight, height, grooming, and lightness of hair and skin.

There may well be a fundamental and ancient human tendency toward adornment. It may well be innocuous and even the basis of all artistic impulse. But what if you don't want to self-adorn? I appreciate the claim Tease-O-Rama proves beyond any doubt that all women regardless of age and size can be glamorous and sexy, but why do we have to be glamorous or sexy? Neo-burlesque doesn't challenge the message that value resides in looks and that women especially should look beautiful – even while it greatly expands the definition of beauty. In its defense, the genre does include among its entertainers Miss Satanica, practitioner of the dying art of light-bulb eating. Although she was dressed in costume, she wasn't trying to look "good" or be visually pleasing to the audience. Among the parade of lovelies, however, she was a minor – albeit loud – note. She was also right when she snarled at us, "Haven't you seen enough tits?" We had, and I, for one, wanted something more, or different. So, does this woman-centered or feminist sex-positivity go far enough? It's hard to tell: would we still delight in strapping ourselves into corsets and high heels if the culture weren't so thoroughly steeped in patriarchal aesthetics?

Tassel-twirling becomes for me a case study on this point. It makes me inwardly cringe, it just looks so torturous, although I have to admit that all of the other women in my afternoon workshop seem to be having a blast. I'm one of the few who doesn't glue on the tassels. I feel too sorry for the nipples. Maybe it's because I've spent two years breast-feeding my child, an experience that was rewarding but also a form of hard labor for the breast. It left me with the sense that you've got to be gentle with them; they need nurturance, support, delicate handling. You can't go swinging them around like a cowgirl looking to rope a steer. A bosom is not a centrifugal lettuce spinner. Satan's Angel delivered something of the same warning in her own workshop – "Ya'll are working too hard," she warns the girls today. She used to affix a fishing lure attachment to her pasties to get more twirl action for less energy output: "It shouldn't take much to make 'em twirl." Her parting words of wisdom are, "Go easy with those breasts. All we ever did in my day was shoulder circles, none of this jumping up and down and tossing them around. Mine still look pretty good in my sixties, but you've got to take care of them." (Of course, she wore asbestos pasties and routinely lit her tassels on fire, but that's another story.)

Would women, free of patriarchy, ever have spontaneously invented tassel-twirling, with noxious glues painted on to delicate body parts? Indigo Blue, as proprietress of Twirly Girl Pasties ("creating exquisite pasties for discriminating nipples"), says that she does it to flout "appalling" laws prohibiting a woman from showing her nipples, as in "Okay, buddy, I can't bare my breasts, so here's a sequined, crystal-beaded, heart-shaped, bright-red propeller-plane eye-catcher instead, as a fuck-you end stop around your laws." These are very tricky questions: what would women's sexuality, fantasy, and exhibitionism look like were it possible for all this to develop unfettered, undeformed, in a postpatriarchal, nonmasculinist world wherein sexual violence wasn't commonplace (if such a utopia were ever to exist)? For that matter, what would men's sexuality be like? We're groping toward answers to these questions, partly through cultural movements such as neo-burlesque, but we simply don't yet know the answers.

I must say that I am most impressed by neo-burlesque when it goes beyond the hot chick, male gaze, classically beautiful. I like Eva von Slut and Miss Satanica; I like the performance art pieces such as the Living Dead Girls as medical patients who strip off their bandages. I want to be convinced that it is women's imagination, fantasy, and sexual agency driving the event, and not just our internalized age-old sense that we've got to look good for the boys. I am more heartened by the Sweet Potato Queens and Tease-O-Rama, by nude biking rallies and goofy nude calendars than I am by CAKE, porno-chic fashion, pop singers and music videos where youth and conventional beauty still rule. I want big women and people of all ages, natural breasts of all shapes and sizes, and more male strippers and burlesque performers. I want tongue-in-cheek humor. I want a wider embrace, less conventionality; less about selling, more about playing. That's the future of striptease culture that I'm looking for: egalitarian, open to critique and exploration of the status quo, to spacious definitions of sexuality, good looks, and sex appeal, but also to mockery and rejection of the whole cult of beauty and sexiness itself. Striptease culture pushes into these boundaries as it experiments with the "neo" of burlesque in all of its theatricality and parody. I do think neo-burlesque is on the right track. I think its explorations have merit. But I don't think striptease culture as a whole is quite there yet.

Another area where we can ask whether striptease culture sex-positivity goes too far, or not yet far enough, is when women aren't just looking or acting sexy (on stage, in the charity calendar or music video, at the workout studio, in fashion choices), but are actually having sex. Is it okay not just to fantasize, to perform, to pretend, but to actually do? Putting both the arguments of sex-positive capitalism and sex-positive feminism into play or into practice as a basis for sexual behavior yields, among other developments, prostitution and nonmonogamy ("promiscuity"). What happens when the stripper or Everywoman's adopted stripper persona becomes the "whore" and the "slut"? The next chapter investigates.

–6–

Strippers, Whores, and Sluts: "Call Off Your Old Tired Ethics"

Sweetheart

A close-up of a couple engaged in anal sex plays out on the giant movie screen in front of me. I'm chatting with the very delightful Sweetheart as she gives me a tour of her club. The porn movie is no doubt as blasé a background to her as elevator music is to an office temp. I'm a little surprised to discover that, by this point, it barely raises an eyebrow for me either.

Awash in stripper culture, I head back to San Francisco – the sex-positive capital of the United States. I am here to spend a warm October week interviewing sex workers (strippers, prostitutes, and a peepshow dancer) and those who organize and advocate on their behalf. The sex-workers' rights movement is another manifestation of the sex-positive trend in contemporary culture, although it turns out that this movement is not enjoying the same success or sexiness quotient as the *Girls Gone Wild* incursions of striptease culture into the mainstream. It may be acceptable now for your average college girl to look like a hooker, but hookers themselves are not necessarily benefiting from this upturn in their popularity. While happy to appropriate the stripper persona and style, we don't seem to care much about the working conditions or on-the-job legal protections of sex workers.

Tonight, I'm at the Mitchell Brothers O'Farrell Theatre in San Francisco. It's quite a famous place in the world of strip clubs and, along with the Lusty Lady, an epicenter of the sex-workers' rights movement for exotic dancers. But while the Lusty Lady is the grand success story for dancers' rights, the lessons of the Mitchell Brothers club are more ambiguous and in some ways represent a tragic failure for the movement. Here's what I hear about the club before we arrive:

> "One of the brothers killed the other one, you know."
> "The owners are just plain greedy – that place is the evil of capitalism."
> "It's basically just a brothel now."

For my escort this evening, I have called up Andy. He is an old friend of my husband's whom I've known for years; the two of them used to work together as flight attendants for the now defunct Pan Am Airlines. After traveling and living all over the world (Andy still speaks German, some French and Japanese, and, courtesy of his émigré parents, Estonian), he eventually settled in San Francisco with a master's degree in international relations and has been making his living as a freelance writer. In short, he seems the perfect worldly escort for an excursion to Mitchell Brothers. Andy is somewhat bemused by this plan for the evening's entertainment. I've explained to him that I'm writing a book on stripping and popular culture, but it's still a bit of a puzzle to him why a female university professor with degrees in religious studies is dragging him off to a notorious strip club. The outing is made all the more curious by the fact that I'm six months pregnant with my second son and sporting a noticeable tummy bulge.

After we pay our cover charge (forty dollars per person, the most I ever pay to enter a club, although there's a two-for-one deal in that a male-female couple counts as just one admission), we pass through the lobby into the club itself. A few near-naked women in standard stripper garb are milling about, working to engage the attentions of the customers, who seem predominantly composed of Japanese male tourists. One dancer in particular notices my entrance right away and sashays up to us to chat.

"Who's the wife? Where's your husband?" she asks me with a warm smile.

"He won't come to a strip club," I laugh.

"So who's this? Your boyfriend?" She's very forthright and perfectly nonjudgmental in her assumption that I have both a husband and a boyfriend.

"No, he's just a friend," I explain.

"Do you like girls?" she asks, running her hand up and down my arm.

She is clearly working very hard to figure out just what a thirty-something woman in flat sandals and a long maternity dress with black cardigan is doing in her club: swinging wife with husband? adulterous wife with boyfriend? lesbian looking for a ménage à trois?

I clear up the mystery for her. "I'm not here for sexual services. I'm actually writing a book and just wanted to have a look around."

She immediately clicks with this new scenario. "Oh, well then, I'm the person you should talk to! I've been here forever. My name's Sweetheart," she says, extending her hand. As we shake hands, I admire her business skills and understand why she's had such a long career. The hardest part about making money in a club, as we've seen, is the hustle. But for those who can project an aura of relaxed confidence and connect emotionally with the customer, then top-earner status opens up. This all takes a certain personality type, and Sweetheart has clearly got it down pat. I'm already reaching into my purse to give her money. I don't ever pay the dancers that I interview in meetings we set up outside the clubs, but this situation is different. Marie has convinced me that if a dancer is spending her time with me in a club, I should generally tip her, and so I do.

Sweetheart has dark blonde shoulder-length hair, wavy and stylishly layered.

She's wearing a thong and an orange net top with long sleeves and a high neck, but with mesh so open that her breasts, festooned with twin silver nipple rings, are clearly visible. Instead of stripper shoes, she's wearing regular street-style white sandals, with heels that are very low for a dancer. She explains apologetically that she's left off her platform shoes tonight since she's on her third double shift in a row, and her feet are killing her. At my request, she takes us on a tour around the club. I had studied the Mitchell Brothers' web site quite thoroughly back in Alabama, so I knew how it was divided into different "rooms," each of which offered specific services and set-ups: peep show, porn-flick screening room (thus the anal sex close-up), main performance stage, bar area, dark room with flashlight show.

This aspect of the club's layout seems somewhat in decline these days, with pretty much the same thing – full-contact private dancing – now available throughout the establishment, along with the possibility of going off with your choice of dancer to the cabanas, booths, curtained alcoves with couches, and very dark corners of the large club. The place's unifying design feature seems to be the myriad boxes of tissues placed next to wastebaskets and scattered everywhere throughout the club. Sweetheart informs us that it's really up to the girls as to what they'll do with the customers: "Strip nude, private lap dance, whatever!" She cultivates a charming, somewhat ditzy demeanor, with a warm and lively personality that has her often smiling, laughing, widening her eyes, tossing her hair, and leaning forward to touch my arm as she asks, "You know what I mean?"

Andy is beginning to look abashed. He might even be blushing, although it's too dark to tell for sure. When he steps away from me, the girls swarm him, although they politely leave him alone if he stays close. Sweetheart explains that she's been at the club for ten years, ever since she herself turned eighteen: "I was waiting to be old enough." She's saved her money, and the real-estate portfolio she's accumulated – several houses in Northern California – is as impressive as her cleavage. She tells us that she tries to advise the younger dancers to invest, "but they don't want to pay taxes, so they stash their money, but then you lose money every year, you know, because it doesn't grow."

After our tour, she introduces us to her friend Alexis, a lovely thin brunette in a white bikini. "She's really smart. Do your talk!" Sweetheart urges. Her friend obligingly quotes Middle English at us from her days earning a literature degree at the University of California at Berkeley ("Here's another profession open to you with a liberal-arts education!" Alexis quips), before the two of them leave to prepare for a show later in the evening. Andy and I head to the main room that has rows of theater-style seating and settle in to watch the stage performance. About to start up is "erotic sex boxing" with gloves and silky mini-shorts but no actual hits and some standard stripper dance routines and pole work. After a while Andy leans over to whisper, amused, that the couple seated next to us – a man accompanied by the only other woman customer in the club – is making eyes at him like they're on the lookout for swinger partners.

The time is ripe, it seems, to hit the road.

Prostitution and the Sex-Workers' Rights Movement

Two things are confirmed for me by my visit to the Mitchell Brothers Theatre. First, the slogan from the upscale strip club Rachel's comes again to mind: sometimes, fantasy really does become reality. At Marie's club, Mr. Lucky doesn't get that lucky. But at some other stripping establishments, he clearly does. There *is* an overlap between the stripping industry and prostitution, and many clubs in recent years have undergone what may be termed a hard-core slide. Clubs have become much more sexually explicit, with many now offering – to the extent of local regulations and sometimes beyond – porn-style feature stage shows, full dancer nudity, grinding lap dances, private rooms of various sorts, and at some of the clubs with some of the dancers, the possibility of negotiating various forms of sex. While the beginning of these changes dates from at least the 1970s – during Tease-O-Rama, Satan's Angel had bemoaned what she termed the "insertion dancers" who came out on stage already "buck naked with one leg on the East coast and one on the West coast" – this trend toward the hard-core has accelerated within the past decade or more.

The change coincides with the rise of striptease culture: as stripping became more mainstream, more women started to enter the profession, the number of clubs increased, and near-nude lap grinding became more acceptable, just like low-slung jeans, *Sex in the City* programming, and the explosion of internet pornography. The resulting culture wars over the meaning of all these changes – whether we're going to hell in a handbasket or finally starting to see the fruits of gender justice and the sexual revolution – may rage in contemporary North American society, but in the strip club the meaning is clear: if you want to maximize your income, take off your clothes and climb in his lap. Lily Burana, in her farewell tour *Strip City*, experiences difficulty while on her cross-country stripping odyssey in maintaining a personal "no-contact" rule against lap dances, titty rubs, and crotch close-ups. "Stripping didn't use to be so touchy-feely," she grumbles, "but in the past ten years, it's become a full-contact sport."[1] Marie experiences this hard-core slide herself, and it is one of the reasons why she eventually retires from the industry: "The clubs were just getting sleazier and the men more aggressive. I didn't want to have to deal with that."

Partly, it's a matter of worker competition. Since management doesn't pay the dancers directly, it has no incentive to limit the number of them working the club at any given time. The girls on the floor then compete with one another for the customers' tips. They often conclude that the more they're willing to do, the more they'll be able to make. In businesses prepared to flout the law or to turn a blind eye, some dancers will offer oral sex, hand-jobs, or intercourse in private areas of the club – in many cases with managers' tacit approval – or, as the dancer Hallie told me, some establishments will put girls in limos with a customer and drive them around the city or allow a worker to leave in the middle of a shift with a customer. I have no idea for what percentage of the clubs this is the case – what percentage are "dirty" as opposed to "clean" – but many of the dancers whom I interview claim or assume that about half of the girls, as they say, "hook on the side." None of my interviewees falls into that half, or at least won't admit it to me, and they complain that such "dirty girls" cut into their income by offering fuller contact services for lower prices: if not some form of sex, then twenty dollar table dances that may include front-straddling a customer, rubbing his crotch with your knee, brushing it with a hand, or kneeling between his legs and letting him play with your breasts. If such services are available to be bought, "Guess which girl's going to get the next dance?" asks Marie.

This phenomenon strikes me as one of the most insidious aspects of the strip-club industry, not necessarily because these types of contact shouldn't be offered, but because women can end up feeling pressured by market competition or by the club managers themselves ("Keep the customers happy!") into having to offer these services. In response to such market pressures, all of the dancers talk about the crucial importance of setting personal boundaries in terms of what you're willing and not willing to do and then sticking with these decisions. The danger of crossing your self-defined line in the sand is another way that the job can become problematic: it can draw you into types of sex work with which you aren't truly comfortable and that can end up eroding your sense of self-respect. This major industry-wide phenomenon of the hard-core slide is in fact at the center of many of the themes that I trace in this book; it expresses the anything-goes, sex-positive mood of pop culture – some would say in its worst manifestations – and has helped inspire in two different forms of counterpoint reaction both the neo-burlesque revival and the sex-workers' rights movement.

One could argue that such club set-ups are simply the inevitable result of sex-positive capitalism allowed free rein. In free-market capitalism, demand creates economic incentive for supply. From a sex-positive perspective, there is nothing to be particularly deplored about the fact that people are sometimes willing to buy and sell sexual services, provided that the transactions occur in a safe and consensual manner. Yet sex-positivity, I've suggested, worked from the capitalist angle alone, seems as empty and ultimately unsatisfying as pure capitalism ever does. There are no values in the marketplace; it provides no meaning or happiness in and of itself, only money. Capitalism is morally inept, unable to protect the marginalized and disempowered other than with bootstrap ("stiletto strap"?) entrepreneurial rhetoric that will simply never work for some. It is out of such concerns that governments introduce regulatory mechanisms into the marketplace in order to protect workers and the public interest.

Thus, the second point confirmed for me by my tour of Mitchell Brothers is the need for the exotic-dancers' rights movement and, more generally, for industry regulation and the labor organization of sex workers. These workers all readily agree with the common cultural evaluation that their jobs are problematic, but they identify the nature of the problem in different terms. For them, the trouble isn't that sex work is necessarily oppressive and immoral in and of itself, but that the work lacks legal, social, and professional support such that abuses can easily occur on the job and are then difficult to rectify. In an attempt to address this situation, activist Margo St. James founded in 1973 an organization dedicated to the aid of other sex workers called COYOTE, a creative acronym that stands for "Call Off Your Old Tired Ethics." The San Francisco-based COYOTE is a lobbying and education group that advocates for the rights of prostitutes, strippers, adult-film actors, phone-sex operators, and other providers of sexual services for pay. While somewhat less active today, it has inspired and continues to work in conjunction with other groups, such as the Exotic Dancers Alliance of San Francisco and the Exotic Dancers Alliance of Toronto, all of which are part of a loose-knit, international advocacy movement in defense of sex-workers' rights.

In specific response to concerns about the exploitation of strippers, the sex-workers' rights movement seeks to protect exotic dancers from the excesses of sex-positive capitalism by adopting the standard goals and rhetoric of the labor movement: the stripping industry needs greater regulation and enforcement of current workplace rules; workers benefit from labor organization and solidarity with others in similar fields; unions and strikes protect workers; there is need for public education, outreach, and greater social sanction for exotic dance. The movement argues at the political and legal level through lawsuits, lobbying efforts, and union organizing that what's dangerous or degrading in the stripping industry can and should be addressed through demands for better working conditions. As movement leaders point out, exotic dance is a legal profession that generates millions annually in tax and licensing revenue for local, state, and national governments. Women who work in this industry are entitled to the fullest extent of the law's protection against unfair hiring and labor practices, health and safety violations in the workplace, racial discrimination, and sexual harassment.

Poor labor conditions do, in fact, abound, as I learn from interviews with Carol Leigh, aka "Scarlot Harlot," a leading organizer in COYOTE as well as a sex worker, artist, and published author in the field; Johanna Breyer, ex-dancer at Mitchell Brothers, social worker, and co-founder in 1993 of the San Francisco-based Exotic Dancers Alliance; and from a later trip to Toronto to meet with Lily, a representative of the Canadian Exotic Dancers Alliance. The problems range from dirty workplaces (no soap in the dancers' bathroom) to sexual harassment by club managers. I hear stories of one manager grabbing at the breasts of a dancer in the change room and of another pressuring a dancer to date a friend of his, with implication in both cases that protests would lead to dismissal. At the Lusty Lady prior to unionization, racial discrimination was practiced by management to limit the number of nonwhite women in the peep show at any one time; if a dancer was unable to make her shift, she had to find a replacement worker for herself of equal or greater breast size and of equal or lighter skin color.[2]

Another big labor issue is the persistent and industry-wide job misclassification of exotic dancers. According to labor law, workers in America are categorized as either employees or independent contractors. Strippers, it turns out, meet all the legal criteria of employee status (house dancers, that is, not the traveling feature performers) but are almost always treated by the clubs as independent contractors. This misclassification allows owners to avoid paying salary, payroll taxes, and benefits, including health plans or sick days. Workers characterized as employees also have much easier options for unionizing and the right to file claims for workers' compensation if injured on the job. All such rights are routinely denied to exotic dancers.[3]

The movement responds to such problems through services such as the St. James Infirmary, a free occupational health and safety clinic for sex workers in San Francisco. In 1999, COYOTE, the Exotic Dancers Alliance, and the San Francisco Health Department jointly established this successful health clinic, where Johanna Breyer now works as Director of Social Services. The labor movement has also had some success with union organizing: the Lusty Lady club in San Francisco became the first unionized strip club in America when they joined the Service Employees International Union and as of 2003 became the first employee-owned establishment ("From busts to boom," read one newspaper headline).[4] During the dramatic unionization campaign, humorously recounted in the documentary *Live Nude Girls Unite!*, the dancers at the Lusty Lady held a "no pink day" in which dancers refused to "show the pink," or display their vulvas, in response to their frustration over stalled contract negotiations. Management retaliated by illegally firing one of the dancers in an attempt at union-busting. A picket line and lock-out then ensued in which dancers marched to cries of "No contract, no pussy" and "2-4-6-8-don't go in to masturbate," before ultimately prevailing in their organizing effort.[5]

Another tactic is the use of class-action lawsuits, as employed by the Exotic Dancers Alliance in the legal battle partly responsible for the notoriety of the Mitchell Brothers club. The issue at Mitchell Brothers revolved around illegal and expensive stage fees charged to the dancers by club management for the right to work at the club. The Exotic Dancers Alliance organized upward of 500 women in a class-action suit against the club for the return of the fees, which the dancers eventually won with a settlement of $2.8 million. However, because there is no monitoring for compliance and no recourse other than new lawsuits when clubs do flout the law, Breyer told me that Mitchell Brothers continues, illegally, to charge dancers stage fees. Such fees then become one of the major contributing factors to the hard-core slide, as women may end up performing more sexually overt services than they'd bargained for in order to make their house fees for the night. As these fees went up throughout the 1990s – from ten dollars a night to reports of more than three hundred dollars a shift now – so did the explicitness of the services for sale: "You are just having to do so much more to make the money than you were even five years ago," laments Breyer, of this problem of economic coercion.

Although the argument of equal protection under the law – a form of worker-friendly, sex-positive capitalism – strikes me as the least controversial claim made by the sex-workers' rights movement, this movement has unfortunately encountered opposition in its attempts to ensure for its members the basic protections to which they are entitled. Even from my students when we discuss these issues in class, I hear some initial responses of laughter and incredulity that a dancer could be sexually harassed: "Well, she's a stripper, what do you expect? Isn't that what her job is all about?" Breyer explains that the monitoring and enforcement of municipal bylaws and of state and national regulations is often lax to nonexistent, partly because strippers tend to be treated as a low priority within the system and partly because the Labor Commission and other agencies are simply very backed up, underfunded, and swamped with similar complaints from day laborers, garment-factory workers, and farm workers. Summarizing her case, Breyer states that "we just really want more enforcement of labor rights and health and safety codes and civil rights and sexual harassment codes."

As a context for the sex-workers' rights movement, this labor perspective constitutes a form of pro-worker, sex-positive capitalism, but it is not necessarily feminist. In fact, it is not even necessarily sex-positive, or is so only in a somewhat restricted sense. The point here is not so much to celebrate diverse sexuality in an open and affirming way as a path to personal empowerment and as liberation from restrictive mores, as is the case with sex-positivity. Instead, the goal is to support sex workers by securing their rights and helping them stay safe as they do their job. Accordingly, people like Breyer, Leigh, and Lily focus on addressing and trying to ameliorate those social forces that lead to oppression in sex work – including the problems of poverty that can force women into such work in the first place – while at the same time nevertheless defending a woman's right to choose this work for herself.

The weighty list of problems in the sex trade, as enumerated to me by Leigh, includes "slavery, trafficking, abuse, social stigma, and low self-esteem." Feminism is not always seen as the best ally in these advocacy efforts, since much of the feminist mainstream has been against sex work. As Breyer tells me, "I always felt that these women who came out against sex-workers weren't really feminists after all, because they weren't really supporting women's choices in terms of what they want to do." Leigh explains this dynamic in terms of a pendulum swing, as "feminism moves between a liberatory and a protectionist perspective." The pendulum action results from the fact that "we do have a lot to protect in terms of our sexual space." Accordingly, feminism in its protectionist mode can end up sounding sex-negative or at least consistently wary about sex as problematic and fraught with danger, Leigh maintains, "and part of that includes telling women they can't have sex without a good reason, such as love or, in certain contexts, lust."

In response, and perhaps in tacit acknowledgement of the limitations of the sex-positive capitalist stance, COYOTE and the other arms of the sex-workers' rights movement agitate for more than just equal protection under the law. They seek to actually change societal attitudes in the direction of greater toleration for sex work, including the legalization of prostitution. Although the advent of striptease culture has altered public perceptions in the last decade, the profession of stripper and certainly that of prostitute are still often disdained in many quarters. The Exotic Dancers Alliance of Toronto sees human rights issues at stake here. Their website reads that "dancers experience inequality as a result of the stigma associated with the profession ... As a result, fear and discrimination restrict exotic dancers from fully participating in society ... These consequences affect the overall well-being of Canadian rights and freedoms."[6] When seeking in this way to spur wider cultural acceptance, the sex-workers' rights movement does often embrace sex-positive feminism, as well as worker-protected sex-positive capitalism. COYOTE's very name makes this point: aren't society's traditional sexual ethics "old" and "tired"? Let's "call off" these ethics, they suggest; let's come up with new ethics that are gender-egalitarian and less sexually restrictive and disciplinary, while still respecting principled norms of human dignity, consent, free choice, and the avoidance of harm.

So, do COYOTE and the other such groups have a point? Are the ethics of both the religious right and of anti-prostitution, anti-raunch feminists "tired" and "old"? Both reject, although for different reasons, stripping and sex work as any sort of fit occupation for women, and both have problems with the easy sexual mores of striptease culture. Are they wrong? As an alternative, is the sex-positive ethic – both capitalist and feminist – on which COYOTE builds its case a solid basis for a defense of striptease culture and of new norms around women's sexuality? Sex-positive culture and the sex-workers' rights movement together raise the issue of the moral status of prostitution and of promiscuity: in the gender upset and *nouveau* sexual revolution of the twenty-first century, is it now okay to be a whore and a slut?

What Makes Sex Ethical?

One ultimate goal of sex-positivity in any of its forms is to expand the traditionally narrow definition of what constitutes ethical sex, to "queer" conventional sexual norms by opening them up in new ways. The time-honored mainstream answer to the question of ethical sex, especially for a woman, is that for sex to be fully legitimate and morally defensible it should be heterosexual, monogamous, married, and preferably procreative in intent. Prostitution and promiscuity, as well as same-sex relationships, are the big challenges to this question. In fact, any type of sex outside marriage – premarital sex, adulterous sex, open marriage swinger sex, group sex, homosexual sex, paid sex – risks various sorts of trouble with mainstream opinion, the job market, religious teaching, and the law.

In recent years, the social movement for LGBT (lesbian, gay, bisexual, transgendered) rights has made the ethical case for same-sex relationships by queering conventional sexual ethics to expand the definition of the family and of what may constitute a morally or socially acceptable way to live one's sexuality and one's life. The availability of reliable birth control and of abortion and various demographic changes have also resulted in the greater prevalence of and higher toleration for heterosexual premarital or non-married sex (e.g., a later age for first marriage, couples living together before or instead of marriage, young adults experimenting with a number of sexual partners before settling down, divorced people returning to the dating game). These social changes are still controversial, however, and in my neck of the Alabama woods, as well as in many other parts of America, they don't always go over well. What really doesn't go over well, however, is the challenge of flagrant promiscuity carried out in the name of either money – as "whores" – or fun – as "sluts."

Sex-positive feminism, as it focuses on women's sexual experience and seeks to expand notions of beauty and sexiness, also makes the claim that women, like men, are sexually desirous beings. Advocating against the historical Madonna/whore split that paints women as either sexually submissive and low in libido or as fallen and even demonic whores, sex-positive feminism instead offers an ethical vision of women's active sexual agency. "Good girls do," is how one pithy newspaper headline summed up the case.[7] This vision holds even if you're not just acting the whore or slut on a strip-club stage or parodying her in neo-burlesque, but actually being her in real life and in your bed. The argument here is stronger than that made by Jeanette and company (sex-positivity is fine as long as you're only pretending for money), and the challenge sharper than that staged by Tease-O-Rama (sex-positivity theatrically performed for fun).

Here instead is an insistence on opening the door to non-normative sex and a defense of such freer sex as still ethical. From this perspective, the full implications of sex-positive feminism begin to be realized: women can or should, if they want, but certainly not as any requirement for liberated womanhood, be able to sleep around with multiple casual sexual partners for lust or for profit, without moral censure. Here is sex-positivity enacted by women in their daily living, for pleasure, for money, sometimes for curiosity or just for the heck of it, maybe sometimes even in error, as part of the "live and learn" experimentation of life. Leading sex-positive author Carol Queen says that she and others like her are trying to "transform the culture one step, one fuck, at a time."[8] The logic behind this provocative mission begins to make sense to me.

The political edge, the social-justice critique, that I found missing in sex-positive capitalism is present in this "one fuck at a time" strategy of sex-positive feminism. For dancers such as Jeanette, Darcy, Andrea, and Mia, the act of endorsing prostitution, even if they themselves don't do it, is simply too radical a move. It challenges too much the rules governing proper female sexual behavior, which, somewhat surprisingly to me, many of the dancers are not willing to do. Instead, they often prefer to maintain the classic good girl/bad girl distinctions, except to move their own work from the bad-girl category to that of the good. They use full-service sex work as a foil – "we're not *hookers*!" they scoff – in order to both define and defend what they do. Jeanette is typical of many of the dancers whom I interviewed, in that she has no sympathy or patience with women who engage in prostitution: "They must be desperate," she told me, "and feel they need money, probably related to drugs, but I make lots of money not doing it." Hookers are the bad girls who go too far, who give away too much, who don't respect that line in the sand defending one's personal integrity and morals. Many exotic dancers show little to no solidarity with other sex workers on this point, and I suspect that many who haven't been involved in the advocacy and rights movement or been otherwise politicized would even feel themselves insulted by the job label of "sex worker."

Before starting the research for this book, I had similarly assumed, without ever really having analysed the issue, that prostitution was wrong and furthermore that I knew what constituted prostitution. But after talking with organizers and leaders in sex-work advocacy, some of whom have also done full-service work themselves, I have occasion to interview three other women who are independent-operating, middle-class, middle-aged "call girls." My initial contact is through Cosi Fabian, the "Holy Whore," whose full story I reserve for next chapter and whom I met through her sex-positive writing in a feminist anthology. Her friend Soleil is a veteran professional with long multicolor braids, and Sunny is a younger protégé with suburban-soccer-mom good looks. All three are well-educated and well-read, with a particularly keen sense of the high calling of the erotic arts, the role of the courtesan in history, and the tragic extent to which sexuality in contemporary culture is shot through with omnipresent shame, exploitation, oppression, and abuse.

By the end of a series of conversations with Cosi and her colleagues, I've spent hours talking to whores. It's their word, not mine, and one that they affectionately use with a tongue-in-cheek playfulness (as also in the case of Carol Leigh, aka "Scarlot Harlot") as well as with political intent to reclaim a derided sphere of women's experience. They tell me about the life journey that brought them to their work, their current practice as skilled artists and devotees of the erotic arts – "There should be a university!" Soleil exclaims – and their philosophical and political take on the historically intertwined denigration of body, sexuality, and the female.

If I had doubts before, I have few afterward, that prostitution – the right type of prostitution, under the right circumstances – can be a fine way to live one's life and earn one's living: fulfilling, challenging, and interesting. My caveat is obviously an important one; I realize that the women I'm talking about represent just one privileged form of sex worker. I'm not talking about child prostitutes, trafficked sex slaves, teen runaways brutalized by pimps, or streetwalkers turning tricks out of the desperation and humiliation of poverty. As Sunny puts it, "there's a big difference between a slave and a farmer who works in her own field." I'm talking about these high-priced, autonomous prostitutes – courtesans, if you will – who advertise discretely, screen their clients carefully, and meet them in the women's own apartments, for fees of around three hundred dollars an hour. I'm talking about women who are in control and are safe. Such prostitution is possible. The biggest threat the women feel is arrest. Their worry stems from the police, not from their clients and not even from public perception. (At least in San Francisco, they laughingly assure me, "It's quite chic now to be a whore, like lesbianism was in the nineties!")

Considering again the opposition and even antipathy that many strippers express toward outright prostitution, I wonder *what exactly does constitute prostitution?* And how is it so different from the work of an exotic dancer? Are the dancers perhaps exaggerating this difference in order to maintain a stance of moral superiority, as others in the general public sometimes maintain this stance over and against them? The standard definition of prostitution entails an exchange of money for sex. But for that matter, what constitutes sex? Questions immediately arise. Some of the dancers say that sex does not occur – Jeanette, Hallie, Mia, Andrea all tell me this – and therefore prostitution does not occur, unless there's penetration or "exchange of bodily fluids." So does orgasm have to happen for an act to qualify as sex? That seems a strangely climax-centered definition. What if a man hires a prostitute for sex but is unable, for whatever reason, to reach climax: does that mean prostitution never took place? What if a man tips a stage dancer after he masturbates under cover of the tip rail or a corner banquette table (a practice more than one dancer confirms happens in dark clubs): is that prostitution? If a friction dance in a thong on a customer's lap for twenty dollars a song does bring him to orgasm – or more typically, naked "hard friction" with her back to him in the privacy of a champagne room – is that sex? Is it then prostitution? Is it sex if she rubs his crotch with her hand through his pants?

To pursue another line of questioning, the goal of pretty much every dancer is to develop one or more regular customers. The regular can lead to the sugar daddy – the long-term customer often seen outside the club who provides gifts and monetary support in return for companionship and, typically, sex. If the barter between dancer and patron involves even just sexually-charged companionship in exchange for mortgage payments, orthodontists' bills, or a car – all stories I hear recounted about generous sugar daddies – is this prostitution? Is there a difference between a mistress and a prostitute? If two people have an ongoing relationship based on sex wherein one is providing financial support for the other, is prostitution going on? Or does the sugar-daddy constitute an exception, on the assumption that he and the dancer have forged some sort of genuine connection that is relational, intimate, caring, and that involves mutual growth? Feminists have famously asked such questions about marriage itself: is it, at least sometimes, not so very different from prostitution, if a woman exchanges her sexual favors for a man's support, especially if there is little love and much calculation of personal benefit in the relationship (the trophy wife, the older rich husband, or even, today, the "boy toy")? What then makes marriage so morally preferable to other arrangements?

It seems to me that either what the dancers are doing is also ethically problematic, or what the prostitutes are doing isn't. From one perspective, everything a dancer does could be seen as a form of prostitution, and this is indeed one basis for a socially conservative, sex-negative critique of exotic dance and of striptease culture – a derisive, "This is all just smut!" I concede to the dancers that there certainly is a difference between aboveboard "clean" stripping and the full-service work of a hooker, but the difference really seems to me more a question of degree than of outright kind. Consider a dancer only half-stripped, bottoms on and nipples covered, dancing at arms' length from a man (the least sexualized or hard-core work identified as exotic dance), compared to a prostitute having full sex with a client. Even the aboveboard exotic dance does seem to blur the line, in a Clinton-esque sort of way: true, it's not sex, but it's not not-sex either. In both scenarios, the customer is paying for a type of sexual engagement or erotically-charged exchange.

All women (and men) can and should have their own clear idea of the kinds of work or services they are comfortable performing, but it seems somewhat disingenuous for the stripper to castigate the hooker. Either the performances of striptease culture and sex-positivity are morally defensible or they're not. If some of them are not defensible – if they go too far – then there needs to be a clearly identifiable and consistently applicable criterion for determining this moral infraction or abuse to be the case. Penetration or exchange of body fluids may go beyond some people's personal comfort zone or sphere of interest, but how does that make such acts for hire, when consensual, universally immoral? I personally am not interested in performing a no-contact semi-nude dance for a stranger (nor am I engaged by the thought of being a stock broker or corporate executive or car salesperson), but I don't thereby conclude from my feelings of distaste or disinterest that such work is immoral.

From a sex-negative perspective, even worse than the "whores" – who at least have a capitalist profit motive on their side – are the "sluts," those who sleep around with multiple partners just for fun or desire or pure whimsy. Their case represents the fullest challenge of sex-positive feminism to conventional sexual mores. Carol Leigh helps me to grasp the import of this challenge by introducing me to a new term that she's coined: *slut-identified*. Men or women who are *slut-identified* or *slut-positive*, she explains, "have transgressive sexuality and aren't afraid to own that. It could be someone who is queer or trans-gendered or a sex-worker and who is identified as deviant by the culture in that way." An important basis for activism and organization is made possible by such a label when the person "then turns around and instead of being ashamed wants to own it and takes on the identity because it becomes such a big part of us." People have the right, she says, to "sell sex if they want to, to have sex with whatever gender they want to." Here, in fact, is the link between the LGBT and the sex-workers' rights movement, since, as Leigh notes, "our natural allies have been lesbians and sex workers together."

Here also is that area where feminism and sex-positivity sometimes part company. In Leigh's characterization, a feminist of a certain stripe may ask incredulously, "What women would want to have sex with a million men?" But for Leigh, there's no reason why a woman-centered, sex-positive feminism need take such a stance, since, as she shrugs and smiles, "it sounds like a very interesting idea to me." The crucial point for her, she explains, is that "if you can't see sex as a ground for experimentation and exploration of people, then of course you're going to think that no woman would want to." To be slut-identified, then, is to value forms of sexuality that lie outside the traditionally acceptable norm of heterosexual monogamous fidelity, especially for women, who have always been more tightly constrained by cultural mores than have men. It is to embrace a wider diversity of sexual practice as within the realm of the morally acceptable, including lesbianism, sex work, and "promiscuity," whether or not one chooses such practices for oneself. It is to joyously celebrate sexuality and especially women's sexuality, even while remaining cognizant of the very real risks and dangers inherent in any life force as powerful as sex.

So, *is* there anything wrong with being a whore or a slut, with sleeping around for money or pleasure? Or with sexual identity and activity played out in flavors not just straight and vanilla but also gay, transgendered, drag, burlesque, group, polygamous, fetishist, BDSM, commercial, artistic, and ritualistic? If so, what exactly is wrong with these other flavors of the sexual rainbow? Wherein lies the sin or ethical infraction? If the problem is simply a violation of traditional patriarchal mores designed to treat women as men's property, then COYOTE and the whores and sluts are right. What then *does* constitute a just criterion for whether or not sex is ethical? If one way to frame the ultimate goal of sex-positivity is the expansion of the definition of ethical sex, then just how far should this expansion go?[9]

The sex-positive answer to all of these questions rests squarely on the issue of consent. All sexual activity needs to be consensual, the sex-positive perspective insists. Such consent means that all parties must agree to the activity, voluntarily and without coercion; that their consent must be an informed one, given by people of sound mind who are old enough to understand and deal with the consequences of their consent and who have thought through issues of sexually transmitted diseases and pregnancy; and that the activity must be carried out in a reasonable expectation of privacy, such that others who have not assented to the activity will not be accidentally exposed to it. If all participants are willing adults practicing safe sex in private space, then pretty much anything goes. From this perspective, rape is the obscenity, not in and of itself the choice of multiple sex partners or non-traditional sexual activity.

As sex-work advocates well know, in order to really deliver on the gender and sexual liberation of the sex-positive promise, this issue of consent needs also to be expanded beyond a matter of mere individual and personal assent to include the material and cultural conditions of our lives which determine the range of choices open to us and to which we can consent. This knowledge is why organizers such as Leigh and Breyer in movements such as COYOTE and the Exotic Dancers Alliance put such emphasis on social issues of poverty, education, and health care. In terms of prostitution, the criterion of full consent as the litmus test for ethical sex (consent that is informed, educated, adult, sane, based on a range of options) involves advocating for a different type of society, one where people have real choice about how to earn their living, where the worst of the problems of poverty, addiction, and failed education are alleviated, and where people aren't forced or coerced into sexual slavery simply in order to survive or to support their families. The fewer the choices in one's life, the less meaningful is the consent that a person gives to any individual one of those choices. My consent, for example, means nothing if I'm offered my pick by a murderer between strangulation and poisoning. Yet as sex-worker advocates point out, it is also true that most work is forced by economic need and as such is beyond our full or free consent, and that much work is dehumanizing at worst or at least occasionally annoying at best. In this context, advocates argues that sex work can be potentially "better" than many other entry-level, women's labor-market jobs.

Accordingly, in terms of prostitution, stripping, and sex work generally, what is most morally problematic and exploitative are the societal conditions of poverty that push women unwillingly into this industry and that render their consent to engage in it less meaningful. As Leigh notes, "Prostitution is something that, if you're a woman, you can do to take care of yourself if you're marginalized, in the most dire situation, in poverty." Obviously, however, if a woman decides to work as a prostitute or a stripper simply out of the desperation of poverty because she sees no other feasible choice open to herself or because her society offers her none, then her "consent" is severely compromised. As a result, Leigh remarks, "the problems of prostitution don't get solved until the problems of poverty get solved."

But how, one can still ask, does a sex-positive perspective defend this definition of ethical sex? If sex-positive capitalists and feminists reject "married" and "heterosexual" as the just and necessary criteria for responsible sex, how do they defend these new criteria that they propose instead of "consensual" and "adult"? On what basis does this perspective allow us to condemn rapists and pedophiles? In fact, on what basis does it "draw a line" at all? The social conservative indignantly playing devil's advocate may toss up her or his hands and ask why consent is important if nothing else is? If we're throwing out heterosexual monogamy, why not let all sex flourish? Aren't you just sliding down that slippery slope where you end up affirming all forms of sexual desire and practice, including rape and kiddie porn and child sexual abuse and those perverts trolling the internet chat rooms to lure out the 10-year-olds?

On this question, the sex-positive answer is the infliction of harm. Rapists and pedophiles are in the wrong because they hurt others. To force sex unwillingly on anyone, to engage a young child in sexual activity, to take sexual advantage of someone who can't freely grant consent, to offer to buy sex from a person who isn't in a position to refuse: all these examples are unethical violations of everything that sex-positivity seeks to celebrate and support. The criterion of informed consent is based on the bedrock moral principle of not causing harm. The purpose of the criterion is to ensure that no one gets hurt. If a sexual activity or desire does harm someone, it is immoral; conversely, if no one is getting hurt, and informed consent is present, then the act of sex is not wrong.

While clear and straightforward, this sex-positive criterion of full consent and no-harm is nevertheless not without its ambiguities and tricky moral quagmires. How, for example, to deal with young teen sex? When exactly does one reach the age of consent? Should a set standard age be applied to all (twelve? fourteen? sixteen? eighteen? twenty-one?) or individual determinations made (by whom?) in each case? What about the issue of harm to a partner through betrayal of marriage vows or other commitments when the services of a sex worker are engaged without that partner's knowledge or assent? (This is an issue to which the prostitutes themselves are not insensitive. Some claim that they aid couples by providing a form of sex education for men or an outlet for unmet sexual needs, while others feel regret and guilt at the deception.[10] Soleil and Sunny suggest that in a different, sex-positive world, single and partnered people alike would all occasionally visit prostitutes – recast as sexual professionals – for celebrations, healing rituals, and advanced-training workshops.) What about "rough sex" in which participants voluntarily risk a certain degree of harm? Does this situation violate the requirement of informed consent and no-harm, or is it no different, for example, from a bunch of guys playing football knowing that one of them might well end up a little bruised or hurt?

Even putting aside such questions, the more central dispute on the stipulation of no-harm revolves around whether the greater social good requires that we maintain the boundaries around the sexually acceptable much more narrowly than the sex-positive advocate would recommend. The social conservative opponent insists that indeed we must, because people do get hurt by the permissiveness of sex-positivity. The moral fabric of society is threatened, family values are undermined, hedonistic and antisocial behavior is encouraged, and children are endangered when sex is too free and easy. Especially because of children's vulnerability, any new norms purporting to better ground an ethics of sex must take special care to protect and nurture children, in terms of both keeping them safe from sexual predation and helping them to develop into sexually healthy and responsible adults.

The Supreme Court of Canada engaged exactly these arguments in a recent decision that garnered much media attention and occasioned further debates on the spread of striptease culture, not just throughout the realm of popular culture, but into the highest legal realm as well. In 2005, the judges of the Canadian Supreme Court held that a conviction of indecency should be overturned for a Montreal business owner who had been operating a sex club or "swingers club" where paying members and their guests could engage in sex and watch others similarly engaged. While the dissenting judges and the lower court judges found that such group sex in commercial establishments was a violation of Canadian social values and standards of tolerance (for example, through "the propagation of a degrading and dehumanizing view of sexuality," "calculated to induce anti-social behaviour in its disregard for moral values"), the high court in the final majority opinion disagreed. The Supreme Court found that no one was harmed and nor was society, since criteria of consent, privacy, and discretion were all met; attendance at the club was limited to those who wanted to be there and all sex acts were voluntary and behind code-locked doors (i.e., no children or unwilling members of the public could be accidentally exposed). While the dissenting judges argued that "it is the tolerance of the general public that counts, not the tolerance of the participants or spectators," the high court essentially replaced this previous test of the "Canadian community standard of tolerance," which it found to be inappropriately subjective, with a new objective harm-based test very similar to that espoused by sex-positive thinking. If the club is hurting no one, it should be allowed to operate. In short, the Court found that group sex wasn't antisocial![11]

From the sex-positive perspective, further desirable public policy implications of this incursion of sex-positive reasoning into the legislative sphere would include the legalization of prostitution (in the context of strict measures against trafficking and sexual slavery, antipoverty efforts, an improved women's labor market, available drug rehabilitation programs, sexually transmitted disease health campaigns, and support programs to keep prostitutes safe); full legal partner rights for same-sex couples, including same-sex civil unions or marriage; extensive programs of accurate and shame-free sexual education in schools, public-health campaigns, and wherever else possible; and generally, higher social tolerance for a broader range of sexual expression, without the stigmatization of some people as "perverts." To what degree these changes will occur remains an open question of great interest to both sex-positive advocates and their opponents. Just where is society going with all this?

I accept the sex-positive judgment that good sex – "good" in the double sense of both ethical and pleasurable – needn't necessarily always be romantic or monogamous. While faithful monogamy is traditionally held up as the key answer to what makes sex ethical – that the relationship must be exclusive – Soleil, for one, argues that that's just patriarchy talking. She is against compulsory monogamy as simply a form of patriarchal ownership: "Thou shall not covet thy neighbor's wife," she quotes for me; and nor, the Biblical text continues, shall you desire "thy neighbor's house, or field, or male or female slave, or ox, or donkey, or anything that belongs to thy neighbor."[12] In my research, I come across estimates of two to three million "swingers" in America and of 2–5 percent of the Canadian population at least occasionally engaging in partner swapping, group sex, or various forms of non-monogamous but nevertheless long-term partnerships.[13] Soleil asserts that she and her male partner of twenty-one years have a wonderful relationship made better without mutual sexual exclusivity. Personally, I have the opposite experience and am contentedly committed to a lifestyle that places me solidly within the most conservative demographic: married, in love, in a long-term monogamous relationship, heterosexual, and mother of children – boys no less. (Monogamy can be sex-positive, too.) But I don't feel that my experience needs to stand for all and given the sex-positive ethical norms of consent and no-harm, I can find no reason to condemn. Truly, why shouldn't adults be able to engage, privately, in whatever consensual sexual practices give them pleasure?

In a class discussion on these issues of sex-positivity and striptease culture one day, Jack, a 21-year-old student majoring in environmental studies, suggests that "it doesn't matter where you get your appetite, as long as you eat at home." Dean, a senior about to graduate in history, adds, "Yeah, it's okay if it gets him aroused, like guys after work going out to a strip club for a couple of beers, if he then goes home and has passionate sex with his wife or girlfriend." We could keep spinning out their metaphor: maybe it doesn't even matter where you eat – and indeed who doesn't like eating out at restaurants now and then? – as long as you do end up going home afterward. But another man whom I interview, a white-collar professional who is a little older and in a settled relationship, objects to the idea of paying another person to whet his appetite. His sexuality, he says, is very focused on his partner, on this one particular beloved person. "I don't want to confuse or dilute that," he insists. "I think guys who are paying for arousal, for this sexual playground, are part of the same industry or mentality that's trying to sell you Pepsi. It's the commercialization of sex, and sex isn't commercial for me, it's individual and relational, focused on this one person whom I love."

His comments raise one final issue that needs to be considered on the question of what makes for ethical sex. Even when the criteria of no-harm and of consent in its fullest sense are completely fulfilled, one can still wonder whether something is lacking in this definition. Not only the social conservative, but even the happily slut-identified whore from within the sex-positive community may point out that there can, and probably sometimes should, be something more. The simple fact that a sex act meets a basic criterion of not being *unethical* does not necessarily mean that the act is a positive good. There has to be something more than just the avoidance of harm to orient our lives. There need also to be positive ethical goals of self-understanding, depth and maturity of character, and caring relationships with others.

Sex, that intimate shock of connectivity, has a certain unique potential to contribute to such growth and flourishing of spirit. It can be, as Leigh noted, a grounds for exploration of both self and other or, as Queen proposed, a path to one-step-at-a-time social revolution. If sluthood were simply to stand for a life of quick and meaningless partners taken on in order to avoid the full jolt of deeper sexual and emotional connection and to hide from the challenges of personal growth, if it meant treating people solely as means instead of also as ends in and of themselves, then there would quite likely be something wrong with such a lifestyle. Shouldn't sex, at least sometimes, or after you've sown your proverbial wild oats, be relational in a way that literally embodies that I-Thou genuine encounter with the other? Such transformative knowledge about self and other does not easily develop through a string of quick fumbles with virtual strangers. Nor, however, is having sex with the same person for fifty years any guarantee either. Romantic love can entail a false myth of "The One True Love," endlessly force-fed to us by the media and popular culture. This narrative about the "true" meaning or purpose of sex is all too often chased, to our detriment, to an end of disappointment, pain, divorce, and shared custody.

Sex is ethical when it is consensual, voluntary, adult, discrete, and causes no harm. Such sex is good; it can give you pleasure or earn you a living; it can add spice to your life and zing a healthy glow into your cheek. But I am intrigued by the possibility that sex can also do a whole lot more. Not only romantic, monogamous, happily-ever-after sex, although it may in some cases take that form. I am intrigued by claims about sex as part of a quest for wholeness and deep personal meaning-making. Neither sex-positive capitalism nor sex-positive feminism insists that sex can or should be part of such a quest. But I suggested earlier that there is a third form of sex-positivity. The last of the three sex-positive arguments, namely sex-positive spirituality, positions itself as one answer to this pursuit of "more." It's time to hear the story of Cosi Fabian, the Holy Whore, who guides me to understand this quest.

–7–

At the Feet of the Goddess: Stripping, Sex, and Spirituality

The Holy Whore

Orange chiffon curtains billow into the room on a warm breeze blowing off San Francisco Bay. "Hello," purrs Cosi, the Holy Whore, in dulcet British tones, "please, do come in."

As we have seen, there are multiple ways to look at the question of meaning in exotic dance and in striptease culture. One last avenue that needs pursuing is that of the dancer and of Everywoman as *goddess*. I was initially surprised when references to goddesses kept popping up in my interviews and readings in the form of suggestions or claims that there is a connection between sex work or striptease culture and spirituality. More specifically, certain strippers and other sex workers were claiming that they were living out a connection between sexuality and spirituality in the embodiment of a goddess-figure who – in some sense, at least some of the time – involves both the sex worker and her clients in an experience that she or they together understand as spiritual, transcendent, transformative, or holy. With my background in the academic study of religion I found such material particularly intriguing, and this led me to develop a set of questions to explore as my final foray into the meaning of both stripping and the broader striptease culture: Is there is a back story of goddess worship that forms part of the popular appeal of contemporary stripping? How, more generally, does religion contribute to people's understandings of the cultural or symbolic meaning of exotic dance and of the identity of a stripper? How do dancers and everyday women participating in striptease culture use goddess images and stories in order to give meaning to what they do? How does "sex-positive spirituality" complement and yet in some important ways challenge the arguments of sex-positive capitalism and sex-positive feminism? I had not initially planned to look for answers to these queries in the world of prostitution, but the most articulate exponent I found of the link between sex work and spirituality happened to be a prostitute. So while in San Francisco interviewing dancers and other people involved in the sex-workers' rights movement, I met also with Cosi Fabian. She is the Holy Whore, and what she tells me about is the power of the Wondrous Vulva.

Cosi (her real name, which she gave me permission to use and under which she publishes) is an elegant and cultured European woman, born in Malta and raised in England. She presently lives and works in San Francisco as a teacher, author, ritualist, devotee of the goddess, high-priced courtesan, and spiritual organizer for other sex workers connecting with what she calls "our noble past as sacred prostitutes." Cosi lives on a quiet street in an affluent, hilltop neighborhood. As I walk up the stairs to her house, I pass a wild rose bush heavy with flowers that are opening – the comparison seems unavoidable – like pink vulvas. Cosi is sleek and sexy in a casual way, a redhead – of course – who greets me at the door barefoot and wrapped in an Indonesian print sarong slung low on her hips. Above it she wears a tight white T-shirt. Although her face is free of makeup, her toenails are painted and her fingernails buffed, and she is adorned with jewelry. She is 55 years old: attractive, with lively and regular features, but clearly into middle age, as evidenced by the facial wrinkles of, she tells me, "a difficult life." Many of her clients are younger men in their twenties and early thirties for whom she fulfills the fantasy role of the glamorous older woman, a British "Mrs. Robinson" as some of her advertising casts her. She calls these clients her "young warriors." In a deep and husky smoker's voice, she informs me that "they lap it up," and I have no doubts.

We spend the afternoon talking about sex work in the context of contemporary women's spirituality and ancient goddess traditions. I interview her in her studio apartment, the same place where she meets her clients. The room is small but brimming with life. In fact, it overflows with art, textiles, books, and flowers. Prints and statuettes of various Mesopotamian, Greek, and Indian goddesses adorn the walls and furniture. A bicycle sits tucked into one corner, half-covered by a red-velour throw. Feminist and religious studies books fill the floor-to-ceiling bookshelves that line one wall. A large floral ironwork circle is suspended from the ceiling. Luxurious textiles hang everywhere: gold, crimson, and exotic prints in velvet, brocade, chiffon, and silk. They festoon the ceiling, walls, and closets. French doors lead to a small balcony with views of the city. I smell incense in the air, mingling with the perfume of fresh flowers artfully arranged in vases around the room: roses, sunflowers, and more. The apartment is, in short, just as I had imagined the home of the Holy Whore to be. She seats me next to "The Bed" – a gorgeous, draped, be-pillowed, altar-like affair – and serves me sparkling water and almonds.

I had contacted her for an interview because of a fascinating essay she wrote in an influential sex-positive feminist anthology titled *Whores and Other Feminists* (which immediately became one of my favorite new books). Her essay is "The Holy Whore: A Woman's Gateway to Power." In it, she *is* the Holy Whore. She recounts how she came to her work (at the age of 42) after years of studying "prepatriarchal models of female sexuality as a noble, even divine power" and how these ancient stories inspired her to see herself in sex work as an embodiment or expression of the goddess. She quotes an ancient Mesopotamian hymn to the Great Goddess Inanna:

> [Inanna] went to the sheepfold, to the shepherd.
> When she leaned against the apple tree, her vulva was wondrous to behold.
> Rejoicing at her wondrous vulva, the young woman Inanna applauded herself.
> She said: "I, the Queen of Heaven, shall visit the God of Wisdom ..."

"There was a time," Cosi Fabian writes, "in fact, throughout most of human history, when the Wondrous Vulva was venerated." As we settle into our interview, I ask her to tell me more about what she's called "this most ancient image of all," that of the Wondrous Vulva.[1]

She leans forward and prepares to light a cigarette. She rolls her own and takes her time adding a filter and licking the paper shut. "To me, I think what it's telling is that when women get together and talk about the Wondrous Vulva, we always laugh. And it's not an ashamed laugh; it's a shared-joke laugh. It seems to be about what women think of their own vulva and its capacity in the world. And so to me that is an element of the cosmic joke – this amazing, expressive, ridiculously powerful part of ourselves." She leans back in her chair, puffs on her cigarette, and smiles. "I think there's a sense that maybe if all else fails, we've always got pussy. Or we women know the ridiculous effect it has on men and the extent to which men will bend themselves out of shape for it." Her hand, silver bangle and jade ring flashing, gestures elegantly in the air at the absurdity of it all: "We were just born to it!" The concept of the Wondrous Vulva, she explains, is meant to express this idea of women "sharing the joke, of women's bawdy humor." Community is important here also. Her biggest fear going into sex work was that she knew she was "moving beyond the pale," and she worried about becoming alienated and without recourse for help if things went wrong. What she found, however, "were so many other women who had created their own autonomous sexuality. At political and social gatherings, we laughingly flirt with each other, really as a way of praising the other person's sexual beauty." And so, she concludes, "the Wondrous Vulva is where all women meet."

When I ask her whether this sense of the wonder and power of the vulva connects to women's fertility and reproductive ability, she hesitates, flicking her ashes and clearly choosing her words with care. "It carries the idea of earthiness, but not in the sort of precious 'goddessy' sense of Mother Earth; it was something much more vital than that." As a woman without children and one who claims her sexuality as a source of great power, Cosi wants to make the point that the Wondrous Vulva isn't just about fertility. "That's been said so much in the last two thousand years," she explains, "that I think we can leave it to others to talk about it. In fact, the Wondrous Vulva has *only* been justified by fertility. So often these old goddesses were called fertility goddesses."

She makes a good point: goddess worship seems less dangerous and is certainly less transgressive of societal norms for women, if it is based on a simple recognition of female reproductive ability. To suggest that women derive power from their ability to give birth, that this function is central to the meaning of femininity, is no different a message than that promulgated by traditional religions such as mainstream Christianity for centuries. To say that women's childbearing conveys on them a quality of the *mysterium tremendum*, a connection to the creative force of the universe, a characteristic of the divine or the holy, is to push the point further in the direction of the woman-centered, but to the extent that this message reduces women's sexuality to reproduction, it still offers a deeply conservative take. Cosi is after something much more radical and more liberating. She wants to emphasize women's sexual pleasure instead of their ability to reproduce, their independence and intellectual creativity instead of their wifely and maternal roles. As she puts it, "Something that I've been concerned with and something that I think has been invisible for so long is the menstrual cycle of women's sexuality rather than the ovulatory: the Lilith instead of Eve. I think the menstrual sexuality is creativity. It's giving birth to ideas, to projects."

Indeed, why is it that feminine sexuality is really only socially sanctioned or revered if it produces children within monogamous heterosexual marriage? Even as – or especially as – a woman who is six months pregnant, sitting there garbed in my maternity dress as I interview Cosi, I agree with her wholeheartedly about the need for society to validate other paths for women. Although I try hard not to judge the life choices that my students make, few things depress me more than seeing my bright young women advisees blaze through college with realistic ambitions of grad school and great careers, only to earn their degrees and then promptly get married, work low-end jobs to support a husband, and postpone their educational and career goals indefinitely to have babies, all by the age of 22. Having seen this scenario repeat itself several times now, I understand better how much pressure these young women are under – from society, family, peers, and, to the extent that they internalize these pressures, from themselves as well – to marry and have children as the definitive sign that they have attained a culturally desired and required wholeness or maturity as women.

I have nothing at all against marriage and children and do indeed feel a sense of deep completion and joy from my life as a wife and mother, but I am also keenly aware of the cost of these roles in terms of time to devote to career and outside interests and personal time for oneself. Even more so, the high rates of divorce and child abuse convince me that these roles of spouse and parent are by no means for everyone and that we need other socially validated paths. Such options seem especially important for young people still forming their identities and with the most to gain – in terms of education, career, and travel – from the freedom and flexibility of the single life. I find myself wanting to urge Cosi on: "Yes, convince my women students that their sexuality means that they are entitled to pleasure, not that they have to be accessible to a man. Convince them that they are complete in themselves, or at least that this completion can take on many forms and is not usually best attempted through marriage at the age of 21. Convince them that motherhood is just one mode among many that their creativity and fulfillment can take." As Cosi says, she wants to present an option; she "wants to see women both young and in their forties think twice, three, or four times" about motherhood achieved through monogamous heterosexual pair-bonding as the only and as the necessary "natural" and "normal" life course for women.

In terms of the connection to spirituality, what interests Cosi is that there are so many female divine figures who are *not* mothers or primarily maternal. Aphrodite is one of her favorite goddesses in this regard. Before a client arrives for a session, Cosi always lights incense and a candle. More importantly, she tells me, she prays to Aphrodite just before the session or when her client first arrives. "I always hug them as soon as they come in. And sometimes you can feel that there is no spark there. And I don't feel like I have a spark that I can draw from, so it is always at that point that I pray to Aphrodite and to all of the women who have come before me as holy whores. The spirit of Aphrodite has never failed me." When I ask her why she focuses on this goddess in particular, Cosi explains that she has found Aphrodite to be very specific for what she calls a "golden spell." "It is the spell of glamour," she clarifies. "And it enables me to find the laughter within myself. I know then that I am projecting enough personality to slam them against the wall. I am moving quickly and lightly. And sometimes," she laughs, "I run out." Her cigarette has burnt down as well, and as she grinds it out she leans forward and looks me in the eye. "And sometimes the person at the end of the session is nothing like the person at the beginning."

This transformation, both of client and of herself, comes about through connection with the energy of the sacred female or the Holy Whore, which is the "quintessence of woman in her ritual, empowered, cosmic aspects."[2] To this extent, there is something healing, transformative, and "magical" about the best of her encounters with clients. "The men have intense loyalty to their wives more than anything else," Cosi maintains. (The student who is transcribing interview tapes for me gets rather incensed at this point. "She's helping men cheat on their wives and then calls herself a goddess! If I were one of those wives, I'd 'goddess' her," Tiffany says threateningly.) "And the ones who don't have wives, who are divorced, they miss waking up next to their wives. They miss the touch of a woman and the smell of a woman. They miss 'Woman.' And that's something I realized: I'm not just a woman, I am Woman. And that doesn't mean that I'm an object and it doesn't mean that I'm less than me. It means I'm something far bigger than I am." Drawing on her earlier language, I offer the comment that it means, "You're the embodiment of the goddess or the sacred female." "Yes," she agrees, "or just that I'm female and that there is integrity to that." Or, as she puts it in her instructor biography for the online Vulva University (an organization offering award-winning "sex wisdom" classes for the past ten years), she is living the archetype of the Sacred Whore.[3]

Eve and Salome at the Strip Club: Sexuality and the Fallen Woman

Cosi's insistence on drawing together sex work and religion helps me to see how, according to at least one reading, the roots of exotic dance and of striptease culture are also quite religious. I'd like to suggest that one way to get at this aspect of religion is through the lens of performance. As we have seen, not only is exotic dance one of the major forms of paid performance in America today, but everyday women now commonly perform stripping personae and styles in their clothing and self-representation. It is rare for me to walk across my university's Quad without seeing a student dressed – except for the shoes – more or less as many of the dancers are costumed in the clubs. And when the students go out to parties and the local bars at night, they assure me, "Oh, yeah, all the girls look like strippers then." If stripping has become such a common mode of body display and of performance for Everywoman, then it behooves us to examine more closely what it is that actual strippers are performing in their work. As I discussed in Chapter 4 in terms of Judith Butler's influential book *Gender Trouble*, exotic dancers are involved in a performance of femininity. What the dancer enacts or performs is gender. She acts out a patriarchal vision of hypersexualized femininity involving her desire for and availability to the (typically) male client. The performance, however, is exactly that: a show, play-acting, a fantasy enacted for the pleasure of the customers and for the enrichment (mainly financial, but emotional as well) of the dancer.

Butler explained that the subject or actor – in this case the dancer – operates under numerous cultural constraints as to what she is allowed to perform without censure or punishment. In other words, while she can bare her breasts, she can't dress in sackcloth or running shoes without losing her job. In order to be culturally intelligible to the audience, her performance has to draw on a limited set of historical possibilities defining femininity and women's sexuality. In the context of the club, she has to maintain a look that is conventionally attractive and she has to be sexual, although she can play out that sexuality in terms of different roles, among which she can switch at will with a change of costume, props, music, and dance styles: flirtatious ingénue schoolgirl, aggressive dominatrix, fresh-faced and fit girl-next-door, sensual temptress. She can even play the lesbian, as long as it is a lesbianism that lets men watch and that invites them to participate. In these ways, all gender performances entail the repetition or what Butler calls the "sedimentation" of meanings and patterns that are already there in the culture.

But to push this analysis further, I want to inquire more specifically about where these performances come from in our culture. On what material do they draw? What are their roots? I want to use the work of Butler to ask: *if gender is a performance, from whence comes its script?* As Butler puts it, gender identity derives not from a psychological core, but has a purely "political and discursive origin."[4] By this she means that gender is constituted by politics, or by rhetoric and ideology that are then naturalized (made to seem "natural," inborn, or divinely ordained), all in the service of power structures and the status quo. Her notion that the origin of gender is *discursive* is very interesting in terms of its connection to the performance category of *the script*. So to extend the theatrical metaphor: the culture provides a repertoire or corpus of scripts from which the performer can draw and within which she can experiment, but only to certain limits, beyond which her performance will no longer make any sense to her audience that is watching and participating.

Inspired by Cosi's work and from the connections to religion and spirituality proposed by other sex workers, I have come to the conviction that *religious scripts* are an important primary source for the gender performances of exotic dance. Such religious scripts seem at the root of much of the meaning of striptease, both in the context of the strip club itself and in the wider social scenes of striptease culture that we have traced. By *religious scripts*, I refer to long-standing stories, images, myths, archetypes, and narratives that originally derived from religious traditions but that have gained currency in the general culture such that people recognize and use these narratives not only inside, but also outside explicitly religious contexts, in order to assign meaning to behavior. In other words, I am suggesting that part of what gives meaning to the striptease experience is its participation in, and active rebellion against, pervasive religious notions still very much alive in our culture about what constitutes ideal femininity. Popular cultural notions about femininity derive, at least in part, from these influential religious narratives embedded in the culture. The narratives, or "scripts," widely known to the audience, then give meaning to the act of stripping.

In particular, I see three such scripts at work in the strip club: (1) *Eve* as the good but fallen woman, (2) *Salome* as the wicked but clever seductress, and (3) the pre-patriarchal *Goddess* figure who claims power and honor in the naked female form. These three religious scripts together help to shape stereotypes and public understandings about exotic dance, but they also more generally represent different ways of characterizing women's sexuality in contemporary America. Again we see that the stripper is Everywoman, and that the way in which she is characterized – and caricatured – holds sway over all women.

In terms of the first narrative, the dancer performs or evokes the fallen woman of the Western religious traditions, in which part of what is responsible for woman's fall is precisely her lust and licentious sexuality. The stripper here conjures up Eve. As David Scott rather gleefully writes in *Behind the G-String*, the exotic dancer "vibrates with the wickedness of the very first temptation, which teetered the divinely inspired order in Eden toward a world chaos of infernal passions."[5] The data on community perceptions of stripping discussed in Chapter 3 supports this perception that, despite the mainstreaming of exotic dance, the public still continues to view women who engage in this occupation as less moral and more promiscuous than other women.

According to this religious script of Eve, the dancer has fallen prey to her sexuality and now tempts man to follow suit. As such, she represents the lure of the passions and of the flesh. That archetypal pink neon sign blinking over the door of the strip club – *Live Nude Girls!!!* – might as well be the fruit in Eve's hand: "Come and partake, for it is good and delightful to the eyes and desirable for gaining wisdom." This Genesis story of Eve is about the link of sexuality, knowledge, and morality. The knowledge offered in the strip club is carnal wisdom, the forbidden knowledge of women's nakedness and hidden mysteries. In a club, a man doesn't have to practice the gentlemanly restraint demanded in normal life. He can ogle to his heart's content. He – Everyman – is enticed into the club with promises of forbidden pleasure and then ensnared as the dancers writhe around him, like the snake in the garden, to the limits of his credit card and the local ordinances.

In this religious script, however, Eve is not forever lost. She and Adam are punished and banished from Eden, but the arc of history in this narrative is one of salvation and redemption. Eve claims she was tricked by the serpent into eating the fruit and offering it to Adam. She strayed not out of real wickedness, but more from curiosity and gullibility. According to this story, both Eve and stripper are the "good girl" whose fundamental role is as companion or "helpmeet" to man, of whom God said in Genesis, "It is not good for him to be alone." Thus the dancers sit with the men, they talk and laugh with them, they make them feel good. Both Eve and the stripper are simply the "good girl gone bad." While the dancer is fallen, she is still redeemable to the extent that she feels shame or was motivated into the profession merely by financial need. The public often views the stripper through this lens as a young woman who is misguided, lured by the promise of easy money, and too immature to know better. She is not really to blame and is not viewed as depraved, as is true of Eve herself, but as merely someone unwise and foolish who has allowed herself to be led down the wrong path. This perception is echoed in the stock character of "the stripper" – or the hooker – "with a heart of gold." Carl Hiassen's novel *Striptease* (1993), made into a movie (1996) starring Demi Moore, follows this narrative: the main character strips as the only way to make enough money to regain custody of her daughter from her crook of an ex-husband; she herself is clever, brave, loving, resourceful, and good. Her stripper persona is very clearly a performance: she tries to eschew lap dancing for stage work only and is renowned at the club for being the only good dancer there.

This archetype of Eve – of woman as innocent turned temptress – is itself rooted in a larger religious context. Much of the practice and teaching of the world's religions is often portrayed as sex-negative or anti-sex, by which is meant an overall stance that is critical or suspicious or shame-filled or guilt-ridden about the role of sexuality in human life. Religious traditions are often especially concerned about sexuality as an impediment to the spiritual life. Monotheistic Western religions, and Christianity in particular, are infamously singled out in this regard as responsible for much of the anti-sex bias of Western culture.[6] From this perspective, religion – by which I mean institutions, texts, people, and practices that use rhetoric commonly called "religious" – has fueled shame and fear, not only around heterosexuality, but also around related issues of menstruation, masturbation, the body, sexual pleasure, sex education, prostitution, and homosexuality.

Religion has played an important role in this regard in constructing cultural value systems that are derogatory and oppressive to women, as well as to people in the lesbian, gay, and bisexual communities (such as issues of discrimination, partner rights, same-sex marriage, and gay ordination). Religion has been used, for example, to constrain women's sexuality within the relatively narrow parameters of heterosexual procreative marriage. Biblical models and Church teachings have historically imposed chastity outside of marriage and monogamy within it as the only two acceptable options for sexual expression, especially for women, and have imposed harsh censure on those – again, especially women – who dared to contravene these norms. Religion has helped shape a negative stance toward birth control, abortion, divorce, and cohabitation, all traditionally seen as sinful and still in many communities seen as shamefully against God's will. Despite several decades of the sexual revolution, these attitudes still endure: why do I – a supposedly liberated and feminist married woman – feel mildly embarrassed to buy condoms?

While all of this is true, it is not the only truth about religion and sex. It strikes me as somewhat too easy to call Christianity sex-negative. Aside from the existence of counterexamples like the intense erotic imagery of the Biblical *Song of Songs* and of the medieval mystics or Protestantism's elevation of married life over a celibate clergy or the current championing of gay rights by a denomination like the United Church of Christ, it may be more appropriate to view Christianity as seeing itself in competition with sexuality for control over human desire. The fourth- to fifth-century Church Father Augustine is probably the most influential example of a Christian thinker who envisioned desire dualistically, as oriented either toward God or toward the world. Sensual delight of all forms, but especially sexual desire and satisfaction, were seen by him and much of the Church as dangerously pulling one away from God and risking the disordered and perverse rule of body over soul, instead of the "proper" rule of soul over body.

Thus historically, in a rather clever move, Christianity has tried to win this competition by requiring sexuality to be constrained within monogamous, heterosexual, married union and by largely painting sex as shameful. Why is sexuality so easily cast in this light? Partly, it is because sexuality *is* a very powerful human force and therefore easily seen as dangerous; it's not hard to make the argument that it is in need of the strictest control. A fuller answer raises a plethora of complex psychosocial issues beyond the scope of this book, including a fundamental human anxiety over losing control; fear of relationality and the vulnerability of opening oneself to another; male fear of women's sexuality rooted in childhood fear of the mother and in the instability of male gender and sexual identity in mother-reared patriarchal societies; women's fear of men's assault in a world that bears witness to the willingness of so many to use rape to humiliate and control; and finally, the sheer chaotic power of the sex drive and the ability of our desire to derail reason.

This nexus of religion, shame, and sex contributes to the continued stigmatization of stripping today and to the enduring Puritanism that marks American culture, despite its nominally sex-positive ways.[7] Religious bias against sexuality supports society's bias against stripping. The practitioner of striptease culture, however, challenges these norms every day with her hip-swiveling erotic license. In particular, the exotic dancer's performance, indeed her very existence, questions the traditional ideal of modest and compliant feminine sexuality. Her performance in this regard becomes an antiperformance, an antiscript, a photographic negative of the image of ideal femininity endorsed in traditional patriarchal religion. Instead of offering her youth and beauty, synonymous with moral innocence, as intangible assets in the marriage market – or passively allowing herself to be so offered in a patriarchal brokerage of father to husband – a dancer quite deliberately does the opposite: she herself profits from her youth and beauty, now equated with moral temptation and fall, as commercial assets in the marketplace of the strip club. In other words, and in terms of my earlier argument, strippers live out a capitalist sex-positive argument in defense of their work.

With the script of Eve, the dancer does not evoke this argument to its fullest extent. She remains somewhat abashed about her profession, too embarrassed to tell her family, a little apologetic – "I'm only doing this to put myself through school" or "until I pay off some debts." But the exotic dancer can also transform the Eve script, or enact another version of it, one in which she feels no shame and in fact claims pleasure and power in her performance. What she then intentionally performs is a very calculated, defiant, shameless, and brazen reversal of the good-girl script. She becomes the mythic figure of a woman who deliberately uses her sexuality against men to beguile and trick them, in order to get what she wants. She instead evokes the whore and the Jezebel. And to the extent that she dances and strips off her clothing while she does so, she enacts another religious script: that of Salome. While both Eve and Salome transgress the traditional religious script of the good girl, they do so in different ways, for while Eve is ultimately repentant, Salome has no regrets. Eve is the good girl gone remorsefully bad, but Salome is the bad girl reveling in her badness.

Although Salome is a popular figure in artistic representation from Roman times through medieval miracle plays and illuminated manuscripts to Renaissance oil paintings, it is only in the last decades of the nineteenth century that what comes to be called a "Salomania" craze takes off. The legend of the alluring princess of Judea as a femme fatale driven by lust and revenge raged throughout Europe at this time. The artistic obsession was best realized in *Salome*, first a play (1893) by Irish writer Oscar Wilde and then an opera (1905) by the German composer Richard Strauss with a libretto based on Wilde's production. It fell to Wilde's scandalous and popular drama – banned in England and performed for the first time in Paris in 1896 – to introduce into the Salome legend what came to be capitalized as "The Dance of the Seven Veils." As Toni Bentley suggests in *Sisters of Salome*, with his stage direction about this dance, Wilde may perhaps even be considered "the unlikely father of modern striptease."[8]

An attentive reading of the New Testament story, however, offers another perspective on this script of a young beauty's power to drive men crazy with desire. The Salome story is recounted in the gospel of Matthew (14:1–12), with a longer and more detailed version in the gospel of Mark (6:14–29). She is not even named in these accounts, although Josephus, the contemporaneous Jewish historian, provides us with her name as the daughter of Herodias. Herod, ruler of Galilee, had imprisoned John the Baptist in his dungeon, both for the unrest his religious ministry was causing and for his critique of Herod's recent marriage to Herodias, the former wife of his brother Philip. Herodias wants to have John executed, but Herod refuses, believing the Baptist to be a "righteous and holy man." During a banquet, Herodias sees her chance when her daughter Salome's dance performance so pleases Herod (her uncle and stepfather), that he swears to her "Whatever you ask me, I will give you, even half of my kingdom." On instruction from her mother, the girl requests the head of John the Baptist.

One salient aspect of this script is Salome's intoxicating youth; its Lolita-like point in this regard is the susceptibility of the older man to seduction and bedazzlement by a girl. Herod's wife does not seem to hold this sexual appeal for him, but Salome's nubile adolescence, the innocence and freshness of her youth coupled with her fledgling erotic charms, renders her both virgin and whore at once and inflames Herod into a panting frenzy of lust, an element much emphasized in Wilde's play. This script, when enacted by the exotic dancers, highlights this irresistible attraction of a girl's blossoming sexuality. When strippers skip around in pleated cheerleader skirts or schoolgirl uniforms, their hair tucked back in ponytails, sucking suggestively on lollipops, they enact this facet of the Salome script.

Wilde further thickens the plot with details that Herod had murdered his brother and that Salome had earlier willfully tried to seduce John and had been spurned, thus explaining her triumphant kiss on the lips of his disembodied head. The playwright thereby increases Salome's agency and turns her into a true femme fatale by giving her a motivation for her seductive dance and macabre request. Such agency is missing in the synoptic gospel account, where Salome dances at the behest of her mother and stepfather and where her only direct words are "What should I ask for?" (to her mother) and "I want you to give me at once the head of John the Baptist on a platter," hardly a very compelling feminist manifesto. She is, in this Biblical version of the narrative, more or less pimped by her mother and offered up in incestuous fashion to Herod. She seems more pawn than power figure.

This narrative is explicitly religious in that Herod's lechery forces him to act contrary to his religious convictions, as he is honor-bound to fulfill his hasty oath and grant Salome's demand. Even more so, the script is religious in that it buys into the competition, the dualistic "either/or," that Christianity sets up between itself and sexuality. Sexual passion in this story is tied up with acts of incest, adultery, murder, revenge, impiety, and impetuosity, all ending with disastrous consequences. No good comes of such passion in this story, and sex is clearly allied here against the ethical and the godly. The moral of the narrative is that a man should know better than to invite a beautiful young woman to dance for him, for she is inevitably manipulative and will beguile him past all reason. In contemporary parlance, Salome is a cock-tease, and no man stands a chance against her.

When applied to the strip club, the message is that men are wrong to go into such places and that at some level they know it, but that they are held captive by their lust and helpless to resist the dancers' allure. Precisely because the Salomes of the world know how to exploit this helplessness and turn it to their advantage, the fault lies ultimately not with the man – mesmerized by her teasing swirl of veil and flesh, who could expect him to act differently? – but with her, with Salome, with the stripper, with Everywoman. We see here the danger of this script for dancers. Woman as sexual and malevolent being is an ancient and perennial trope stretching far beyond the figure of Salome; when a woman seeks to make her living as a stripper, like it or not, she exposes her performance to be read in terms of this wider script.

This close reading gives one pause. The old questions resurface: do the dancers remain pawns, are they deluding themselves, is the capitalist sex-positive argument flawed? In trying to play the men's power game of capitalist patriarchy yet turn the tables against them, do the dancers merely succeed in trapping themselves within tired notions that women are just sexual and conniving beings? In the Biblical form of this script, it is not clear how Salome herself benefits from her dance, and Wilde's version ends with her slain on the orders of Herod, now repulsed by her monstrosity. A third religious script, as well as another argument evoked by the sex-workers' rights movement and by striptease culture, attempts to address the sense that there may be something insidious and ultimately self-defeating about the stripping industry's reduction of sexuality to a market commodity. Here, finally, enters the script of the Goddess and the argument of spiritual sex-positive feminism.

Stripping and the Goddess

On a return visit to Mr. Lucky's one night, I notice that the management has sprayed some sort of stucco finish on the outside of the club building and painted it black. It's a strange effect that makes the walls look rather like particle board, but Mr.

Lucky's was never geared toward the most upscale crowd anyway. Adding to the renovations is a new, large Venus de Milo statue greeting visitors just inside the entrance door. Although this is the first time that I notice a goddess motif in connection with stripping, I soon note the association springing up repeatedly. The Peek-a-boo Club down the highway from Mr. Lucky's has four identical versions of a classical goddess statue lined up in front of its building: a coy Artemis, interrupted at her bath. A Montreal-area club calls itself "Les Déesses," or "The Goddesses." In other researchers' published interviews and in some that I conduct myself with sex workers, women talk about their job and their self-understanding in terms of goddess spirituality. Again, I ask myself, what does it mean to be a stripper? She embodies the fantasy of unbridled sexuality and acts out the scripts of both Eve and Salome. Does she also enact a script of the Goddess, the magical female being whose sexuality is life-giving and healing? In terms of the wider implications of exotic dance for contemporary understandings of sexuality and gender relations, part of the current appeal of striptease culture seems precisely that women, through it, get to "become the Goddess." To put it another way, a third line of defense for striptease culture, apart from the arguments of sex-positive capitalism and sex-positive feminism discussed in the last two chapters, is sex-positive spirituality.

While much of the practice and teaching of the major world religions, and of the Western monotheistic religions in particular, does bear strong marks of the sex-negative, there are other religious traditions that do not fear uninhibited sexuality as inevitably leading to disorder and immorality and that do not fuel shame around sexual enjoyment. Alternative traditions to the more recent Western monotheistic ones, such as the ancient goddess traditions, may more easily celebrate the power and pleasure of woman's sexuality, including its expression outside monogamous procreative marriage in forms that have usually earned women labels of "fallen," "whore," or "slut." Similar to Cosi's embrace of such goddess religion as the inspiration for her work as a prostitute, some strippers claim to connect with these traditions of ancient goddess religion in their dancing. The dancer here performs according to a religious script even older than the biblical stories of Eve and Salome, namely that of the powerful, sexual, female divine.

Seen through this lens, the dancer enacts or conjures up prepatriarchal goddess figures and temple priestesses that proclaim power and honor in the naked female form. This script raises questions about the pagan (Aphroditic or Dionysian) "sacred" nature of stripping and sex. According to the controversial feminist critic Camille Paglia on the topic of pornography (from a guest article in *Playboy*, no less), pornography is "a pagan arena of beauty, vitality, and brutality, of the archaic vigor of nature. It should break every rule, offend all morality. Pornography represents absolute freedom of imagination … It lets the body live in pagan glory, the lush disorderly fullness of the flesh."[9]

I start to think about these issues in terms of Cosi's celebration of the Wondrous Vulva. Strippers shave their pubic areas – either entirely or partially, as do adult-film actresses and centerfold models, as well as many women in bathing suits at the pool or beach – and then dance in ways that highlight and display the Wondrous Vulva. Depending on local laws, the norms of the club, and the personal preference of the dancers themselves, they may keep their vulva covered in a G-string or thong – a style that itself is a way of highlighting the pubis. They will inevitably dance or move onstage in a sexually suggestive manner that has them rocking and rotating their hips to draw attention to the pelvis. And they may well do pole or floor work that involves splaying their legs and displaying their vulva, either by wrapping themselves around the stage pole or by performing splits and rolls on the floor that can bring them within scant feet of those customers seated at the tip rail around the stage. The vulva, like the breasts, clearly has great power.

Pulling these ideas together, one could argue that men come into strip clubs as into pagan temples. The patrons of the club are devotees of Cosi Fabian's sacred cult of the Wondrous Vulva. The modern-day stripper is the goddess. As she dances onstage, men worship – literally at the feet of the goddess. (Gyno Row takes on new meaning here.) In this context, the popularity of strip clubs today becomes a testament to the timeless fascination and perennial appeal of the naked female body: mysterious, soft and sensuously curved, magically able to create and also to creatively renew life through the primordial power of female sexuality. Stripping and striptease culture are then one important part of popular culture in which women can use this power playfully, erotically – and even religiously – for their own financial, emotional, and spiritual fulfillment. The dancers' gracious erotic display of breast and vulva brings men in droves into the clubs in an exchange that according to at least some dancers makes them feel in some sense like "goddesses."

Sometimes, women use this goddess language metaphorically and tongue-in-cheek. A "goddess" can simply be synonymous with a woman who is powerful, out-spoken, and self-confident. Mattson, for example, in *Ivy League Stripper*, adopts such a style of self-expression when she describes her persona at the Foxy Lady, "playing the goddess to their twenty-dollar bills … I had my goddess attitude switched on high, as usual. 'I deserve tons of money, I deserve adoration' …"[10] Similarly, to be "worshipped" can mean to revel in the attention garnered by a healthy and humorous exhibitionism. Brandy, the ex-lawyer and dancer at the Lusty Lady told me, "I definitely get the feeling that I'm being worshipped. The customers stare with big wide eyes, like little boys. They say things like 'You're so beautiful, you have such beautiful eyes or breasts.' I never feel quite like a goddess, though; there's always that cellulite! A goddess probably doesn't have cellulite on her butt." Cosi laughingly assures me later, "The Goddess in us simply doesn't care!"

Sheila Kelley's popular "S-Factor" stripper workout program for everyday women draws freely on this type of goddess imagery, featuring moves labeled the "Prancing Goddess" and the "Goddess Rising." In her book, she supplies a goddess quiz to determine one's "erotic personality," with role models ranging from Oya, the African river goddess; to Gaia, the classical Greek Earth Mother; to Lilith, the Mesopotamian seductress and first wife of Adam. All women have an inner sex goddess, Kelley argues, a "hidden erotic creature, a center of sexual power and self-knowledge."[11] When dancers and women who play with the ways of striptease culture use this language, a "goddess attitude" implies a strong sense of self as well as a sense of entitlement to pleasure. It's about a woman strutting her stuff and having a great time being delightfully naughty.

Without explicitly evoking goddess language, some dancers draw on a similar vocabulary to more generally characterize the stripper experience in terms of a creative life force. Rita Rhinestone, for example, when interviewed in Scott's *Behind the G-String* about her work as a dancer, maintains that "the female nude does have a lot of impact onstage. People can be mesmerized by it. And I think some of that is the power of the female nude as the symbol of creation. There's a lot of fear around that ... When a performer creates that moment of being super alive and superhuman, expressed so fully, so vividly, then everyone in the crowd identifies with that person; everyone in the crowd feels more possibilities in life."[12] In Rita's account, the dancer is not necessarily a "goddess" but, in her nudity and anonymous womanhood, she does represent creativity, possibility, and a type of vivid, unmasked life force. By taking off her clothes, she pares herself down to the – literally – bare essentials of her personhood. As Rita says, there can be fear in this moment, for both dancer and audience: fear arising from shame, guilt, vulnerability, and rejection. But in the liminality of the moment, in its deliberate breach of the sometimes stultifying bulwarks erected to protect and enforce conventional sexuality, it can also be a space of great creative freedom.

Other sex workers evoke goddess language quite explicitly as a way to understand the appeal of what they offer. Hyapatia Lee, a Native American porn star, dancer, and rock-and-roll recording artist sees "the adult materials and the display of the nude female body as a throwback to the goddess-worshipping days, where forms of nude women – particularly pregnant women, the many-breasted Isis, all these fertility figures – were everywhere, and they were worshipped. When I'm dancing and somebody's giving me money in my garter, what is everybody giving me these dollars to see?" Lee asks. Her answer? "Where all life comes from. That's what we're looking at in the movies – how life is originally started. That's what the sexual act, basically, originally, had as its most important function."[13] In this interpretation, "goddess" signifies women's reproductive power. Female sexuality is magical, mysterious, and transformative precisely because its power is that of creating, not just symbolic possibility, as Rita had suggested, but actual new life.

Some sex workers draw on such religious language in order deliberately to combine in their work a sex-positive approach with a spiritual one. Tara, for example, is a Lusty Lady dancer featured in the documentary *Live Nude Girls Unite!* about the peep show's unionization campaign. Tara explains that she sees "sex work as a sacred act, even in the most base context like this pornographic peep show. There's life force in it, and it is healthy. And I consider myself to be providing a spiritual service, a sexual spiritual service." The nature of the service provided here is often understood as one of *healing*: healing the hypocrisies, abuse, condemnations, and fearful restrictions imposed by the sex-negative culture underlying much of the ostensibly sex-positive ways of contemporary America.

Nina Hartley, a well-known porn star and sex educator, illustrates this point: "Instead of being viewed as a trailblazer, many of my sisters views me as (at best) misguided and brainwashed or (at worst) as a traitor and rapist. Luckily for Eros and Aphrodite (the Greek gods of erotic love and passion), there exists a small but growing parallel universe, occupied by sex-positive feminists and the people who love them. Among this crowd, I have learned that there are many people out there who get what I'm giving in the spirit it's intended: the joy of sex offered by a humble handmaiden of Aphrodite ... The pleasure I invoke can work ... healing magic."[14] Or note the bold proclamation of sex-positive theorist and sometime-whore Carol Queen: "To guide another person to orgasm, to hold and caress, to provide companionship and initiation to new forms of sex, to embody the Divine and embrace the seeker – these are healing and holy acts ... In our collective extraordinary experience we prostitutes have healed even those who do not honor us. Were the attack on us over, we could begin to heal the whole world."[15]

In both Hartley's and Queen's comments we see, as with Cosi, a sex worker's explicit self-identification, through this category of healing, with ancient goddess traditions and with a claimed connection to these traditions through contemporary neo-paganism or Wicca (modern-day witchcraft, not to be confused with Satanism). We see as well an explicit link made between an embrace of sex-positive feminism and an alternative pagan religiosity; the two stances are seen to complement each other in providing a foundational philosophy or worldview to undergird a woman's choice of sex work as career. (Much of this thinking and practice goes on, as one may guess, in the San Francisco Bay area, that crucible of all things sex-positive, from gay rights to Tantric sex priestesses to dominatrix clubs.)

In this alternative, woman-centered, and sex-friendly spirituality, sex workers find greater acceptance for a freer, healthier expression and exploration of women's sexuality. The prostitute, the exotic dancer, the Everywoman prancing through her stripper workout routine at home identifies with, or feels herself to be embodying, a goddess figure: a prepatriarchal and in some cases prehistorical expression of the feminine divine. She becomes – symbolically, literally, or tongue-in-cheek jokingly – an expression of this goddess. These women talk about their sexuality in terms of goddess imagery, for reasons of the fertility or joy or creativity or pleasure or healing or life force or beauty that they experience as associated with their female bodies. Such goddess spirituality finds in women's sexuality and in the naked female form a playful, powerful, healthy, creative, and curative force – a type of magic, if you will. What emerges from these associations is a spiritual sex-positive interpretation not only of exotic dance and sex work, but also of women's sexuality in America today.

To me, this material offers some of the most intriguing interpretations from my foray into the world of stripping. From this perspective of sex-positive spirituality, the invitation of Mr. Lucky's DJ Bill that I recounted in Chapter 1 takes on a whole new meaning: "Get those titties in your face," he had said in a phrase that stuck with me ever since, "and life is good." The exotic dancer here reenacts the experience of the breast as the source of life, of creative and even divine power to make and sustain new life. The stripper recalls the mother, but also the Great Mother. She is a remnant, or a modern reenactment of the Great Goddess, the Earth Mother, the original, primal religious figure of all humanity. "In the beginning was the breast," writes the feminist scholar Marilyn Yalom in her book-length history of the breast.[16] Indeed some of the earliest human art and artifacts are stone carvings and figurines of the naked female form from Old Europe, dating back to thirty thousand years ago. Often called "Venuses," these are stylized figurines of a woman's body, with large fleshly breasts, belly, hips, and buttocks. These Venuses appear to be humanity's first focus of religious devotion.

One can situate contemporary sex work within a context of goddess spirituality by continuing to trace a historical lineage in order to link up the Venuses with the present-day practitioners of striptease culture. David Scott, in his *Behind the G-String*, maps out these links especially well. He views the stripper as one contemporary manifestation of what he calls the "quintessential male fantasy image" of the goddess. The goddess, in his account, is the female nude portrayed as "physically enchanting, available, unambivalent, sexually willing, and a tireless servant of one's personal preferences." This goddess appears as a religious form and/or an art form in an ancient line of fantasy females that he traces stretching down from the Venus figures, through classical Greco-Roman statuary, to Renaissance allegorical oil paintings, nineteenth-century nude tableaux vivants, and twentieth-century American vaudeville and burlesque, all the way to the modern strip club.[17] Bentley, whose work *Sisters of Salome* I discussed earlier, helpfully adds the nineteenth-century "Salomania" movement as another important precursor in this chain of "goddesses."

Other goddesses in the stripper family tree include Uzume, the Japanese Shinto shamanic goddess of merriment, who according to legend performs the first ever "striptease" for an audience of myriad delighted goddesses and gods in order to lure the sun goddess Amaterasu out of hiding and out of a deep depression. In a similar story from ancient Greece, Baubo – belly goddess, wise crone, court jester and nurse to Demeter – teases Demeter, who is grieving over the loss of her daughter Persephone, to laughter when Baubo lifts her own skirts and displays her belly and vulva. Both these stories echo Cosi's point about how the celebration of the vulva is not necessarily in relation to fertility or arousal, but can also be about joke and shared laughter among women.[18]

This perennial fantasy of the sexual goddess has a further deep historical context in the widespread ancient tradition of sacred-temple prostitution. The powerful sacred prostitutes, seen as handmaidens or priestesses of various goddesses, played an honorable role in the religious life of classical Greece, Rome, the Near East, and India. The temple dances they would perform and other ancient traditions of body work such as belly dancing may be seen as a deep root of contemporary exotic dance. The *devadasi* of Hindu temples in India; the *hierodule* in Greece, servants of goddesses such as Aphrodite and Inanna; the *qadeshet* of the Great Goddess Ishtar, Mother of Harlots, in ancient Mesopotamia; and the *horae* of Ptolemaic Egypt (from whose name derives one etymology of "whore") were all generally understood as handmaidens and embodiments of their patron goddess. They were often well-educated and of high social status. Ritual sexual union with them apparently carried various meanings of joyful worship, ceremonial purification, and even "sacramental replay of the divine act of creation," as sacred whore and man lying together mirrored the *hieros gamos*, or sacred marriage of the Great Goddess and her consort, the reenactment of which bestowed kingship and ensured the fertility and prosperity of the land.[19] This tradition is celebrated today as Cosi, along with other prostitutes, appropriates the *qadeshet* for inspiration in her work. Other sex-positive supporters adopt Asian sexual practices of Tantra, a philosophy of consciousness emphasizing breath and pathways of subtle body energy. This tradition is seen also in the central dictum of contemporary Wicca, repeated by its practitioners and attributed to the Goddess, "All acts of love and pleasure are My rituals."

To say that this message about sexuality is different from that promulgated by Christianity is an understatement, to say the least. The core and central point of all this language about goddesses and sacred prostitutes is that sex and religion needn't be enemies. Carol Queen, commenting on her participation in a performance art piece that staged (in San Francisco, of course) a creative reimagination of the sexual rituals of ancient temple prostitutes, marvels, "If this is what the 'heathen' Goddess-worshipers were doing before the new religion came along, no wonder Christianity has tried so hard (and relatively successfully) to colonize sex. This stuff would be big, *big* competition."[20] In other words, a necessary tactic in the triumph of the newer monotheistic, male-god patriarchal religions (Christianity, but also Judaism and Islam) over the older pagan, goddess religions was to control the public perception of sex. To dethrone the Goddess – to turn the "The Great Whore of Babylon" from an honorific title of Ishtar into a dire insult – Christianity had to change sex from sacrament to sin.

These various forms of the Goddess script, in their context of contemporary spiritual sex-positive feminism, add another dimension to the scripts of Eve and Salome. While Eve, reaching for her forbidden fruit, is a narrative about the desire for knowledge, sexuality in her story carries a negative moral valence as linked with a forbidden knowledge that ushers into the human realm lust, shame, sin, and even death. Yet the Goddess script turns this moral valence on its head: yes, sex is knowledge, and the Biblical metaphor "to know" another is an apt description for carnal union, but such knowledge is not forbidden and lust is not synonymous with fall and sin. Instead, to explore one's sexuality is to gain important self-knowledge that can lead to wholeness, personal growth, and holistic healing. In a contemporary striptease-culture example, Kelley offers affirmations to repeat out loud as part of her goddess-tinged, stripper aerobic program: "In expressing my sexuality, I channel spiritual energy" and "Discovering my physical sensuality is the pathway to embracing my whole self."[21]

We see here that the Goddess script of sex-positive spirituality adds an element of critique to the arguments of sex-positive capitalism. The goal is no longer just to make money, but to "embrace the whole self." As Cosi explains, when she became a prostitute, "the immediate impetus was unemployment and disgust at the women's labor market, but my deeper motivation was the continuation of my quest for wholeness and meaning."[22] Eve is just trying to survive in the sexual economy into which she has unwittingly stumbled, and Salome has quite deliberately sashayed her way in and is determined to thrive there at whatever cost. The Salome script in particular is ultimately an amoral, or immoral, one: get what you can out of the marketplace, by whatever means are available to you. There is little to no room for moral considerations in sex-positive capitalism. But while Eve and Salome are just trying to make the world work for them, the Goddess – ahh, the Goddess! – she is trying to make the world a better place, and her goal is to heal.

As was the case with sex-positive feminism, one form that this healing takes is a critique of common social norms of female beauty. According to sex-positive spirituality, all women have an inner sex goddess and any woman can be a goddess. Central to this script is a rejection of patriarchal or consumer-oriented notions of women's beauty that claim such appeal necessarily involves youth, slimness, conventional good looks, and a body groomed at great expenditure of time and money. Being a goddess is not dependent on being 5'10" and 120 pounds, or 22 years old, or gorgeous in any sense endorsed by *Cosmo* magazine, Madison Avenue, or MTV. It is instead a matter of attitude, of projecting an inner conviction of beauty and desirability, as indeed any stripper or Sweet Potato Queen knows well.

One may wonder to what extent this language of "sacred whore" and "embodying the goddess" is real or just rhetoric. Is it just a clever marketing campaign that uses religious language to pretty up prostitution or to make the self-abasements of raunch culture seem acceptable to women now duped by talk of their inner goddess into stripping for undeserving husbands? Are dancers just using this language as a way to claim respectability or to kid themselves about their empowerment in a profession still marginalized despite its wayward popularity? Is there an archetype and quintessence of "Woman as Sacred Whore" or is there just gender performance, à la Judith Butler? From one perspective, these two ways of talking are very different. The former implies a preexisting, ontological category or essence of being that one can embody: "Goddess" or "Sacred Whore" channeled by today's woman. Does this stance risk glamorizing, idealizing, or romanticizing sex work?

Butler's notion of performance is the opposite: there is no essence of Woman, only discourse, politics, and rhetoric. Butler's concern that the essentialism of the first stance conceals the political power agenda behind it may be somewhat mitigated by the fact that women are quite gleefully doing the political and rhetorical construction of these sexual identities for themselves. Yet her work still fruitfully directs us to deconstruct the rhetoric, to examine the contemporary material conditions (social, economic, political) that lead some women to make these goddess claims. Sex workers today have a political stake in designating "the Goddess" as the inspiration for their career choice. From this perspective, "Holy Whore" as an identity category is not the *origin* and *cause* of the sex workers' identity or work; this category is instead the *effect* of various institutions, practices, and discourses with points of origin in patriarchy and compulsory heterosexuality.[23] Here, the Goddess script may even be more about creative imagination and invention than about memory or historical accuracy.

To my way of thinking, the point of this debate isn't whether or not contemporary sex work and striptease culture have "actual" historical roots in sacred temple prostitution and ancient goddess worship. Either way, as part of striptease culture today, people are now exploring the possibility of a very different model of human sexuality, particularly of women's sexuality, and of the relationship between sex and religion. A new day may be dawning. As Carol Queen proclaims, "After seven thousand years of oppression, I declare this the time to bring back our temple."[24]

Sex-Positive Religion?

As I drive back over the Golden Gate Bridge after my interview with Cosi, the setting sun lights up the sky and I am reminded of Alice Walker's powerful and disturbing novel *Possessing the Secret of Joy*. The novel is about, among other things, female genital mutilation. Walker dedicates the novel "With Tenderness and Respect To the Blameless Vulva." This is perhaps the only such literary dedication that this key body part has ever received. I am aware of my own vulva, engorged now with the blood of pregnancy, starting to flower with the pressure of the baby's head in my third trimester. I remember too a feature dancer whom I saw perform one night at Mr. Lucky's. Part of her act involved bestowing close-up looks at her vulva to the patrons at the tip rail, as she lay on her back and inched her way around the stage, spreading her legs for public view. It struck me as both bizarre – do men really want to stare at women's vulvas? Isn't that a curiosity that wears off after high school? – and oddly touching as an offering or ritualized unveiling of that which is normally hidden, mysterious, and taboo. I thought of a priestess dispensing grace.

I thought of public viewings of saints' relics as they are carried in procession around the village square. All of these images are revelatory of the various moods and modes of the vulva, but where do they lead?

I realized that I was being ushered toward a large open-ended question that I will pose, in order to be maximally provocative, in its most extreme form using the nomenclature taught me by Carol Leigh, aka Scarlot Harlot: *Can religion be "slut-identified"?* Can it be truly sex-positive, any day soon? Can it endorse stripping? Sex work? "Promiscuity," as in consensual unmarried sex? Everywoman's search for her inner sex goddess? By "religion" here, I have in mind traditional institutional religion, not just the California New-Age pagans or the feminist witches. Is it possible to develop a broad-based mainstream religious consensus in America around a sex-positive ethic, as part of an overall religious vision that embraces difference, resists oppression, celebrates the body and sensuality, honors the erotic nature of our human being, and supports the moral development of the full human person? If so, what would this ethic look like? Jesus's words (John 8:1–11) to the adulteress whom he saves from stoning are "Go, and sin no more." This story has at least a whiff of the sex-positive about it, in that he could have agreed with the scribes and the Pharisees that the woman's act was so egregious that execution was the only response. But how about a divine charge to "Go, and have great sex"?

I have in mind a commandment to seek out sex that honors the creative life urge and the force of love; a mandate to share pleasure and the sensual delights of our physical embodiment with each other; a directive to experience sex as a drive toward intimacy and healing and away from our stubborn, lonely, fearful self-centeredness. What about a command, through sex, to breach the boundaries of ego and to transcend our separateness for transformative relationality with another, ultimately in order to experience the oneness of all life and the possibility of attaining compassion and wisdom? And behind all must be a command not to limit the expression of human sexuality, other than that sex should be consensual, safe, adult, and respect privacy. Do what you will, as the Wiccans say – be it gay, lesbian, straight, bisexual, transgendered, drag, burlesque, group, polygamous, fetishistic, BDSM, commercial, artistic, ritualistic, or transcendent – and harm none. While humans are clearly all too capable of misusing sexuality in instances of abuse and rape, from a theological point of view, this potential for misuse – for sliding into sin – is true of all human capacities and is the tragically inevitable concomitant of free will. If one wants to use such theological language, what is the Incarnation – that claimed embodiment of the divine in human or fleshly form – if not the creative life force of sexuality? Where in this world do we see evidence of the divine more than in the experience of connectivity, in the orgasmic dissolution of self, and in the fruits of new life that can arise through human sexuality?[25]

I'm very intrigued by the possibility these questions raise of a sex-positive, explicitly religious interpretation of what exotic dancing and prostitution can be, at their best. I am especially intrigued by the prospect of drawing conclusions and making applications outside the world of sex work to the wider context of human sexuality and in the development of truly sex-positive religion. Overall, I am intrigued by the conviction that there is a "more," that sex isn't just about making money or exercising one's lust, but that it can be part of a personal exploration of depth and meaning in life. This suggestion doesn't have to imply that you become a devotee of Ishtar or Aphrodite or a Tantrika practitioner or call yourself a Holy Whore – although it might. This quest for holistic growth doesn't have to be "spiritual" at all. It can be a wholly secular, this-worldly pursuit: instead of sex-positive spirituality, sex-positive ethical humanism. The point is simply that sex is powerful, ripe with both pleasure and danger. We can squander this power, fritter it away, and miss the opportunities it presents (like we do with so many other realms of our lives, watching too much television, letting petty annoyances fester, passing up opportunities to learn new things because we're comfortable in our ruts). But we can also take advantage of these opportunities for seeking wholeness and depth through I-Thou connection with others, or with one beloved other.

Just where are we as a society going with all this? Where is striptease culture taking us? Can we arrive at a vision that sees sexuality for what the sex-positive spirituality people claim it ideally to be: a healthy, creative, playful, transformative, healing good, capable of taking on many more different forms than those traditionally sanctioned? These are questions that ultimately reach beyond the scope of this book, but the project has left me with them, and so I now pass them on to my readers.

Conclusion: Take It Off!

The closest I ever come to a stripper moment myself occurs years before I even start this project, when I was called upon to perform an obscure French-Canadian ritual called the Sock Dance. I'm still not sure whether Danielle, my sister-in-law, simply made this up, but she swore to me that it is a time-honored tradition and indeed a requirement for any older, unmarried sister of the family to perform a dance in her socks at the wedding of a younger sibling. In other words, if Big Sis is still single at the time of a brother or sister's nuptials, she gets one last chance to catch the eye of a potential mate by dancing in a somewhat suggestive state of semi-undress. When my younger brother and Danielle were married, my own wedding was in fact already planned for just two months later. Nevertheless, Danielle insisted that tradition be upheld. Her brother-in-law the Scottish bagpiper provided thick woolen socks that came up to my thighs. I danced at the reception – I can't remember to what song, but it was some three-minute top-40 hit – and I must admit, I loved it. The sense of ritual requirement freed me from self-consciousness, and people whooped and cheered me on. It didn't feel sexy so much as fun. I didn't feel desired, but celebrated. Maybe I am more of an exhibitionist than I realize.

Lesson? There is definitely a pleasure to dance, to being centered in one's body, to celebrating the joy and sensuality of movement, and maybe even to being the center of attention while doing so. While this project didn't get me onto the strip club stage, it did inspire me to take belly-dancing classes, which I've greatly enjoyed, and even to buy a pair of high heels (gorgeous Italian black leather with sturdy three-and-a-half inch heels, in mint condition for just seven dollars at Salvation Army). I wear them now, even sometimes to walk to work, and manage to feel both virtuous in my frugality and sexy at the same time. In the end, then, what other stripper lessons have I learned, and what do I make of all of this material? How, finally, are we to evaluate this phenomenon of striptease culture, in order to measure its gains and costs? In answer, I offer certain research moments that have stayed with me, and the final questions that they raise.

One lesson concerns the varieties of dismay encountered while working on this project. First is the dismay of "good men" trying to do the right thing, reading in my work a message that they should treat women as sex objects and that that's what the women themselves want. A couple of male colleagues reacted this way to my project, with confusion and even frustration at what they perceived as the mixed messages of the feminist movement. Another brand of dismay is that experienced by feminists firmly opposed to sex work: one woman at an academic conference at which I presented a paper objected to my admittedly flippant comment that I was having more fun with this project than with any of my previous research. While I think that their respective stances fail to take into account the full complexities and ambiguities surrounding exotic dance and sex work, still, I see their points. I have wondered myself at times, am I betraying something or someone here? I never fully resolve these issues of dismay, and don't, in fact, think that they can be resolved, or at least not yet. They are part of the ongoing debate in our sex-positive, yet also sex-negative society as to what to make of new possibilities for gender roles and sexual norms. Striptease culture has become a key test site for experimenting with what constitutes sexually "liberated" and "enlightened" in the twenty-first century, but the answers are still far from clear.

So what do *I* think about stripping? In the end, I am aware of a certain disconnect: most of the dancers with whom I talk report that they are happy enough with their jobs – although they have bad shifts and job annoyances like anyone else – but I also hear warnings that it won't work out for many of them as well as they hope, or that only a small percentage use it well. The long-term dancers tell me that many, and maybe even most, of the girls to some extent do get lost in the profession: they forget about, or fail to accomplish, the long-term educational, financial, or career goals that they laid out for themselves when they started dancing (which of course may be true for many of us in our jobs: life doesn't always turn out the way we hope) or they get consumed by the party scene. Partly, this book dispels negative stereotypes about dancers, but the pop culture already does this work, and probably all too well. The tale here could then be cautionary: while strippers do certainly belie stereotypes of the drugged-out airhead or moral degenerate, the work is by no means as empowering as an episode of *Stripperella* might make it out to be. It's a risky profession: most dancers won't make as much money as they initially hoped, and even the fantasy pleasure of the experience can come at a high emotional cost. You are, after all, always on show, every naked inch of you constantly being evaluated and judged and, as often as not, rejected in favor of a different girl or another beer.

Even when it does work out well – high steady income; safe work environment; creative fantasy play; attention, praise, and gratification; good friends among co-workers – there is still the question of the function of stripping in society. The job can clearly benefit some individual women, but what effect does this industry have on women overall, on gender relations and attitudes toward sexuality? As I've said before, if the name of the game is patriarchy, stripping *is* one way for a young woman to win the game, by using that which society values against those guys willing to spend money in the clubs. But a critic, such as Ariel Levy in *Female Chauvinist Pigs*, will argue that the problem here is that stripping doesn't *change* the game. In this regard, I think of two women whom I interview some years after they had quit dancing, one now a lawyer with her own practice and the other a tenured university professor in the humanities. While neither regrets her time dancing and both feel that they learned important lessons, they did have caveats about the value of their experience. The professor recounted how she had danced as an edgy and liberating challenge to staid stereotypes about women's docile sexuality, but ultimately felt the effort was often wasted up against male customers' stereotypes of woman-as-whore: "I realized that I could feel as empowered and sex-positive feminist as I wanted, but to the majority of the guys there, I was just another pussy." The lawyer, with whom I talked about goddess spirituality, in which she had participated for a while, told me, "I feel more like a goddess now, as a successful woman lawyer earning respect in my profession."

So are such critics right: does stripping fail to change the game? Judith Butler writes that "sexual practice has the power to destabilize gender."[1] Do strippers create such useful "gender trouble" that serves to shake up and break down patriarchal culture patterns? More generally, as the stripping industry feeds into broader cultural patterns now taking hold, does striptease culture change the game? This is the book's ultimate question, and one on which the jury is still out: is striptease culture becoming an effective force in the spread of sex-positive attitudes throughout the pop culture? Is the current popularity of all things stripperesque changing in a positive way how we think about gender and sexuality in the twenty-first century? Will it create better attitudes – less hypocritical, freer of double standards, more democratic and just – toward sexuality for all of us: woman, man, and child?

This case of children and young people poses an important test for striptease culture in the future: to the extent that it can be a force for productively opening up discussion of sex and improving sex education, it will be sex-positive. The question here is how to support the healthy development of a young person's sexual identity? Through parenting, school, and extracurriculars, we support our youth's emotional, physical, financial, and intellectual development, yet seem almost paralyzed when it comes to their sexual development. One of my students told me that her mother warned her that she, my student, would die – literally die – if she had sex before marriage. Many parents and the U.S. federal government seem most comfortable with sex education that simply admonishes young people to chastity. We struggle to talk comfortably to our children about sex, and mostly, we're just afraid for them. Sex *is* dangerous: it can get you hurt, it can break your heart, it can leave you sick for life or pregnant. Yet we have drawn the boundaries of sexual ethics far too narrowly, to the great and unfair detriment of those then deemed "perverse," while at the same time fostering a culture that produces a great deal of sexual violence and abuse. We instead need sex education at home, at school, and in the media that is extensive, well-rounded, shame-free, and that stresses consent, safety, responsibility, and the possibility of sex as a path to self-discovery, deep connection to others, and personal growth. The test of such sex-positive education will be the extent to which it results in lower rates of unwanted pregnancy, sexually transmitted disease, and sexual violence.

This issue of young people, and especially of young girls, presents a sharp challenge to sex-positive feminism and to sex-positivity in general. Here is a deep memory, one that I had quite forgotten until I was well into my research on this project. When I was 12 or 13 and at a friend's house with a group of girls, our ringleader, Patricia, made a crank call to a local Ottawa strip club called Pandora's Box. She pretended to be 10 years older and looking for a job: "Yes, I've got green eyes and long brown hair … I can come down for an interview this weekend." We collapsed in giggles after her call, impressed by her boldness, captivated by the thought of this place, fascinated by the sense that we were on the cusp of having at our command something that we couldn't quite understand, but that we could tell was powerful, as well as dangerous. We were about to have something that the boys were going to desire.

We want girls and women to take charge of their own sexual lives, to own and direct their desire. But what exactly would that look like? Is striptease culture helping, or just making it worse by sexualizing girls prematurely? Abercrombie & Fitch's thong-marketing campaign for 12-year-old girls comes again to mind (although they are by no means the only retailers to do so, now that "porno-tot" fashion is a trend). One doesn't have to be a conservative right-wing moralist to find this problematic. But Cosi and her friend Soleil, the "sacred whore" prostitutes of San Francisco, helped me to think about this issue differently. Soleil told me a story of watching a 14-year-old girl perform an erotic dance, spontaneously, on a table at a party. The girl was a virgin, but was reveling in her budding sexuality and captivated the people there. Cosi suggests that we should teach girls aged 8–12 the stories of the temple prostitutes, of the Goddess and her sacred vulva. Who more than a 10-year-old girl, asks Soleil, is curious and interested in a thong? They may well be right, although this case study of "stripper tweens" is a discomforting one that makes me somewhat relieved I have boys.

Girls and women are presently allowed to be more sexual than has previously been the case (since goddess days?). That is a real freedom and power. They aren't necessarily always handling it well, but I expect missteps along this path. This is new territory. As Carol Queen provocatively puts is, "Slut stigma and its meaning are in the process of some social reconstruction – many men and women (some of them feminist) no longer devalue a woman who fucks for fun and pleasure."[2] There is obviously an appeal to this new license to be as raunchy and sexual and promiscuous – or at least to pretend to be – as men and boys have traditionally been allowed to be. There is also lots of room for abuse here, for things going wrong and people getting hurt. A woman's teens and twenties are a crucial although clearly vulnerable time for figuring out issues of sexual identity and, as Cosi puts it, for learning the erotic arts. Part of that learning experience means making mistakes and going too far. Sometimes it means acting like an idiot and regretting it later.

To the extent that there is now more latitude than ever before, let's not waste it on replicating tired, old notions of sexy fun. Sex-positivity means nothing if we're all simply empowered to act like a traditional, narrow-lensed version of a sexist man. If we're going to have sex-positive culture, let's have it be really sex-positive, not tamed to a patriarchal aesthetic. If there are going to be "Golf Pros and Tennis Ho's" parties (as are held among the sororities and fraternities of my campus), let's have "Female CEO and Pool Boy" parties as well. Let's have guys stripping down. If you want to embrace stripping as within the morally acceptable, you have to also embrace a pluralistic and democratic sexual ethic based on full-consent and no-harm that allows the expression of a wide range of sexual styles, preferences, and fantasies; you have to give up on patriarchal control of women's sexuality; you have to celebrate the beauty of our many sizes and shapes and stages of life; you have to condemn rape and child sexual abuse and sexual harassment as the worst violations.

If striptease culture simply means that girls and women are now under pressure to prove that they're hip by allowing themselves to be made into – or making themselves into – trite and one-dimensional sex objects, then I don't want to dance in that parade. I don't want stripper-style to only mean candy-pink thongs with big breasts and shaved flesh. I want room for hair and goth and leather, for deviance and defiance. The point isn't to push a good girl image of the stripper, docile in her conformance to a plastic Barbie look. Let's not be unimaginative. But nor, obviously, is the point that we all become strippers, or wear thongs, or sleep around. The point is choice and acceptance. Sex-positive means something different for everyone, including the choice of heterosexual monogamy. Let's not lose the possibility of this cultural moment to really open things up in a positive way. There is a real risk that the present sex-positive mood will not support the flourishing of women's sexuality, but merely redomesticate it. As one of my students asks, "Is buying in the same as selling out?" A case in point is another recent A&F offering in the form of a T-shirt that reads across the chest, "Who needs a brain when you have these?"[3] A woman striding down the street in this T-shirt may boldly mock such a sexist attitude by daring to flaunt it, but if so, it's another example of the parody being subtle, probably too subtle for most people to see past the surface sexism.

As to my interviewees themselves, where they are now? Marie ended up dancing for about five years, to the age of 38. She is now contentedly employed at the Kinsey Institute for Research in Sex, Gender, and Reproduction at Indiana University, as a part-time assistant in communications. She and Jeff are still happily together. Laura remains out of contact, but the last Marie knew, was working as a waitress in West Palm. Mr. Lucky's is still there, with a new coat of paint and DJ Bill still revving the crowd and Jeannette hustling the floor. Business is all right, although not back to pre-9/11 levels (a big reason why Marie left, as economic pressures had turned the club sleazier). Her final thoughts about dancing are that she found it at the right time in her life, when she was mature enough for the job's taxing emotional demands. She appreciates it for serving an important purpose as a stage in her personal growth: it gave her contact with people and life experiences far broader than she might otherwise have had and "it also unlocked an entirely new dimension of my sexuality and gave my 'feminist' relationship with my body a deeper complexity." Hallie has moved from Atlanta to California, where she is now back to work as an engineer, and recently married a man whom she met while stripping. She reports that she "doesn't regret one day of dancing": it financed her degree, taught her to be her own boss, and made her some life-long friends (one of whom was a bridesmaid in her wedding). Cosi is largely retired from prostitution and is doing some teaching these days at local universities ("Blood and Sex: The Holy Whore as Metaform.") She also reports that she has quit smoking and that, "with planning, becoming a non-smoker is easier than we're told!"

As I have said before, stripping isn't just about strippers, but is in the end about Everywoman, whom exotic dancers illuminate as a more curvaceous version of her. Similarly, this book isn't just about stripping, but is about the ultimate impact of this cultural bump and grind on contemporary society. If the call is to "Take it off!" what exactly are we taking off? Stultifying inhibitions of shame, guilt, fear, and ignorance; unjust gender bias and oppression of those who enjoy consensual sex in forms outside the norm; ridiculously narrow definitions of beauty and sexiness? Or are we taking off and shedding our common sense and moral decency, our hard-won feminist gains that women (and men) are not sexual objects to be ogled and bought and that sexual intimacy shouldn't carry a price tag? Is it both? Is it neither? Just where *are* we heading?

The question is still open.

It is for you to decide.

Go on. Figure out for yourself what to take off.

Notes

Chapter 1 Stripping: Demeaning and/or Empowering?

1. Lily Burana, *Strip City: A Stripper's Farewell Journey Across America* (New York: Talk Miramax Books, 2001), p. 44.
2. Statistics come from Eric Schlosser, "The Business of Pornography," *US News and World Report*, February 10, 1997; Burana, *Strip City*, p. 44; Judith Hanna, "Undressing the First Amendment and Corseting the Strip Tease Dancer," *The Drama Review* 42:2 (Summer 1998): 38–59; Katherine Frank, *G-Strings and Sympathy: Strip Club Regulars and Male Desire* (Durham and London: Duke University Press, 2002), p. xxi. The 15-billion-dollar figure comes from Dave Manack, publisher of *Exotic Dancer* magazine, as quoted in an Associated Press story in the *Tuscaloosa News*, May 21, 2004.
3. Sut Jhally, "Advertising and the End of the World." Northampton, MA: Media Education Foundation video, 1998.
4. Elisabeth Eaves, *Bare: On Women, Dancing, Sex, and Power* (New York: Alfred A. Knopf, 2002), pp. 288, 292.
5. Hervey Colette, "Pay gap widens for female managers in 90s," *The Tuscaloosa News*, January 24, 2002; data from a U.S. congressional study by the General Accounting Office.
6. Mary Pipher, *Reviving Ophelia: Saving the Selves of Adolescent Girls* (New York: Ballantine, 1994), p. 224.
7. David A. Scott, *Behind the G-String: An Exploration of the Stripper's Image, Her Person, and Her Meaning* (Jefferson, NC: McFarland, 1996), pp. 232–33.
8. Kitten on the Keys, "Pony Girl," *(It's not a) Pretty Princess Day* (Rug Burn Records, 2004).

Chapter 2 The Work of a Stripper: Six-inch Heels and Pole Tricks

1. Carol Queen, *Real Live Nude Girl: Chronicles of Sex-Positive Culture*, 2nd edn (Pittsburgh: Cleis, 2002), p. 200; Kim, quoted in Eaves, *Bare*, p. 103.
2. Sheila Kelley, *The S Factor: Strip Workouts for Every Woman* (New York: Workman, 2003), p. 167.

Chapter 3 "A Lot of Guys Just Want to Talk" and (Other) Reality Costs of Stripping

1. Arlie Hochschild, *The Managing Heart: Commercialization of Human Feeling*, 2nd edn (Berkeley: University of California Press, 2003 [1983]).
2. Heidi Mattson, *Ivy League Stripper* (New York: Arcade Publishing, 1995), p. 264.
3. "Girl expelled because mom is a stripper," *Tuscaloosa News*, May 18, 2002.
4. See Alice Miller, *The Drama of the Gifted Child* (New York: Basic, 1981).

Chapter 4 Where Fantasy Becomes Reality

1. Frank, *G-Strings and Sympathy*, pp. 234–36.
2. Mattson, *Ivy League Stripper*, p. 265.
3. Julia Query and Vicky Funari, directors. *Live Nude Girls Unite!* First Run Features, 2000.
4. Erika Langley, *The Lusty Lady: Photographs and Texts* (Zurich: Scalo, 1997), p. 155.
5. Judith Butler, *Gender Trouble: Feminism and the Subversion of Identity* (New York: Routledge, 1999 [1991]). All quotes in this section come from her pp. 172–80.
6. Scott, *Behind the G-String*, pp. 90, 95.
7. Carole S. Vance, ed., *Pleasure and Danger: Exploring Female Sexuality* (Boston: Routledge & Kegan Paul, 1984).

Chapter 5 Striptease Culture: Thongs for Everywoman

1. *Rolling Stone*, Issue 883/884, December 6–13, 2001. In an interview inside, she opines, "I think it's a beautiful thing to be sexy, and I think women should be proud of their bodies. And if I wanna show my belly in a video or show a little bit of cleavage, I just don't see anything wrong with that" (p. 88).
2. Smuin Ballet premiered *Bluegrass/Slyde* in company with other works at the Palace of Fine Arts Theatre, San Francisco. The program was reviewed in "Pole dancing and bluegrass intertwine in Smuin Ballet," *San Francisco Chronicle*, October 3, 2005.
3. http://blogthings.com/exoticdancernamegenerator/ accessed on November 16, 2006.
4. Alison Pollet and Page Hurwitz, "Strip till you drop: teen girls are the target market for a new wave of stripper-inspired merchandise," *Nation*, January 12, 2004; Karen von Hahn, "Peeping Thong," *Globe and Mail*, July 20, 2002; Janelle Brown, "Shake your Bootie," *Ottawa Citizen*, June 8, 2002.

5. Mattson, *Ivy League Stripper*, p. 138.
6. Lily Burana, quoted in "Stripping's new side," *USA Today*, October 28, 2003.
7. Pollet and Hurwitz, "Strip till you drop."
8. "Fitness trend off to sizzling start," *Ottawa Citizen*, September 10, 2005; "Exercise in feelin' sexy," *Ottawa Sun*, February 1, 2004; "Good girls do," *Globe and Mail*, April 8, 2006; "Polates: A Workout Class With a Lot of Attitude," *Tusk*, November 17, 2006; *Ottawa Recreation Guide*, Spring/Summer 2006.
9. Ariel Levy, *Female Chauvinist Pigs: Women and the Rise of Raunch Culture* (New York: Free Press, 2005), ch.1.
10. Jill Conner Browne, *The Sweet Potato Queens' Book of Love* (New York: Three Rivers Press, 1999); *The Sweet Potato Queens' Wedding Planner/Divorce Guide* (New York: Crown, 2005). See also www.sweetpotatoqueens.com.
11. Levy, *Female Chauvinist Pigs*, pp. 70–74; Virginia Vitzthum, "Stripped of our Senses," *Elle*, December 2003.
12. *Maclean's* magazine, March 28, 2005.
13. "Mayor takes it all off for charity," *Ottawa Citizen*, December 21, 2003. See also "Happy Nude Year," *Birmingham News*, December 5, 2004; "Calendar attempts sweeping exposure," *Ottawa Citizen*, November 1, 2005.
14. "Online casino goes over the top," *Ottawa Citizen*, July 4, 2003.
15. Liz Highleyman, "Professional Dominance: Power, Money, and Identity," in *Whores and Other Feminists*, ed. Jill Nagle (New York: Routledge, 1997), p. 148.
16. "Ad in campus paper promises free tuition for strippers," *Ottawa Citizen*, August 29, 2003.
17. Vitzthum, "Stripped of our Senses," *Elle*; Levy, *Female Chauvinist Pigs*, back cover flap and p. 82. For an example of the media's discussion of Levy's book and the issues she raises, see the cover story of *Maclean's* magazine, September 26, 2005, by Judith Timson, "Girls gone raunch: Why are young women treating themselves like pieces of meat?"
18. Tawnya Dudash, "Peepshow Feminism," in *Whores and Other Feminists*, ed. Nagle, p. 111.
19. Lola the Vamp, quoted in Suzanne Pullen, "What a Tease!" *San Francisco Chronicle*, September 18, 2005.
20. Carol Queen, "Sex Radical Politics, Sex-Positive Feminist Thought, and Whore Stigma," in *Whores and Other Feminists*, ed. Nagle, p. 127. See Highleyman, "Professional Dominance," in *Whores and Other Feminists*, ed. Nagle, for a discussion of the role-playing and erotic power exchange of BDSM.
21. Paul Ricoeur, *The Symbolism of Evil*, trans. Emerson Buchanan (New York: Harper and Row, 1967); also his *The Rule of Metaphor: Multi-disciplinary*

Studies of the Creation of Meaning in Language, trans. Robert Czerny, with K. McLaughlin and J. Costello (Toronto: University of Toronto Press, 1977).
22. Levy, *Female Chauvinist Pigs*, p. 82.

Chapter 6 Strippers, Whores, and Sluts: "Call Off Your Old Tired Ethics"

1. Burana, *Strip City*, p. 68.
2. Julia Query and Vicky Funari, directors, *Live Nude Girls Unite!* First Run Features, 2000.
3. For further discussion, see Burana, *Strip City*, chs 14–15.
4. "From busts to boom," *Ottawa Citizen*, June 27, 2003.
5. Query and Funari, *Live Nude Girls Unite!*
6. Taken November 8, 2002, from the website for the Exotic Dancers' Alliance, http://groups.msn.com/ExoticDancersAlliance/abouttheeda.msnw.
7. "Good girls do," *Globe and Mail*, April 8, 2006.
8. Queen, *Real Live Nude Girl*, p.165.
9. Much of my discussion is influenced by Gayle Rubin's seminal article, "Thinking Sex: Notes for a Radical Theory of the Politics of Sexuality," in *Pleasure and Danger*, ed. Carole S. Vance.
10. See, for example, Highleyman, in *Whores and Other Feminists*, ed. Nagle, pp. 153–4.
11. R. v. Labaye, [2005] 3 S.C.R. 728. Supreme Court of Canada judgment rendered December 21, 2005.
12. Deuteronomy 5:21; compare Exodus 20:17.
13. Expert testimony included in R. v. Labaye, [2005] 3 S.C.R. 728.

Chapter 7 At the Feet of the Goddess: Stripping, Sex, and Spirituality

1. Cosi Fabian, "The Holy Whore: A Woman's Gateway to Power," in *Whores and Other Feminists*, ed. Nagle, pp. 45–6, 52.
2. Fabian, "Holy Whore," p. 47.
3. Vulva University can be accessed at www.houseochicks.com/vulvauniversity.
4. Butler, *Gender Trouble*, p. 174.
5. Scott, *Behind the G-String*, p. 232.
6. See, for example, Patricia Beattie Jung, Mary E. Hunt, and Radhika Balakrishnan, eds., *Good Sex: Feminist Perspectives from the World's Religions* (New Brunswick, NJ: Rutgers University Press, 2001); Marvin M. Ellison and Sylvia Thorson-Smith, eds., *Body and Soul: Rethinking Sexuality as Justice-Love* (Cleveland: Pilgrim Press, 2003).

7. See, for example, Tracy Fessenden, Nicholas F. Radel, and Magdalena J. Zaborowska, eds., *The Puritan Origins of American Sex: Religion, Sexuality, and National Identity in American Literature* (New York: Routledge, 2001).
8. Toni Bentley, *Sisters of Salome* (New Haven: Yale University Press, 2002), p. 31.
9. Camille Paglia, "Guest Opinion: The Return of Carry Nation," *Playboy* October 1992, p. 38.
10. Mattson, *Ivy League Stripper*, pp. 203, 264.
11. Kelley, *The S Factor*, p. 3 and all of ch. 4, "The Goddess Rising."
12. Scott, *Behind the G-String*, p. 80.
13. Hyapatia Lee, in an interview by David Bradford, "Comings and Goings: Hyapatia Lee on Movies, Music, Feminism, Pornography, and Power," *The Ryder Magazine*, September 9–23, 1994, p. 60.
14. Nina Hartley, "In the Flesh: A Porn Star's Journey," in *Whores and Other Feminists*, ed. Nagle, pp. 60, 61.
15. Queen, *Real Live Nude Girl*, pp. 204–5.
16. Marilyn Yalom, *A History of the Breast* (New York: Ballantine, 1997), p. 9.
17. Scott, *Behind the G-String*, p. 90 and his chapters 6 and 7.
18. Shahrukh Husain, *The Goddess: Power, Sexuality, and the Feminine Divine* (Ann Arbor: University of Michigan, 2003), pp. 64–6; Trina Robbins, *Eternally Bad: Goddesses with Attitude* (Berkeley, CA: Conari Press, 2001), pp. 61–7.
19. Husain, *Goddess*, p. 92 and all her ch. "The Sexual Life of the Goddess." See also Fabian, "Holy Whore"; Georg Feuerstein, *Sacred Sexuality: The Erotic Spirit in the World's Great Religions* (Rochester, VT: Inner Traditions, 2003 [1992]), ch. 5; and Barbara Walker, *Woman's Encyclopedia of Myths and Secrets* (San Francisco: Harper and Row, 1983).
20. Queen, *Real Live Nude Girl*, pp. 92–3.
21. Kelley, *The S Factor*, p. 216.
22. Fabian, "Holy Whore," p. 44.
23. Adapted from Butler, *Gender Trouble*, p. xxix.
24. Queen, *Real Live Nude Girl*, p. 205.
25. We're just beginning to see work in this area as religious studies scholars challenge sex-negative traditions and come up with sex-positive interpretations within Christianity and other major religions. See, for example, Carter Heyward, *Touching our Strength: The Erotic as Power and the Love of God* (HarperSanFrancisco, 1989); David Guy, *The Red Thread of Passion: Spirituality and the Paradox of Sex* (Boston: Shambhala, 1999); Marcella Althaus-Reid, *Indecent Theology: Theological Perversions in Sex, Gender, and Politics* (London: Routledge, 2000); Feuerstein, *Sacred Sexuality*; recent anthologies such as Jung et al., *Good Sex*; Ellison and Thorson-Smith, eds., *Body and Soul*; and Scott Thumma and Edward R. Gray, eds., *Gay Religion*

(Walnut Creek, CA: AltaMira Press, 2005). See also the carefully sex-positive work of the ecumenical Religious Institute on Sexual Morality, Justice, and Healing.

Conclusion: Take It Off!

1. Butler, *Gender Trouble*, p. xi.
2. Queen, *Real Live Nude Girl*, p. 177.
3. As quoted by Bob Herbert, "Why Aren't We Shocked?" *New York Times*, October 16, 2006.

APPENDIX: Tables of responses to questionnaire

The data in the tables below was obtained through telephone surveys with 484 Alabama respondents, representative of the state population as a whole, on public perceptions about women who work as exotic dancers. The survey was conducted in 2002 by the Capstone Poll, Institute for Social Science Research of The University of Alabama. I thank Michael Conaway, Project Coordinator of the Capstone Poll, for producing this survey research.

SEX OF RESPONDENT

		Frequency	*Percent*	*Valid Percent*	*Cumulative Percent*
Valid	**MALE**	233	48.1	48.1	48.1
	FEMALE	251	51.9	51.9	100.0
	Total	484	100.0	100.0	

Q1: Do you feel that it is acceptable or unacceptable for a man to visit a club where strippers perform?

		Frequency	*Percent*	*Valid Percent*	*Cumulative Percent*
Valid	**ACCEPTABLE**	182	37.6	37.8	37.8
	UNACCEPTABLE	227	47.0	47.2	85.0
	DEPENDS	46	9.5	9.6	94.5
	DON'T KNOW/ NO ANSWER	18	3.7	3.7	98.2
	REFUSED TO ANSWER ANY MORE QUESTIONS ABOUT STRIPPING	8	1.7	1.8	100.0
	Total	481	99.6	100.0	
Missing	**System**	2	.4		
Total	484	100.0			

Q2: Do you feel that stripping as an occupation for a woman is acceptable or unacceptable?

		Frequency	*Percent*	*Valid Percent*	*Cumulative Percent*
Valid	**ACCEPTABLE**	163	33.6	34.4	34.4
	UNACCEPTABLE	261	53.9	55.1	89.5
	DEPENDS	38	7.8	8.0	97.4
	DON'T KNOW/NO ANSWER	11	2.4	2.4	99.8
	REFUSED TO ANSWER ANY MORE QUESTIONS ABOUT STRIPPING	1	.2	.2	100.0
	Total	473	97.8	100.0	
Missing	**System**	11	2.2		
Total		484	100.0		

Q3: Do you think that today's society as a whole finds stripping as an occupation for a woman to be acceptable or unacceptable?

		Frequency	*Percent*	*Valid Percent*	*Cumulative Percent*
Valid	**ACCEPTABLE**	223	46.2	47.4	47.4
	UNACCEPTABLE	215	44.5	45.7	93.1
	DEPENDS	15	3.0	3.1	96.2
	DON'T KNOW/NO ANSWER	18	3.7	3.8	100.0
	Total	471	97.4	100.0	
Missing	**System**	12	2.6		
Total		484	100.0		

Q4: Do you think that today's society views stripping as an occupation for a woman to be more acceptable today than ten years ago, less acceptable today, or no different from ten years ago?

		Frequency	*Percent*	*Valid Percent*	*Cumulative Percent*
Valid	**MORE**	344	71.1	73.0	73.0
	LESS	20	4.2	4.3	77.3
	NO DIFFERENT	94	19.4	20.0	97.3
	DON'T KNOW/NO ANSWER	13	2.7	2.7	100.0
	Total	471	97.4	100.0	
Missing	**System**	12	2.6		
Total		484	100.0		

Q5: Stripping as an occupation is degrading or demeaning to the women who do it.

		Frequency	*Percent*	*Valid Percent*	*Cumulative Percent*
Valid	**1-STRONGLY DISAGREE**	81	16.8	17.2	17.2
	2	37	7.6	7.8	25.0
	3	90	18.7	19.2	44.2
	4	34	7.0	7.2	51.3
	5-STRONGLY AGREE	213	44.0	45.1	96.4
	COULD NOT USE SCALE	5	1.0	1.0	97.5
	DON'T KNOW/NO ANSWER	12	2.5	2.5	100.0
	Total	471	97.4	100.0	
Missing	**System**	12	2.6		
Total		484	100.0		

Q6: Compared to women in general, do you think women who strip as an occupation are more sexually promiscuous or loose, less sexually promiscuous, or the same?

		Frequency	*Percent*	*Valid Percent*	*Cumulative Percent*
Valid	**MORE**	245	50.7	52.3	52.3
	LESS	31	6.3	6.5	58.8
	SAME	155	32.0	33.0	91.8
	DON'T KNOW/NO ANSWER	38	7.8	8.1	99.8
	REFUSED TO ANSWER ANY MORE QUESTIONS ABOUT STRIPPING	1	.2	.2	100.0
	Total	469	97.0	100.0	
Missing	**System**	14	3.0		
Total		484	100.0		

Q7: Compared to women in general, do you think women who strip as an occupation are more intelligent, less intelligent, or the same?

		Frequency	*Percent*	*Valid Percent*	*Cumulative Percent*
Valid	**MORE**	24	4.9	5.1	5.1
	LESS	139	28.7	29.6	34.7
	SAME	291	60.2	62.1	96.8
	DON'T KNOW/NO ANSWER	15	3.1	3.2	100.0
	Total	468	96.9	100.0	
Missing	**System**	15	3.1		
Total		484	100.0		

Q8: Compared to women in general, do you think women who strip as an occupation are more likely to be drug users, less likely, or the same?

		Frequency	*Percent*	*Valid Percent*	*Cumulative Percent*
Valid	**MORE**	249	51.5	53.3	53.3
	LESS	29	5.9	6.1	59.4
	SAME	157	32.4	33.6	93.0
	DON'T KNOW/NO ANSWER	33	6.8	7.0	100.0
	Total	467	96.7	100.0	
Missing	**System**	16	3.3		
Total		484	100.0		

Q9: Compared to women in general, do you think women who strip as an occupation are more likely to be taken advantage of or exploited, less likely, or the same?

		Frequency	*Percent*	*Valid Percent*	*Cumulative Percent*
Valid	**MORE**	341	70.5	72.9	72.9
	LESS	34	7.0	7.2	80.1
	SAME	78	16.1	16.7	96.8
	DON'T KNOW/NO ANSWER	13	2.7	2.8	99.6
	REFUSED TO ANSWER ANY MORE QUESTIONS ABOUT STRIPPING	2	.4	.4	100.0
	Total	467	96.7	100.0	
Missing	**System**	16	3.3		
Total		484	100.0		

Q10: Compared to women in general, do you think women who strip as an occupation are more immoral, less immoral, or the same?

		Frequency	*Percent*	*Valid Percent*	*Cumulative Percent*
Valid	**MORE**	154	31.8	32.9	32.9
	LESS	76	15.8	16.4	49.3
	SAME	212	43.7	45.3	94.5
	DON'T KNOW/NO ANSWER	24	4.9	5.1	99.6
	REFUSED TO ANSWER ANY MORE QUESTIONS ABOUT STRIPPING	2	.4	.4	100.0
	Total	467	96.7	100.0	
Missing	**System**	16	3.3		
Total		484	100.0		

Select Bibliography and Further Reading

Albert, Alexa. *Brothel: Mustang Ranch and Its Women*. New York: Random House, 2001.

Althaus-Reid, Marcella. *Indecent Theology: Theological Perversions in Sex, Gender, and Politics*. London: Routledge, 2000.

Barton, Bernadette. *Stripped: Inside the Lives of Exotic Dancers*. New York: New York University Press, 2006.

Bentley, Toni. *Sisters of Salome*. New Haven: Yale University Press, 2002.

Bruckert, Chris. Taking *It Off, Putting It On: Women in the Strip Trade*. Toronto: Women's Press, 2002.

Burana, Lily. *Strip City: A Stripper's Farewell Journey Across America*. New York: Talk Miramax Books/Hyperion, 2001.

Butler, Judith. *Gender Trouble: Feminism and the Subversion of Identity*. New York: Routledge, 1999 [1990].

Delacoste, Frederique and Priscilla Alexander, eds. *Sex Work: Writings by Women in the Sex Industry*, 2nd edn. San Francisco: Cleis Press, 1998.

Dudash, Tawnya. "Peepshow Feminism." In *Whores and Other Feminists*, ed. Jill Nagle. New York: Routledge, 1997.

Eaves, Elizabeth. *Bare: On Women, Dancing, Sex, and Power*. New York: Knopf, 2002.

Egan, R. Danielle, Katherine Frank, and Merri Lisa Johnson, eds. *Flesh For Fantasy: Producing and Consuming Exotic Dance*. New York: Thunder's Mouth Press, 2006.

Fabian, Cosi. "The Holy Whore: A Woman's Gateway to Power." In *Whores and Other Feminists*, ed. Jill Nagle. New York: Routledge, 1997.

Fessenden, Tracy, Nicholas F. Radel, and Magdalena J. Zaborowska, eds. *The Puritan Origins of American Sex: Religion, Sexuality, and National Identity in American Literature*. New York: Routledge, 2001.

Feuerstein, Georg. *Sacred Sexuality: The Erotic Spirit in the World's Great Religions*. Rochester, VT: Inner Traditions, 2003 [1992].

Frank, Katherine. *G Strings and Sympathy: Strip Club Regulars and Male Desire*. Duke University Press, 2002.

Futterman, Marilyn Suriani. *Dancing Naked in the Material World*. Buffalo, NY: Prometheus Books, 1992.

Guy, David. *The Red Thread of Passion: Spirituality and the Paradox of Sex*. Boston: Shambhala, 1999.

Hartley, Nina. "In the Flesh: A Porn Star's Journey." In *Whores and Other Feminists,* ed. Jill Nagle. New York: Routledge, 1997.

Heyward, Carter. *Touching our Strength: The Erotic as Power and the Love of God*. HarperSanFrancisco, 1989.

Highleyman, Liz. "Professional Dominance: Power, Money, and Identity." In *Whores and Other Feminists*, ed. Jill Nagle. New York: Routledge, 1997.

Hochschild, Arlie. *The Managed Heart: Commercialization of Human Feeling*, 2nd edn. Berkeley: University of California Press, 2003 [1983].

Husain, Shahrukh. *The Goddess: Power, Sexuality, and the Feminine Divine*. Ann Arbor: University of Michigan Press, 2003.

Jung, Patricia Beattie, Mary E. Hunt, and Radhika Balakrishnan, eds. *Good Sex: Feminist Perspectives from the World's Religions*. New Brunswick, NJ: Rutgers University Press, 2001.

Kelley, Sheila. *The S Factor: Strip Workouts for Every Woman*. New York: Workman, 2003.

Langley, Erika. *The Lusty Lady: Photographs and Texts*. Zurich: Scalo, 1997.

Lee, Gypsy Rose. *Gypsy: Memoirs of America's Most Celebrated Stripper*, with an afterword by Erik Lee Preminger. Berkeley, CA: Frog, Ltd, 1999 (1957).

Levy, Ariel. *Female Chauvinist Pigs: Women and the Rise of Raunch Culture*. New York: Free Press, 2005.

Liepe-Levinson, Katherine. *Strip Show: Performances of Gender and Desire*. New York: Routledge, 2002.

Maglin, Nan Bauer and Donna Perry, eds. *"Bad Girls"/"Good Girls": Women, Sex, and Power in the Nineties*. New Brunswick, NJ: Rutgers University Press, 1996.

Mattson, Heidi. *Ivy League Stripper*. New York: Arcade Publishing, 1995.

McNair, Brian. *Striptease Culture: Sex, Media, and Democratisation of Desire*. New York: Routledge, 2002.

Nagle, Jill, ed. *Whores and Other Feminists*. New York: Routledge, 1997.

Naked Truth, An Information Resource for Exotic Dancers in Ontario, The. Published by the Exotic Dancers Alliance (Canada). www.jumpstartcommunications.com/NakedTruth/Naked.

Pipher, Mary. *Reviving Ophelia: Saving the Selves of Adolescent Girls*. New York: Ballantine, 1994.

Queen, Carol. *Real Live Nude Girl: Chronicles of Sex-Positive Culture*, 2nd edn. Pittsburg: Cleis Press, 2002.

Queen, Carol. "Sex Radical Politics, Sex-Positive Feminist Thought, and Whore Stigma." In *Whores and Other Feminists*, ed. Jill Nagle. New York: Routledge, 1997.

Query, Julia and Vicky Funari, directors. *Live Nude Girls Unite!* First Run Features, 2000.

Robbins, Trina. *Eternally Bad: Goddesses with Attitude*. Berkeley, CA: Conari Press, 2001.

Ronai, Carol Rambo. "Sketching with Derrida: an Ethnography of a Researcher/Erotic dancer." *Qualitative Inquiry* 4(3), September 1998.

Ronai, Carol Rambo and Carolyn Ellis. "Turn-ons for Money: Interactional Strategies of the Table Dancer." *Journal of Contemporary Ethnography* 18(3), October 1989.

Rubin, Gayle. "Thinking Sex: Notes for a Radical Theory of the Politics of Sexuality." In *Pleasure and Danger: Exploring Female Sexuality*, ed. Carole S. Vance. Boston: Routledge & Kegan Paul, 1984.

Schweitzer, Dahlia. "Striptease: The Art of Spectacle and Transgression." *Journal of Popular Culture* 34(1), Summer 2000: 65–75.

Scott, David A. *Behind the G-String: An Exploration of the Stripper's Image, Her Person, and Her Meaning*. Jefferson, NC: McFarland, 1996.

Shteir, Rachel. *Striptease: The Untold History of the Girlie Show*. Oxford: Oxford University Press, 2004.

Vance, Carole S. ed. *Pleasure and Danger: Exploring Female Sexuality.* Boston: Routledge & Kegan Paul, 1984.

Wood, Elizabeth Anne. "Working in the Fantasy Factory: The Attention Hypothesis and the Enacting of Masculine Power in Strip Clubs." *Journal of Contemporary Ethnography* 29(1), February 2000.

Yalom, Marilyn. *A History of the Breast*. New York: Ballantine, 1997.

Index